"Win Bl[...]
very be[...]

"For the [...] of the early West, it is good entertainment
with lots of color, suspense, and excitement."

       —*The Denver Post*
     on *Give Your Heart to the Hawks*

"Blevins has done his research and knows the mountain men
as well as anyone could—to read this tale is to get a true
sense of what their ordeal and adventures must have been
like."   —*Library Journal*
     on *Dancing with the Golden Bear*

"A rousing installment in a fine epic of the American frontier."
     —*Publishers Weekly* on *Beauty for Ashes*

"His gritty fiction brings to mind the fur-trade novels of
Frederick Manfred (*Lord Grizzly,* 1954) and Vardis Fisher
(*Mountain Man*). . . . The glory years of frontier life, fresh
and rich."   —*Kirkus Reviews* on *Beauty for Ashes*

"Win Blevins's novel about venturesome Sam Morgan and
the fur trade and mountain men of the 1820s is both authen-
tic and entertaining. It will be a welcome addition to any
collection of Western fiction."

   —*The Dallas Morning News* on *So Wild a Dream*

"Author Blevins, an expert on early American fur trade,
introduces his Rendezvous series with this entertaining,
vivid portrait of frontier America as seen through the eyes
of an impressionable youth."

        —*Booklist* on *So Wild a Dream*

ALSO BY WIN BLEVINS

Give Your
HEART
to the
HAWKS

A TRIBUTE TO
THE MOUNTAIN MEN

Win Blevins

FORGE®

A TOM DOHERTY ASSOCIATES BOOK
NEW YORK

GIVE YOUR HEART TO THE HAWKS

The title *Give Your Heart to the Hawks* is borrowed from the poem and book by Robinson Jeffers, published in 1933.

Map by Mark Stein Studios

A Forge Book
Published by Tom Doherty Associates
175 Fifth Avenue
New York, NY 10010

www.tor-forge.com

Forge® is a registered trademark of Macmillan Publishing Group, LLC.

ISBN 978-0-7653-5290-3

Our books may be purchased in bulk for promotional, educational, or business use. Please contact your local bookseller or the Macmillan Corporate and Premium Sales Department at 1-800-221-7945, extension 5442, or by email at MacmillanSpecialMarkets@macmillan.com.

First Forge Edition: November 2005
First Forge Mass Market Edition: May 2018

Printed in the United States of America

0 9 8 7 6 5 4 3 2 1

for Thomas Blevins

I write as though I were speaking directly
to an ideal reader with whom I share basic values.
Because we worked out those values together,
because we are friends more than brothers,
and because, in the day-by-day writing
these words were spoken to your ears,
this book is dedicated to you.

CONTENTS

ACKNOWLEDGMENTS

I am indebted first to Thomas Blevins, who listened patiently to the thinking through of this book and who read the manuscript and made useful suggestions. Then to Craig Stinson for reading the manuscript perceptively. And to the Henry E. Huntington Library for making its excellent resources available to me.

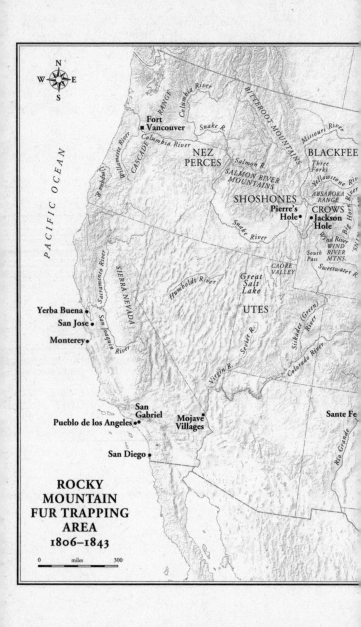

ROCKY
MOUNTAIN
FUR TRAPPING
AREA
1806–1843

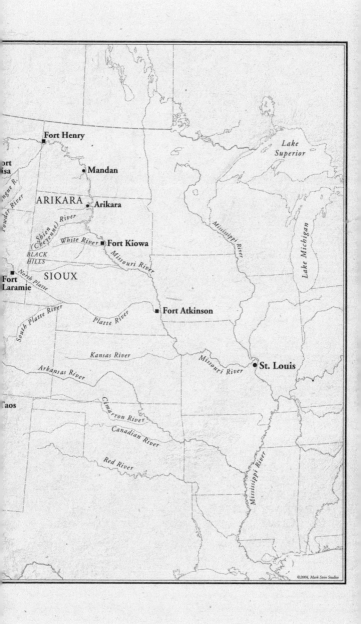

INTRODUCTION

The credit for this book's longevity—in print for more than thirty years, thanks to my readers—belongs to the men it celebrates, the fellows we call the mountain men. They are our nation's half-known, half-regarded, half-scorned heroes.

Their accomplishments were huge. In 1805 the Lewis and Clark men came back. In 1843 the first big migration struck out across the Oregon Trail. In the thirty-eight intervening years, the mountain men roamed the landscape between the Missouri River and the Sierra Nevada. Hundreds of miles from the nearest store, outside the authority of any sheriff, beyond the help of the U.S. cavalry or anyone else back in the States, all the way off the map, they rode, walked, floated, and crawled virtually every inch of the West. They learned the plains down to the last buffalo wallow, the mountains down to the last side canyon, the deserts to the last hidden spring. They lived, hunted, trapped, married, raised children, raised huzzahs to life, and died in the West.

More: They found the trails for their successors to follow. (Frémont, the Pathfinder, was guided by mountain men.) They found out how to survive, and what would get you killed, and handed down the knowledge. In their pitifully small numbers, they learned how to make peace with the Native tribes: A brigade of two dozen men does not march among tens of thousands of Indians looking for a fight.

Unfortunately, the Indian agents and officers of the United States Army did not walk the peaceful path, in Indian relations, that the mountain men had blazed.

Unfortunately again, the mountain men were still in the prime of life when the first wagon trains headed for the paradise of Oregon, or of California. The wagon people looked down their noses at the men in buckskins. "Half Injun," they said. "Squaw man." "Dirty half-breed." So in the 1840s the mountain men gave up and went to farming, or disappeared into Lakota tipis, or deeper into the mountains, and left the settling of the West to their inferiors.

The story of the next half century was sadder, and far bloodier, than it need have been.

My first acquaintance with them came when my great teacher, John G. Neihardt, the author of *Black Elk Speaks*, told marvelous stories about them. Hugh Glass crawling toward the Missouri River and leaving blood in his hand prints. Jedediah Smith setting out for the Pacific shore with no idea where it was, or what terrible deserts and mountains stood in the way.

Adventure stories, sure. Heroic stories, yes. Stories of the courage of individuals, and at the same time of the bond between men in danger. Ordinary life piddles—these stories strut.

When I began writing this book, the stories were personal to me. I was spending every possible day climbing mountains. I started on the highest peak in Europe, Mont

Blanc, and climbed avidly in the dry mountains of the Mojave Desert, in the grand Sierra Nevada, in the glacial Northwest, in high, cold Colorado, and in the redrock country of the Four Corners.

I wasn't necessarily brave. Usually I got the willies, especially on the ground before we started. But I learned about life. I experienced the partnership of the rope, the link between you and your partner, each literally holding the other's life in his hands. I learned about doing what was necessary. I learned to keep a sharp eye on weather, rock formations, and everything around us. I learned to find more inside than I knew was there. I learned about fearing death and choosing life. Most of all, I learned how it felt to *live*. The soul does not cry out, "I made the summit." You suck in the air, relish the feel of the sun on your skin, and exult quietly, "I am alive."

Such blood awareness made me feel in step with the mountain men. They understood that you never feel so alive as when you risk everything. They understood complete loyalty to your partners. Understood that when something has to be done, no matter how hard, you do it. So they felt like kinsmen.

I haven't climbed in years. But courage, loyalty, awareness, commitment, willingness to take a chance, and love of life are good companions elsewhere.

So here are the stories of America's mountain men, once again.

Note: We do not, in this book, see the mountain men as part of the history of America, or even the West. Instead we enter into their lives as they experienced them. We stand knee-deep in cold creeks with them, hear the whir of an arrow past the ear as they did, get parched with them on dry crossings, even whoop it up with their whiskey. This is history for the heart and gut, not the head.

Further note: Many readers have congratulated me on this "wonderful book of fiction." But every one of these stories is known to be true. They come from the journals of men who were there, from newspapers of the day, from books written or told by participants. Though I've dramatized them, I haven't made them up.

That's the breathtaking thing about the mountain men: The stories are true.

WIN BLEVINS
Canyonlands, March 2005

PREFACE

I have not attempted here to write a history of the era of the mountain men. A history would have to be much more comprehensive than this book is; it would have to treat its characters with something like their importance in the perspective to time; it would have to analyze causes and consequences; it would be obliged to put the mountain men into a larger view of American history.

Instead, I have selected men and events that seem to me suggestive of the whole. For instance, I have dealt with Jed Smith, Jim Bridger, Tom Fitzpatrick, and Bill Williams in some detail, but have almost excluded figures of perhaps equal importance—like Kit Carson, Joe Walker, Manuel Lisa, and Josiah Gregg. This book does proceed chronologically from the beginning of the period of the mountain men to roughly its end; but I do not want to delude the reader that all of its major action is included. I only hope that the flavor of the men and their time is evoked fully enough that readers can grasp the large picture without some of its specifics.

History as a record of large movements, the working out of abstractions like mercantilism, imperialism, or

Manifest Destiny, does not interest me much. What does interest me—fascinates me—is history as a rendering of felt experience. When I read, I want to know what it felt like to be the first European to see the New World, or what it felt like to be a tinker in London during the Age of Enlightenment. History does not exist as an abstraction; it exists, and existed, only in personal perspective, as actual people lived and experienced it.

This book deals with actual people and actual doings. Every substantial event in it is verified by newspapers, journals, documents, or books that recorded actual statements of trappers. None of that is invented. But I have gone beyond the objective events into the subjective sphere: I have tried to tell not only what they did, but how they felt about what they did, what their lives were like on a day-to-day, experiential basis. That is the other half of any reality.

Naturally, that kind of recreating involves a certain amount of creating. We may not know whether a man experienced fear in terms of violent nausea or of a sharp constriction of the throat; we may not know what the expression on his face was when he heard thieves among his horses. In defense of that kind of dramatic re-creation, I can only plead a long and intimate acquaintance with mountains, immersion in the material, strong identification with the characters, and a common humanity that permits us to feel with another man in situations he faced. Many of the details I have invented may be inaccurate; I am confident that the moods and feelings they suggest are right.

I have tried to take the trappers' perspective on their lives: their knowledge and ignorance of the West they lived in, their attitudes toward Indians and greenhorns, their convictions about their lifestyles. And I ask the reader to enter into their point of view. One procedure will help here: The mountain men thought of the West topographically, not in terms of political boundaries or man-made landmarks, which did not exist. So I have used their names for the places of the West. The maps will help the reader who thinks of the West in terms of its modern states; occasionally, when complete disorientation seemed to threaten, I have helped out with a modern geographical reference. But the reader will see the West more nearly as the mountain men did if his conceptions are topographic and not political. He will also do well to remember that while we might think of the trappers as agents of Manifest Destiny in a westwarding nation, they certainly did not.

In form, this book is a succession of stories, roughly chronological, about the doings of mountain men. Small essays, called interludes, are interspersed between the stories to provide background that seemed critical to understanding. The stories stand independent of the interludes, but not of each other.

Give Your

HEART

to the

HAWKS

I

The First Mountain Man

JOHN COLTER KNEW THAT THEY WERE GOING TO ask. He had been answering their questions all day—about where beaver were to be found; which Indians were the most peaceable; where mild weather was to be had for wintering; where game jumped out of every gully, and where, in a whole plain, not one living creature might be seen; what parts would likely thirst a man to death and what parts give him easy living. Colter was not a man to spend many words on anything. His years in the woods and mountains had honed his tongue to a tool he used sparingly and exactly. So he had answered their questions about the Rocky Mountains slowly, seriously, learning as much about them as they could from him, volunteering nothing. He might have been explaining the workings of a lathe.

But he thought the things he didn't speak. He turned them around and around in his head—his two years out there in the mountains, and beyond, on the Pacific. He didn't stick words like labels onto his memories; they belonged to his whole body: The roiling of creeks in the spring fret. The little quickening of the blood to be shoved aside immediately when he heard elk hooves clapping along a dense hillside. The bone cold that actually split trees in the winter. The quiet, smooth V widening through the water before a beaver as he swims, his black nose at the surface. The sky of the alpine night, with ten times as many stars as he could see from the flats, big and pointy as thistle balls. The strong, sweet smell of buffalo chips on a fire. The violent, hurting cold of a swallow from a high creek. The strange mingling of fear, servile friendship, and hostility in an Indian camp. The scorch of alkali dust in his nostrils. The crystalline aloneness of day after day of hunting away from the expedition, unbroken and somehow awesome, the solitude so real he might have touched it. The taste of hump ribs, and of beaver tail. The plain hugeness of high country. He knew the words, Bible words mostly, that men in settlements put on that high country, but he didn't use them. The Rocky Mountains were too particular in his memories for those words to carry anything.

He looked at Dixon over the rim of his tin cup when the word came.

"Want to go up and trap with us?"

Colter didn't answer right off, so Dixon and Hancock took turns persuading him. "Beaver's worth ten dollars a plew in St. Louis." "The three of us'll be partners. We've got the equipment." "We can make ourselves rich."

He said he'd talk to Lewis and Clark about it.

Lewis and Clark both thought that John Colter had it coming. They wondered that after two years of pushing through unknown country, over the mountains and all the way to the Pacific, he didn't want to see folks, sleep on a bed, and be with his people in Virginia. But he had served well, had proven to be one of the most dependable hunters and all-around hands they had taken on the expedition. They saw he took to the mountains naturally. So they gave him permission to muster out and go back to the Rockies to trap beaver with the first followers in the wake of the Lewis and Clark expedition, Dixon and Hancock.

John Colter had set out to join the expedition in 1803. Leaving his home in Virginia, he traveled across roadless wilderness, and caught up with Lewis and Clark in Ohio.

Since he claimed to be a good hunter, they took him on. They left St. Louis in 1804, executed their mission with astonishing success, and were now in the Dakota country, at the Mandan villages, on the way back to St. Louis to report their findings. If one man wanted to stay in the mountains, why not?

Later, Nicholas Biddle, the chronicler of the expedition, would charge Colter with a lack of human feeling, and suggest that something dangerous lurked in the mind of a man who would shun civilization. Others probably saw something romantically adolescent in a man of such wild and wayward spirit. Colter, in his mid-thirties, didn't give a damn about either conviction. When his employers asked why he wanted to go back, he allowed only that it was a good business proposition. He didn't mention the memories; Lewis and Clark had them too.

Hancock and Dixon had a windfall in Colter. They were the first to penetrate the West in search of fur, and Colter was one of a handful of whites who knew the country. But, somehow, the enterprise petered out. Hancock and Dixon were never heard from again. And, a year later, Colter was headed down the Missouri in a canoe, alone and empty-handed.

At the mouth of the Platte River, he met the second expedition to go up the Missouri for beaver, led by Manuel Lisa. Lisa realized that Colter's knowledge of the area was invaluable, so he made him a proposition. Colter was more realistic now about the fortunes to be made in mountain fur. Still, he turned away from home for the second time within a year, and headed back to the mountains.

Lisa was outfitted on a bigger scale than Hancock and Dixon had been. He had more men, and he had trading goods for the Indians. He didn't plan to get most of his pelts (called plews) by trapping, but through trading, as the law required him to do. He would build a fort among friendly Indians and persuade them to come in and exchange their furs for blankets, cloth, and various doodads they fancied. So Colter led him into the center of Crow country, at the confluence of the Big Horn and Yellowstone, and the men put up four walls of pickets. Colter knew this country—he had trapped it the previous year—and the experience of the Lewis and Clark expedition suggested that the Crows would be more peaceable than the Blackfeet, who inhabited the upper Missouri.

Lisa wanted someone to roam out among the Crows and tell them about the fort and the goods they could get. Colter volunteered to go alone.

He set out with only his possible sack (the trappers' term for a bag crammed with survival equipment like flint, steel, powder, and balls), and spent the better part of a year making a great circle through the Rockies to spread the news. Getting tips about the country from the Crows he met, he traveled south, up the Big Horn almost to the continental divide, and then up the Wind River to the favorite Crow wintering spot, where he sat out the season of the worst cold and snow. Then he crossed the continental divide and moved into the spectacularly beautiful place later named Jackson Hole. From there he turned homeward and walked straight into the area around Yellowstone Lake, which was to become Yellowstone National Park. He gaped at the shore of the lake, where springs of hot clay bubbled and from time to time erupted into geysers, where a man could smell sulphur and suspect that he heard devils under his feet. From Yellowstone he picked his way, with his sharp mountain sense, straight back to Fort Lisa.

The men scoffed at his tale about the back door to hell. But he had done the job for Lisa. He knew that he had also brought off a major exploration of the Stony Mountains. If he ever got back to the settlements, Lewis and Clark would be glad to get his knowledge for their map. He had also traveled the better part of a thousand miles alone through hostile country, surviving by his wits. That was all right with Colter. He liked to be alone.

Lisa had another lone mission for him. They had secured the Crow trade, and now Lisa wanted to open the Blackfoot trade. So Colter headed for the Three Forks of the Missouri, where the Jefferson, the Madison, and the Gallatin forks join to form the big river, traveling this time with a band of Crows and Flatheads. Unfortunately, Crows and Flatheads were ancient enemies of Blackfeet, so, at the Three Forks, the hostile tribes fought a big battle. Colter, fighting with his own side, was shot in the leg and was noticed by the Blackfeet. The next morning, his Indian friends had moved on and left him. No sense in approaching the Blackfeet now that he had fought against them. So he hobbled some three hundred miles, again alone, to Fort Lisa.

Lisa could see that this Colter was a graduate mountain man. He could survive anywhere by his woodsmanship. So he sent him back to the Blackfeet, along with a trapper named Potts. They canoed up the Missouri to the Three Forks. Seeing no Indians at first, they did some trapping while they waited.

While they were gathering their catch one morning in a creek about six miles from Jefferson Fork, Colter felt himself getting edgy. He felt it in his body, in a tension and a sliver of jumpiness. He was in the habit of listening to his body when it knew something he didn't. He paid attention to it while he slipped the canoe toward the deeper water where the next trap was set.

The sun was up. He could see it, where the fog had

thinned, catching the tops of the cottonwoods. Soon it would bc up far cnough to slant between the steep banks of the creek and reveal the canoe. Right now the light morning fog gave them some protection. In twenty minutes, maybe, they would have sunlight on the water surface.

Colter saw the trap stick floating near the big rock by the deep hole. He steered the canoe, with one imperceptible motion, to the stick, reached into the icy water, grabbed the chain, and pulled the trap and the drowned beaver into the canoe. Silently, he slid the beaver beside the others, floated the canoe to a better spot, locked the trap open, set it on the bottom, dipped the thin stick into his stoppered horn of beaver medicine, and drove the thick stick through the trap chain and into the creek bottom.

Potts grinned, and Colter thought he nearly spoke. It was a good morning's take. But Potts knew better, barely, than to talk without need. Blackfeet could flush them at any time. They had set and checked their traps in the twilight of the dawn and at dusk for a week, and lain hidden during the daylight hours. Meeting the Blackfeet would be touchy even at a time and place Colter chose. Being surprised by Blackfeet would be risky—especially since they might remember him from the Crow battle. Now they were dangerously late. They had two more traps to check out, and it was nearly full light.

At first Colter gave no sign that he had heard anything. Only by his particular stillness, and an extra touch of straightness, could Potts tell that Colter was listening intently. Quickly, Colter slid the canoe under an overhanging branch. It sounded like hooves to Potts, lots of them, trampling along the bank. Potts saw Colter looking hard at the top of the high bank opposite, in a way that was too calm.

"Indians," Colter said. "Let's cache."

But he didn't sound quite sure. So Potts said, "Indians, hell. Buffler. Buffler trompin' around."

Colter listened again, but the sound had gone. His mind couldn't be sure, but his body said "Indians." He hesitated.

"We're almost done," Potts added. "Them's buffler." He grinned at Colter. "You sure are queer lately." He paused, half turned away, and said, "Gone skittish, seems like."

Colter knew what Potts was doing. With one stroke he sent the canoe gliding toward the next trap. If he wanted to bother getting square with Potts, he could do that later.

He saw them, sprouting up on both banks, before he heard anything more. Several hundred Indians, Blackfeet, painted. He even saw women and children poking their heads through. One motioned him to bring the canoe to shore. When he headed in, Potts started a little. Colter didn't know whether Potts had just noticed the Indians, or was badly rattled. Colter felt his whole body become a set of nerve endings to get hold of this situation, to feel its medicine, to grasp the mood of the Blackfeet, and to figure out what to say, what to do. Maybe they would just be robbed. This was not a war party. Quietly, with one hand, he slipped his traps over the side and dropped them to the bottom of the creek. The traps cost ten dollars apiece.

He put the canoe in to shore, stepped out, and made the sign that he came in peace. Potts got halfway out of the bow, holding his rifle like he didn't know what to do with it. A husky Indian snatched it from him. Instantly Colter grabbed the rifle and handed it back to Potts, who still had one foot in the canoe. Potts abruptly pushed from shore and sat in the canoe in midstream.

"Put in," Colter said firmly in English, "right now. There's nowhere you can go now. Put in, show them you aren't afraid of them."

"You crazy?" Potts answered with a weird laugh. "Look at 'em. You can see they're gonna kill us. Torture us first. Don't make any difference what we do."

An arrow cut off the last word with a thock. Potts doubled over, and Colter could see the notched end sticking out of Potts's hip. Colter heard the sound before he realized what was happening. From his clutched-over position. Potts came up with his rifle and shot the Indian who had seized it. The man fell. The answering sounds were as soft as Potts's sound had been loud, the nasty whir of arrows and the little slapping sounds when they hit. A couple of rifles sounded late, tagging after. Potts's body was made a riddle of.

Immediately the whooping and wailing started. Some braves charged into the water to get Potts's body and drag it to shore. The others uttered the strange cries that meant vengeance. The squaws sent up their ululations of grief. Colter had heard it often enough to know to shut off most of the sound, which could drive him crazy, and let in only the information: The Blackfeet were fully riled—in a mood to get even for their death of the tribesman with a slow, ritual revenge.

Colter felt the hands on him, and did not flinch or protest. Women and children ripped his own clothing away until he stood naked. Others were hacking at Potts's body with their hatchets and knives. He looked away. Several dozen of them crowded around him to gawk at his white skin. Some of them touched cautiously. Some jabbed him. Colter stood straight and looked directly at them, making no move to stop anything. He could see, out of the corner of his eye, braves and squaws still cutting at Potts, and beating the body with clubs.

A squaw stood in front of Colter looking directly into his eyes. He hadn't noticed her coming. The racket died down a little as the other Blackfeet watched. She held something bloody up in front of Colter's face: Potts's genitals. Then, from less than two feet in front of him, she threw the bloody mess into his face letting out a fierce scream. The whoops soared again. Colter didn't need to look to know what was happening. He forced himself to keep his eyes open as he felt the slaps of organs and chunks of flesh against his chest and face.

When he let his eyes see again, several braves were pushing toward him, tomahawks in hand. But others held them back. They're going to make a ceremony of it, he thought. Maybe Potts was right. Colter stood still as a tree. At least they were going to take some time about it. He didn't have to worry about an arrow in the back at the moment. Whatever chance he had lay in being calm, showing no fear, and thinking.

A dozen braves, important-looking ones, sat down and began to talk. Colter wondered if they would let him speak at the council. He decided to use what little Blackfoot language he knew. He spoke the Crow language better, but he couldn't take the chance of reminding them of their age-old enemies right now. If he did that, they might even remember seeing him with the Crows.

He understood enough to know that some braves were proposing to set him up as a mark to shoot at. Others were arguing for a more lingering death by tomahawk. He waited.

Finally a chief came over to him and asked if he was a fast runner. Colter took his time. It didn't do to hurry formal palaver with the Indians, though this wasn't exactly negotiation. He guessed that they were thinking of letting him run for his life. Some chance, with 500 angry braves on his tail, and him running through the cactus naked and barefoot. But a chance.

He spoke deliberately and ambiguously. "The Long Knife is a poor runner, and not swift," he said. "He is considered by the other Long Knives to be very swift, but he is not." A half challenge. The chief returned to council.

When he came back, he signaled Colter to follow him onto the plain. After they walked twenty or thirty yards, the old chief said, "Walk further, past the large boulder, and then you must run to try to save yourself." Then he went back to the party. Colter could see the young men getting rid of their blankets and leggings, preparing for the race. He walked slowly and calmly, passed the boulder and kept walking. He intended to walk as far as possible, because they would come as soon as he started running. Finally he heard a series of whoops, glanced back to see that the braves were starting, and let his own legs go into motion.

His legs turned toward the Jefferson Fork. From where he was, the creek arched down to the Jefferson, like a bow. He would run as the bowstring would go. It was maybe five, six miles to the Jefferson that way. He knew he had no chance. He didn't know how far along that straight line he would get. But his legs ran toward the Jefferson Fork because that was his only pretense of a chance. He could not get away from the Blackfeet on land. They knew the country and they were expert trackers. Alone and unarmed, he had no hope of standing them off if they caught up. His only hope was to get into the river so that it would destroy his trail, and then hide. Except that he had no hope.

Plains and hills, plains and hills, as far as he could see. He noticed the pain in his right foot first. His feet were not missing all of the low, gnarly cactus. He let his eyes stay focused on the ground, his eyes cooperating with his legs on taking him over and converting his body into one long motion of running.

He liked the feel of the running. He felt his breath coming full and deep, sucking in the thin air, bellowing it out, regular as the pendulum of a clock. He felt his legs following one after the other on the sandy earth automatically, in a loping motion. He didn't feel the steps one at a time, but blended into a kind of glide. He was surprised at how fast that motion was carrying him. He was running as fast as he could run for a long time. But he felt that if he needed a little more speed he would have it for a while.

He deliberately did not look back. He wondered how far he had run. A couple of miles, at the most. He put his pursuers out of his mind, and turned back to the feeling of the running.

Colter gave himself up to his legs, and his mind floated. Images of herds of running horses came into his mind, horses spread across a plain. Buffalo passed through, huge in foreshortening. The water-wheel of a mill drifted in, turning steadily with the flow of a wide, Virginia creek, as it had turned for years. A stick slid along, frictionless, on ice covered with a thin layer of water. And, underneath, he felt the evenness of his own slide. He loved the feeling of the running. He would run until he died.

How close were they? He felt he had to look back, just a quick glance. They were scattered all over the plain, most of them straggling far behind. Only one was close. He was no more than a hundred yards behind, and carrying a spear. He had been gaining.

That glance had made Colter feel a sort of quickening.

Maybe he did have a chance. Now was the time for that extra speed he thought he had. He forced his legs to pick up the pace, and then let them settle into their own faster rhythm. It must still be two or three miles to the river.

He felt his breath coming faster now, maybe twice as fast, and it rasped in his throat. He ignored the rasp, and the pain that was growing in his chest, and tried just to feel his legs moving and moving. The rest of his body was getting loggy, as though only his legs were still alive.

When he snapped to, he realized that he had been dizzy for a moment. Dizzy! He fixed his eyes on the ground and made a point of holding them open. The dizziness came back in slow waves, and with it came nausea. He merely watched as his body let both pass and his legs kept moving relentlessly. For a couple of minutes he let the waves pass, observing himself dispassionately. Once he choked off the feeling that his bowels would let go, then ignored it. He snatched huge chunks of air into his lungs and forced himself on.

Maybe he had left the Indian behind. He decided to look back quickly. He knew that his body would not stand much more of this punishment. He was afraid that it would just shut down, on its own. He looked. The Indian was only about twenty yards back, and now had the spear lifted high for the moment when he would be close enough to throw it. Colter forced his legs a little harder.

He gradually became aware of something on his knees, as they pumped in and out of view. Blood. He looked down. The whole front of his body was covered with blood. He felt it now on his lips, sticky and salty. My God, blood was gushing out of his nose.

Colter wondered whether, in the surprise of the blood, he might have slowed down. Then he began to think that the area between his shoulder blades might be hit by that spear any moment. He wished he could shake that feeling off, like an itch you can't reach. But it was getting to him.

All right. He hadn't much chance. He couldn't outrun this Blackfoot.

Abruptly, he stopped, turned around, spread his arms, and called to the Indian in the Crow language to spare his life. Startled, maybe by the suddenness, or by the plea, or by the blood, the Indian tried to stop and to throw his spear at the same time. He stumbled, just at the moment when his arm started forward, and his body pitched toward the earth. The spear stuck in the ground, and broke off in his hand.

Colter pounced. He grabbed the head of the spear and, as the Indian pleaded for mercy, drove it into his stomach.

He waited, and took about six deep breaths. Suddenly, he felt as though he had enough energy left to run to St. Louis. His legs tingled with new blood. Not an Indian in sight. Yet. He started toward the river with the loping motion he liked. Before long he heard one whoop, and then a series of whoops, as the Blackfeet found their dead comrade. He must be no more than a mile from the river, he thought. He was going to make it. Maybe. He let his legs take over again, long and easy.

Only one step shorter than the others broke the rhythm as he shifted from run to dive. The water was a blast of ice. His head reeled as he came up. He had to spot the top of the island again. The strokes took him just above it and he slipped beaverlike, beneath the surface. Both hands groped for some kind of space between the logs. He couldn't see anything, and his breath was running out. He turned around, and a moment later his head eased above the surface of the water about where he had dived.

He looked for a long moment at the big pile of driftwood lodged at the top of the island. Somewhere under those logs must be a place he could get his head up.

On his second try he stuck his arm through a hole between logs, right off. He couldn't see anything, but he put his head through. His shoulders didn't even touch. A big hole. And he must be under five or six feet of wood. He could see out of small chinks sideways, and, straight up, he could see, through the crevices, blue and a cottonwood branch moving lazily in the wind. It would do. It would do in a pinch, definitely. Colter grinned, and then laughed noiselessly, scarcely believing.

The Blackfeet soon began to splash in the water and prance along the bank. Colter watched them without moving. They were yelling and screeching like devils. Several swam across to the island and trampled all over it, sounding like they thought noise would help them trap their prey. One stepped out onto the raft of driftwood, and Colter slipped back under water. He didn't think any had tried to swim under it. If one did, and found him, he could strangle the man. Now that he had a hiding place, he felt strong—bull strong.

An hour later the Blackfeet were still crisscrossing the area. Colter wondered what they were thinking, now that they had lost his track. They must have known, by then, that his trail didn't come out the river for quite a distance, upstream or down. He had a sudden thought, and it chilled him. What if they decided to set fire to the driftwood. He stopped himself. They wouldn't. No reason.

Then he realized where the chill came from. He was still up to his chest in this icy water, which was melted snow spilled down from the continental divide. He intended to stay here until the Blackfeet went away. It could be a couple of days if they were stubborn. But if he stayed in this water, he might never get out of it. Men who lay injured in creeks too long didn't make it. He figured a way to prop and wedge up, mostly out of the water. It was tiring, but he could do it.

It had been dark for two or three hours when he decided to risk getting out. He had heard no sound of Indians for quite a while by then. Without a sound he swam under the raft and came up alongside the island. Then, keeping his hands in the water so he wouldn't make any noise, he swam slowly downstream. He went a long way. They still might check again for his track leaving the river. Then he walked all night to make sure.

At dawn he clambered onto some rocks, and walked trackless a ways, and lay down to sleep at the bottom of a rock chimney. His feet were bleeding from the night's beating. Though his face was leathered, his body was white as the underside of a fish. He wouldn't be able to expose it to much sun.

Well, he had done it before. Traveled alone from the Three Forks to Fort Lisa after that other tangle with the Blackfeet. That time he had had a wounded leg. This time he was naked, so his feet would go raw. They were already cut. That made it about even. But the first time he had had his knife and gun. This time he was bare-handed. He could survive, he thought, on roots and bark. More than two hundred miles—a long walk.

When John Colter approached Fort Lisa, eleven days later, the man at the gate didn't recognize him. His face was gaunt, his body emaciated and covered with scratches and dried blood. Only the beard identified him for sure as a white man.

When he told his story, some believed it, others scoffed. He didn't take much notice either way. One, a veteran, decided not to travel with Colter any more. The man was plaguey bad luck. Another, a newcomer, didn't sympathize much because Colter seemed such a queer fellow, talking as though he were seeing faraway places and didn't care if anyone listened anyway. Lisa wondered why Colter seemed to take to these lone odysseys. Anyway, thought Lisa, Colter seemed to be a man born to the mountains.

The man born to the mountains surprised Manuel Lisa, when the ice broke up on the river early in 1810, by announcing that he was going back to civilization. Storming into the fort one day, after a new encounter with the Blackfeet, he threw down his hat and declared, "If God will only forgive me this time and let me off I will leave this Godforsaken country day after tomorrow—and be damned if I ever come into it again," wrote a trapper who was there.[1]

With two other trappers he set out downriver, had another brush with the Blackfeet and, by traveling at night and hiding in the daytime, made it to St. Louis in May. There he gave William Clark information for the forthcoming map and talked considerably around town about his adventures. (Meriwether Lewis had died under mysterious circumstances—a victim of suicide or murder.) Colter's stories earned him a reputation as a confirmed liar, and he was not vindicated for some years.

Soon he got himself a piece of land at Charette, Missouri, along the great river, and got married. By the next year he had mountain fever again. The Astoria expedition made a stop to talk with him and invited him to join them. He was reluctant to see them move on without him, but he was too recently married to go along.

Two years later the first mountain man, who had left the mountains because it was hazardous to his health, died of jaundice in the settlements.

The Great American Desert

IN 1803, WHEN THOMAS JEFFERSON BOUGHT THE *Louisiana Territory from France, neither the President nor the American people knew what they got in the bargain. Except for the part along the Mississippi River, Louisiana was largely a blank space on the map. Jefferson persuaded Congress to outfit a military expedition, headed by Meriwether Lewis and William Clark, to do some exploring.*

Jefferson had several goals in mind: to find an overland route to the Pacific that might be a key to trade with the Orient and commerce in the northern Pacific; to bring back a map of what they found to fill in that blank space; to secure the friendship of the Indians of the West for their new rulers, the government of the United States; to improve the American claim to the territory of Oregon; and to open a way for the American fur trade to get the pelts of its own land—the British had been stealing down from Canada to take Louisiana Territory beaver.

Nowadays, Americans are inclined to believe that the drive for westward movement raged in early America like an incurable fever. It didn't. Some Americans did believe that in the West, just over the next hill, stretched ground so fertile you had to be careful of what you planted; they expected that somewhere out there lay a Kentuck of a place, the Promised Land, with the Fountain of Youth bubbling evermore. Just as many scoffed at whatever might be west of the Hudson River, or whatever river they happened to live east of. Some of these people even proposed legislation to make venturing west of the settlements a crime. (Benjamin Franklin had countered shrewdly that it makes no sense to pass laws that can't be enforced.) These people feared the effect of the wilderness on civilized man. Man had been nurtured, they thought, by Christianity and the work ethic out of a state of savagery and depravity; if men returned to the wilderness, if they left the civilizing persuasions of society, they would again become as beasts.

Lewis and Clark executed their mission superbly, guided over the Rockies by an Indian woman, Sacajwea—The Bird Woman. They made a long and dangerous journey into unknown territory with the loss of only a single man (and him by illness). But their findings lent strength to the anti-westering forces. What Lewis and Clark had found, people said, was that the country west of the frontier at St. Louis was one huge desert. They had crossed over the Rocky Mountains, or Stony Mountains or Shining Mountains as they were variously called, but they had found a country that no man could live in—arid, uncultivable, oppressive. Nomads might exist there, buffalo and antelope might thrive there, but no civilized man—no white man—would want to.

And so was born the myth of the Great American Desert. The other early reports confirmed it. They spoke consistently of desert, of steppes, of the Sahara and Tartary.

Myth can grow in ground that supports nothing, and it did. While some white men were living in the Rocky Mountains, the myth that the West was unhabitable thrived. While some white men went all over the West as familiarly as other men went to the post office, the map-makers continued to label it UNEXPLORED TERRITORY and to invent lakes, rivers, and mountains that bore no relation-

ship to facts. While any tavern conversation in St. Louis could have provided accurate information about the West, most Easterners stuck to their land of fable—poisonous fable. Even in 1844, a year after thousands of emigrants had traveled the Oregon Trail, this kind of speech was common enough to be attributed to Daniel Webster and to be believed:

What do we want with the vast, worthless area, this region of savages and wild beasts, of deserts, of shifting sands, and whirlwinds of dust, of cactus and prairie dogs? To what use could we ever hope to put these great deserts or endless mountain ranges, impenetrable and covered to their base with eternal snow? . . . I will never vote one cent from the public treasury to place the Pacific coast one inch nearer to Boston than it now is.[1]

While most Americans were wondering to what use such a worthless area could be put, a very few men asked a different question and got an answer: They asked what kind of living could be made in the West, and answered their own question by building a life they loved. Caring nothing for the myth of the Great American Desert, they had found their Promised Land smack in the middle of it. Caring nothing for an Easterner's civilization or a Midwesterner's agricultural society, they created a culture around beaver, buffalo, antelope, and wild places.

Their progenitor was a single man who left the Lewis and Clark expedition. While Meriwether Lewis and William Clark went home to report to the government, and their brigade made its way to the settlements, one man, John Colter, had turned back and gone to live in the Shining Mountains.

II

Mountain Skill, Mountain Luck

THE STORY OF HUGH GLASS SOUNDS LIKE SOME yarn spun by a veteran and carried all over the plains by some green listeners who told it without understanding the game. Maybe part of the story is a yarn, the part before old Glass met up with a grizzly in South Dakota one September morning. After that, it has a lot of wise hands to vouch for it. And it was too good for even mountain men to improve on.

Glass is said to have been a sailor, perhaps even an officer, working the Caribbean in the years just after the war with the British. In 1817, he had the bad luck to encounter Jean Laffite, the pirate who saved Andrew Jackson at New Orleans and then returned to piracy. Laffite captured Glass's ship and its crew. He gave Glass the choice of becoming a pirate or being dispatched instantly to another world. Glass made the prudent choice, and was taken to Laffite's current lair, Galveston Island. After perhaps a year of pirating, Glass could stand it no longer, rebelled at doing something especially repulsive, and was told he would be executed. With a friend, he decided to swim for it. Their chief worry was cannibalistic Indians over on the mainland. But if they could stay hidden and work their way northeast, they could join an outpost of Americans in Texas near the Louisiana border.

They swam and managed to escape the Karankawas, but, somehow, they managed to misread the sun enough to travel more northwest than northeast. Instead of getting to Louisiana, they ended up in western Kansas, in Pawnee country. The Pawnees captured the two and promptly made a human sacrifice of Glass's friend. As Glass was about to help placate the Pawnee gods as well, he handed the Pawnee chief some vermilion. The impressionable fellow was so taken with this gift that he not only spared Hugh's life, but adopted him as a son.

So, in 1818 or 1819, Glass became a Pawnee and began to master plains craft as he had mastered marine craft. At some later time, his adopted father made a journey to St. Louis, to see William Clark, now Superintendent of Indian Affairs. Hugh went along, and, in St. Louis, he again became a white man.[1]

Perhaps Hugh's story is fanciful to this point. But from here on, it is well substantiated and even more fabulous.

In the spring of 1823, Glass enlisted with the Ashley-Henry men who were going up the Missouri River to trap in the mountains. General Ashley, an important political figure in the new state of Missouri, had already sent brigades to the mountains last year, and St. Louis was aflurry with reports that these men were going to bring back a fortune greater than the wealth of the mines of Peru. People said that any man who was enterprising, didn't mind a little hardship, and didn't quail at danger, ought to have a try. Glass, who had been a wanderer and adventurer on the seas, had fallen for the plains and decided to have a go with Ashley.

Ashley led the band upriver to the Arikara villages, where they were attacked by this unpredictable tribe, and forced back down. Fifteen men were killed in the battle, and Hugh was wounded in the leg. It was the worst defeat any American trappers had suffered to date. Ashley realized that he had to take some action to keep the river route to the Stony Mountains open; the Arikaras would be even more dangerous after this heady victory. So he secured the help, not only of the rival fur company, but of the U. S. Army. These Rees (as the Arikaras were also called) must be made to know their place.

Unfortunately, the commander of the expedition against the Rees, Colonel Leavenworth, turned the affair into a comic opera of miscalculations. He let the Rees get away scot-free, so they were not chastened but aroused and encouraged to thumb their noses at the ineffective white men.

Ashley and his field leader, Major Andrew Henry, led their men downriver in great discouragement. The river route was now closed. They had to get to the mountains, and their only choice was a land expedition. At Fort Kiowa they scrounged up a few horses—not enough so that the men could ride, but enough to get the supplies to Fort Henry at the mouth of the Yellowstone. Major Henry would lead one small land party, very carefully. The Rees had disappeared after the farcical campaign against them; no one knew where they were, and now would not be a good time to find out by accident.

Henry's party of thirteen left Fort Kiowa in mid-August, moving up the Missouri and then due west up the Grand River. The plains of South Dakota were scrubby, nearly barren, flat, dry, unaccommodating. Henry put men out ahead and to the side to watch for buffalo and for Rees. But on one of the first few nights, an Indian attack left two men dead and two more wounded.

Glass was not a leader in the party. He was a new man, relatively speaking, and the party counted on veterans like Black Harris and Hiram Allen. So, five days and probably a couple of hundred miles out of Fort Kiowa, two old hands were ahead of the main party, hunting. Glass, at about forty, had been his own master too long to traipse along docilely with the others. He liked to be by himself, and he was as stubborn, insubordinate, and independent as any mountain man. He was out ahead, against discipline, looking for some berries, when he stumbled into a thicket and onto a huge grizzly and her two cubs.

Old Ephraim charged, and Hugh knew what he was in for. He didn't take off running because he knew where his best chance lay. When the grizzly reached him, she stopped long enough to raise up on her hind legs so that she could swat him with her forepaws. Hugh waited, shoved his fear out of the way of his vision, and, when she exposed her chest, shot directly at her heart. Then he dropped his gun and ran desperately, screaming for help at the top of his lungs. (The rifles of the mountain men, unfortunately, fired just once. Then it took thirty seconds to get more powder and another ball in place.)

The grizzly caught Hugh after a dozen or two steps and with one swipe sent him sprawling. Then she hit the limp body again. Then she tore off a piece of flesh and carried it back to her cubs.

Black Harris was the first to get there. When he burst into the thicket, one of the cubs took after him and chased him into the river. From chest-deep water Harris shot and killed the cub. The rest of the party ran toward the snarling she-grizzly. They found Glass gamely slashing at her with his knife, but she was mangling him with every swat. When she knocked him down and started to pounce on him again, several men fired balls into her. Finally, from Hugh's original shot, or from the new shots, she keeled over next to Glass's body.

When they turned Glass over, they were surprised to find him breathing at all. His face was partly raked away to the bones, His ribs were crushed. An awful tear in his throat bubbled every time he breathed. His body was littered with gashes. Any one of fifteen wounds was enough to kill him. The men smiled a little, sadly, but admiringly, at the gumption of a man who could live even for a few minutes after having gotten so torn up. They hovered, waiting for the old man to die. After a few minutes, they decided to make camp. After the burying, there wouldn't be time to move that day, anyway. Strangely, when dark came and they turned in, old Glass was still hanging on.

And in the morning he was still hanging on. Now the whole thing was beginning to get embarrassing. For Glass to live a little while was touching, but for him to survive the night was dangerous.

Henry did what he had to do. The Rees could be anywhere, and it was essential to get out of their territory as quickly as possible. It made absolutely no sense to risk ten lives waiting for another man to die so that they could go through some ritual of duty. The men were already antsy. But, still, Henry could not bring himself to abandon a man who still clung to life. That was something a decent man just didn't do. So he compromised. He asked for two volunteers to stay with Glass until the old man gave up, bury him, and hightail it after the main party.

Right off the kid volunteered, a gangly nineteen-year-old of no particular account named Jim Bridger. This wasn't the sort of man you left almost alone in a hostile country. Henry looked at the other men. He was an old hand at the mountains and at leading men, so he didn't berate them. He just told them that the job had to be done, and asked who was willing to do it. John Fitzgerald spoke up. It wasn't fair, he said. A man would be daring the Rees to take his scalp, would get nothing done with the dare, and would get nothing for his trouble in the end. Might even come out behind, 'cause he might miss the fall hunt if he couldn't get to the fort quick enough. Maybe, if Henry made it worth a man's while. . . .

At least Fitzgerald had been around a little. Maybe he could get this boy back with all his hair on his head. Henry declared the company would go forty dollars a man to stay behind, if Fitzgerald would stay. Fitzgerald allowed that he would. Forty dollars was two or three months' pay.

They broke camp quickly, all of them fidgety about having hung around so long and uneasy about making their way to the mouth of the Yellowstone with just the eight men left. Henry noticed young Bridger standing around self-consciously straight, like he thought everyone was looking at him. Henry had a nagging feeling that Bridger might pay dearly for his chance to look good. He shrugged the feeling off. In this situation he couldn't afford it. They cleared out.

Bridger didn't really pay any mind to Fitzgerald or the mauled body he was guarding for an hour or two. He sat and stared at his rifle, his mind back home in Missouri where he had been bonded to a blacksmith and hated the life. He imagined the surprise and envy in the blacksmith's eyes if he could see his bound boy now. He remembered when, slaving on his folks' farm on the river above St. Louis, he had watched the keelboats headed upriver, into wilderness country, where a man might show that he could do brave things, the kind of things that other men told stories about. He had longed, at twelve, to go up one of the two great rivers with those men and be one of them. He smiled to himself.

He needed a moment to take in that Fitzgerald was talking to him. "I'm gonna have a look around," he said. "Why don't you see what you can do for him?"

"Do for him." It hadn't quite struck Bridger that they would have to do for old Glass until he went under. He guessed they would. They had to give him his fair chance, even if he didn't have none. He stood over the body and looked down at it. It looked peaceful, asleep, and maybe resting. Bridger looked at the awful wounds, half bound with strips of Glass's dirty shirt but still showing raw for all that. He felt a little nauseated. He picked a piece of rag from the shirt lying next to Glass, stepped over to the spring to soak it, and poked it into Glass's open mouth. Glass's eyelids fluttered a little, and he sucked on the rag. Well, they would just wait, that's all. At least they had water without even going the twenty steps to the creek, and enough dried meat without having to shoot and make a ruckus that could be heard. There were even buffler berries for a change, if they wanted one. He wondered where Fitzgerald was. He himself wouldn't even have left the thicket to check for Rees. They had all they needed right here and could sit tight and not be seen till the job was done.

The mouth had stopped sucking, he noticed, and he reached out for the rag. Fitzgerald spoke before Bridger saw him standing behind. "How's his breathing?"

Bridger felt around the nose and mouth for the air. "Feeble," he answered. "And fitful."

It seemed callous to say more, but Fitzgerald did. "Won't be long then, and it's a good thing. This country makes a man uncomfortable alone."

Bridger felt a twinge of resentment. Fitzgerald wasn't alone, was he? He walked over and got a handful of berries, crushed them, and put them in Glass's mouth one by one. He wasn't afraid to stick the job out. Fitzgerald sat and waited, not paying any mind to Bridger or Glass. Bridger could sense that Fitzgerald's sitting was uneasy.

They got into their buffalo robes early that night, since they couldn't build a fire. Bridger wished to hell Fitzgerald would say something—just anything, just talk, to show that they were two human beings and not something else. He forgot: *three* human beings, though one couldn't talk and wasn't any company. He guessed Glass would be gone by morning. Bridger had seen more than a few dead men, since he'd been in the mountains a year and a half. So that didn't bother him. He turned his head and peered through the darkness toward the black shape, no more than ten feet away. It was a funny notion, the idea of sleeping practically next to a body that might be alive and might be dead.

Come morning, Glass was still alive. Fitzgerald checked him and said that the fever had come up in him and he wouldn't stand against it long. If the tearing up and the losing blood didn't get him, the fever would take him off pretty quick. Bridger was ashamed of it, but he felt a little relieved. Why, what if old Glass held out for a couple of weeks? What could they do about that?

He took his turn walking out to check around that day, going slow and quiet and turning himself into all eyes and all ears. This country wasn't fat, like the upper Missouri country, at least not this time of year. It was decidedly thin. The sun had dried the sandy soil almost into a crust, like it had been in an oven. Sun and wind had got the sagebrush and the cottonwoods crackling dry, and had turned what little green there was to gray. The Dakota country swept away in scrubby hills as far as he could see, and as far as he could imagine anybody seeing. Back in Illinois and Missouri the hills didn't reach so far but hedged in more. Out here everything seemed to be about twice as big, as though proportion had gotten out of hand and everything was twice as far or twice as broad, or twice as high, like the country had been made for men of double size. Bridger didn't have any words for how big it was or how empty it was, but he could feel the bigness and the emptiness inside.

When he lay in his robes that evening, he thought of the great sweep of plain around him, and this thicket the only place that was somehow sheltered, and they just one small spot against it all.

On the third morning Glass was still alive. Now he seemed delirious. He opened his eyes sometimes, although he didn't seem to see with them, and babbled things Bridger couldn't understand. He sat and waited, and listened to Fitzgerald muttering and cursing. It was amazing to him that Fitzgerald could have spent three days with him and not really spoken to him, just talked to himself or talked at Bridger. Some mountain men, Bridger noticed, got to be almost dumb brutes, after a while, that couldn't talk at all.

On the fourth morning Bridger wasn't sure for a while whether Glass was alive or dead. The chest didn't seem to move, and there were only the barest stirrings around the nose and mouth. He seemed to have gone into a sleep that was near to death. The fever was down some, though.

It was that afternoon that Fitzgerald finally talked to him. Suddenly friendly, he started hinting that he and Bridger were mighty good fellows to have stayed so long with Glass, risking their own necks. They had certainly gone more than forty dollars worth. They had done it because they were not the kind of niggurs that would walk off and leave a dying man and not try to help. But it would be terrible and not right if it turned out they'd have to stay a week or two weeks or goddamn knows how long until old Glass gave up. Nothing for it, of course, but it still wasn't right.

He kept on like that, gentle but clear, that day and evening. Glass stayed in the sleep that seemed near death. Perhaps he would just ease over to being dead any time now, without making a sign. The next morning he was the same. Fitzgerald kept angling back to how unfair it was, but gentle, because Bridger didn't take up his line. He knew where Fitzgerald was headed. That evening Glass was the same.

The next morning the stubborn old fellow opened his eyes. They were glazed, and at first Bridger wasn't sure whether he could see. Then he knew Glass could, and he told Fitzgerald.

"I'm glad he can see," answered Fitzgerald, "because he's going to need it."

He started packing up. "This niggur's getting out of here, Bridger. I think we've overstayed our time. Henry didn't mean for us to have to wait five days anyway, just for forty dollars. He thought we'd be right along. This ain't reasonable." He was lashing his gear to their one horse. "We used up our medicine, staying this long. This child ain't crazy."

Bridger didn't say anything. He looked at Glass. His head was wagging back and forth. Might just be delirious. But Bridger thought he could see what was happening, and probably could hear, too. Bridger stared at him.

"I'm ready," Fitzgerald said flatly. "You coming or staying?"

"I can't go," Bridger answered dully.

"Boy, I ain't gonna argue with you. It don't make no mind to me. But you know what they're gonna do to you, don't you? Maybe stick slivers of pine into you and light 'em, so you burn slow. Maybe skin you alive. This ain't no joke, boy, and no time for fancy notions." Bridger said nothing. "Get the hell off your ass and let's move. You ain't ready to throw it all away yet, not for a corpse."

Bridger felt like his body was moving, not himself, like his legs were part of someone else and had their own orders. His whole body felt very, very heavy.

"Get his gear on there quick. I want to move." Bridger looked at Fitzgerald, unbelieving. Fitzgerald barked, "Get the gun and the knife and everything else put up here. You don't leave a dead man's things when you bury him. You take 'em along. And we buried old Glass. Remember that, boy."

Bridger didn't look at Glass, but a glimpse out of the corner of one eye hinted that maybe Glass was trying to make a movement. He turned away. He walked alongside the horse in a stupor, and they were miles away before Bridger thought or felt anything again. Then he was violently angry, and maybe a little sick.

When Bridger and Fitzgerald left, Glass passed out. He didn't know how many days went by before he woke up. At first he wanted to holler and get them to come running back. But he knew it had been too long.

His body felt hot and he was aching for water. His tongue was dry and swollen, filling his mouth. He started to roll toward the spring, felt pain hit him like a club, and almost lost consciousness. He rested for a long time. Then he calculated slowly how he could do it. He rolled once, hard. The pain took his breath away. Then, lying on his stomach, he pivoted slowly until his face slid into wetness. He thought later that he might have slept a little before he drank. He noticed that the movements had gotten the bleeding started in thin trickles. He couldn't feel the gashes separately. His whole body pained him, and it must be pain that was keeping half his consciousness away. He slept.

He woke up alive, and thought that was a good start. He wanted food. Another good sign: Dying men aren't hungry. A half-dozen buffalo berries hung low enough to reach, after he rolled onto his back. He would wait until tomorrow to try for more.

The next day Glass felt clearer in his head. First the berries: He had an idea. He would scoot to the base of the bush and put his weight on the branches, forcing them to the ground and breaking them so they would stay. Afterwards he felt like he had been trampled by a horse. He rested a long time before he scooted out to get the berries and spent the rest of the day in a kind of daydream. He kept seeing Fitzgerald and Bridger leaving. He could go backwards some in his mind, and hear the words they said before they left—not all of them, and not clearly, but some of the words. Then he saw Bridger taking off his possibles and the two of them leave him empty-handed. When he woke up the next morning, Glass knew for the first time what had happened to him. He could put it in order in his mind. He spoke his first words, and they made him sure of it: "Son of a bitches went off and left me to die. Took everything I had." He spent the rest of the day mulling over that. Come morning, he had decided that he was going to get out of this hole, get up the river, and square accounts with Bridger and Fitzgerald. The ache to get square came on him like a new fever.

On the following day the desire for vengeance got a lucky break. Waking up from a nap, he saw a rattlesnake lazing nearby. It had just eaten a bird, and was swollen in the middle to the size of a man's fist. Hugh knew that he wouldn't even have to be especially agile. He slammed the rock down just in back of the rattler's head four or five times, cutting it in half. Then he shredded the meat, soaked the pieces in water, and fed himself like a baby. His medicine was good.

And when the sun came up one morning, just far

enough to begin to warm things, he decided: He might as well move today as any day. He felt pretty good. He didn't know how many days had gone by since he met the grizzly, but enough of them. He might as well start for Fort Kiowa today.

Fort Kiowa it would have to be. That was a lot closer than Fort Henry. It was also generally downhill. And he could follow the river. A man who couldn't walk had best stay next to his water and not set out across country toward the Yellowstone.

Because Hugh couldn't walk yet. He figured that if he waited till he could, his wait would outlast his food. Eating was his biggest worry. A lone man could make out in the Dakota, even if he was crawling, if he had a gun to shoot buffler and a knife to cut it with. But those son of a bitches had taken both his knife and his rifle. Well, he would eat roots. Living with the Pawnees and knowing their ways came in handy sometimes.

Before that day was half over, he collapsed with weariness. He had begun by crawling along the creek. With every movement one of his wounds opened and bled. He nearly passed out a couple of times from the pain and was so weak that he felt like he was carrying a mule on his back. He had only been able to make about a mile all day, and he told himself that he would have to do better tomorrow because he didn't figure to get any stronger just eating roots. But telling himself didn't help. He wasn't sure that he could move at all tomorrow.

He did move, though. Another mile, and it felt about the same. On the third day he thought he went somewhat farther. But he would never make two hundred and fifty miles this way.

A couple of days later he heard wolves yipping close

by on the plain. He crawled up the bank to take a look. They were harassing a buffalo calf. He watched with desperate hope while they brought the calf down and began to tear away the flesh ravenously. He waited and waited, calculating what he was going to do, until the calf was nearly half gone. He had to have that meat. But he had no hope of scaring off the wolves if he went up on all fours. They would see that he was a crippled man and would attack, as a predator will attack any crippled enemy. He bided his time and got set in his mind.

At last the wolves slowed down in their gorging. They were full now, feeling heavy of belly and sluggish. Glass, taking along his driftwood club, crawled to within fifty yards of the carcass. Already the wolves had noticed him and were beginning to stir. He couldn't wait any longer. Leaning heavily on the club, he tried to stand up for the first time since Old Ephraim downed him. His mind reeled, and he felt like his body must be swaying like an old bull shot and about to fall. When he began to be steady, he held onto the club and cut loose with a fantastic screech, a Pawnee war cry. The wolves scattered a few feet and then began to ease back toward the calf. He walked straight forward now, depending on the club, letting loose with the screech again and again, rocking like a dinghy pitching on a heavy sea. The wolves slunk off.

When he reached the calf, Glass knelt down slowly, clinging to his crutch, trying not to break his wounds open any worse. What blood he was losing, he thought, he would get back right here. He tore at the raw flesh, and he stuffed great chunks into his mouth. I'm gonna live, he thought, I'm gonna live.

Hugh stayed by the carcass for several days, sleeping on the lee side at night, gorging himself on liver and heart and blood and intestine during the day. He stayed until the flesh began to go so bad that even he could smell it, used to it as he was.

When he left that spot, he was walking upright. It made him feel like a lord. Now he was high enough to see over the scrub brush that covered the plains. He could watch for bears, or Indians. He might be able to kill a rabbit or a badger if he was quick and lucky. But most of all it just felt different with his head up. Instead of staring into the sandy soil all the time, he could look around from horizon to horizon. He felt like a man again, not a four-legged crittur.

His wounds were better now. They all seemed to be on the way to healing, except for a bad one that was infected high on his back where he couldn't reach it. If he went slow and steady, he could make ten miles in a day now. He did go slow and steady. His mind bounced between jubilation at being alive to ornery vengefulness at having been left to die alone. The two drove him down the Grand to where it meets the Missouri and south along the great river toward Fort Kiowa. There Ashley was known and an Ashley man's credit would be good. He would get a new outfit, gun, knife, flint, powder, ball, and other possibles. And from there he would turn around, head up-river, and get the men who abandoned him.

He made Fort Kiowa in the second week of October. It had been seven weeks since the grizzly had had her whacks at him. He had survived six of those weeks alone, and had risen from the state of near-corpse to crawl and walk some two hundred and fifty miles through hostile territory with no way to get meat and no protection from the marauding Rees. It astounded the trader Cayewa Brazeau, who ran Fort Kiowa.

Hugh was proud, but he was not enough impressed

with himself to give his battered body a rest. Brazeau was outfitting a mackinaw to go up to the Mandan villages. The wilderness grapevine reported that the Rees had bought a village from the Mandans, who lived in permanent huts and not tipis. The Rees had given the peaceful Mandans a promise of good behavior. Brazeau thought that now might be the time for a peaceful mission to re-establish trade with both tribes. He had six men, led by Antoine Citoleux and including the famous Charboneau, of the Lewis and Clark expedition, to make the journey. He was glad to add a seventh hand, Hugh Glass—though he must have thought the fellow was a bit queer, starting right out like that. After what Hugh had been through, though, it didn't seem like such a big deal. He'd made up his mind to the thing.

Citoleux was nervous. He made his will, just in case. The party began to get close to the Mandan villages, in what is now North Dakota, in the fourth week of November. Abruptly Charboneau decided to get out and walk. The Ree village was a mile south of the Mandan village, and Tilton's Fort was up by the Mandans. Charboneau wanted to circle around the Ree village on the west bank and go directly into Tilton's Fort. His medicine told him something. He trusted the Mandans, but not the Rees. The Frenchmen who made up the boat's crew just laughed. The next day Glass also put in to shore. The Missouri makes a considerable bend just below the villages. Hugh had no business at the villages or the fort. He could move faster and over a shorter route by himself cutting overland. So he set out.

A few miles across he saw several squaws. Rees, he noticed. They disappeared quickly. Glass figured they had gone for their men and started running. His wounds still bothered him some, and he couldn't make much

time. Soon several braves came after him, mounted and
screeching. Hugh saw he didn't have a chance. Maybe his
luck, which had gotten him through two impossible situations, had just played out. Just when the Rees were within
rifle shot. Glass heard hooves from the opposite direction. Mandans. Being ridden down from two sides, Hugh
just stood and waited for whatever was going to happen.
One of the Mandans pulled him up on the horse behind,
and sprinted off toward the upper village.

The Rees had attracted the Mandans' attention with
their whooping. The Mandans were tired of the Rees'
troublemaking, and afraid that the whites might take their
revenge against both tribes. So they delivered Hugh to
their village, where he found Charboneau. That evening,
at the fort, they got the news that the party in the mackinaw had been slaughtered on the river by the Rees.

Hugh figured, with what he had come through, he didn't
have much to worry about traveling on to Fort Henry. The
next day he took off, only taking the precaution of walking along the east bank of the Missouri where he was less
likely to run into Rees, Assiniboins, or Blackfeet. Most
tribes were unpredictable; the Blackfeet, alone among the
plains tribes, were always hostile to whites. Had been,
since John Colter had run away from them. Last time he
heard, they had been plaguing Fort Henry like devils.

The snow was a foot deep now. Sometimes the wind
swept down cuttingly from the north. The Missouri here
flows through country bare of timber, and the wind could
run unobstructed for miles. He hunted along the way, spent
some cold nights, and got within sight of Fort Henry, 300
river miles from the Mandans, in less than three weeks.
He tied some logs together with bark to cross the icy
river. But he had already begun to suspect that something
was wrong. In the fort he found only some friendly Sioux,

exercising squatters' rights. The Henry brigade had gone up the Yellowstone, they said, to the Big Horn. That doubled the length of Hugh's lone journey, and took him still higher into mountain country. He started straight out through the snow.

On the night of December 31, 1823, Andrew Henry's brigade was celebrating the new year inside the new Fort Henry. They had reason: They had relocated from Blackfoot country to Crow country, after losing life after life to the Blackfeet. The Crows seemed nothing but friendly. The trapping in the fall hunt had equaled the Missouri trapping, if not topped it. They were finally about to take some beaver and make some money. They had found Indians who would trade pelts instead of stealing them. The country was good, sheltered enough, and with plenty of buffalo for the long winter. The life looked good.

They barely heard the pounding on the gate above the howling wind. Someone stumbled through the driving snow to open for whatever Indians might be there. What he saw he couldn't believe for a moment: the grizzled, hoar-frosted ghost of Hugh Glass, his hair, beard, and buckskins whitened by caked ice. Glass strode on into the room where the men were celebrating. The debauch stopped dead. "It's Glass you're seeing," Hugh said bluntly, "where's Fitzgerald and Bridger?" One man edged forward and touched Hugh to see if he was solid. The others barraged him with questions he couldn't sort out, much less answer. "It's Glass," he said. "Fitzgerald and Bridger went off and left me, goddamn 'em. Even took my rifle and my possibles. I been to Kiowa and the Mandans and I come to square with them. Where are they?"

Henry said that Fitzgerald was gone—gone downriver—given up and returned to the settlements. Why, Glass must have passed him on the river, him and Black Harris, going down in a canoe. Henry stalled a bit. Harris was taking an express down to Ashley, he went on, and Fitzgerald and another fellow went with him—mustered out, just quit. Looks like Fitzgerald wasn't much account anyway.

"Don't back me off," Glass snapped. "Where in hell's Bridger?"

Stuck, Henry just pointed into a corner. Bridger had been shrinking there since Glass materialized from the dead. He had been shouldering a secret, festering wrong all these months, relieved only by the knowledge that dead men tell no tales. And here stood a dead man, sent back by the devils of hell against Jim Bridger, who more than half believed in ghosts. Stunned, he could hardly keep his mind conscious against the welling of guilt, hardly considering whether this specter were dead or alive.

Hugh stared at the man he had pursued for a thousand miles. Bridger had the look of a man ready to be killed and go to hell for his mortal sin. He wasn't going to say anything. He looked pathetic, and pathetically young.

One of the two men he had pursued, Glass corrected himself. He remembered the scene of the two leaving him, and Bridger coming over and taking the rifle and knife. He hated Bridger. He remembered what he could of the words Fitzgerald had hit Bridger with at the time, words that struck fear into the boy. Glass wavered. Bridger had committed the unpardonable sin, not of God, but of the mountain man: Never skip out on your friends in a fix. Glass glared at him. But he was just a boy.

"It's Glass, Bridger—the one you left to die, and not only left, but robbed. Robbed of them things as might have helped him survive, alone and crippled, on them plains. I came back because I swore I'd put you under. I had that notion in front of me when I crawled across the prairie starving and walked up the river alone, just to get this one job done, to make you a dead niggur like you tried to make me. But I see you're ashamed and sorry. I think you might have stayed by me if Fitzgerald hadn't got on you. You don't have to be afraid of me. I forgive you. You're just a kid."

Bridger's face didn't show relief, or anything else in particular. He looked dazed or maybe sick. Glass felt lighter and easier, having gotten all those words out at once. He sat down, someone handed him a glass of whisky, and within a few minutes he had passed out.

Bridger felt almost nauseated with guilt and shame. He had been let off because he was a kid. He'd rather have been put under there and then.

When Glass woke up, he lazed around, thinking of starting downriver after Fitzgerald. The laze stretched on for several days. The idea didn't seem to be goading him quite as hard now. He told himself that it was a bad winter, and he might as well wait for better weather. And he listened to himself.

In a few more days Glass found his vendetta route: Henry wanted to send a dispatch to Ashley. He intended to tell Ashley about the abandoning of the original Fort Henry, the new post among the Crows, and the upswing in business. And he wanted to add some bad news—that Ashley had better find another partner. Major Andrew Henry, who had been run out of the mountains by Blackfeet in 1810, had lost a lot of men and horses to the Blackfeet the last two years, and had had five casualties among thirteen men on last autumn's cross-country to the mouth of the Yellowstone, didn't care that business was looking good. Henry was the unluckiest brigade captain who ever led men into the mountains. He meant to quit the business, and fast—as soon as spring broke up the ice and he could get a boat down the Missouri.

Who better to take the message down to Ashley than Hugh Glass, who was demonstrably the luckiest man in the mountains and kept coming up when he should have gone down? As for Hugh, it meant he would be paid handsomely to make a trip he was going to make anyway, to get his revenge. The dispatch had to go to Fort Atkinson, where it could be taken by government courier to Ashley in St. Louis. At the fort, Hugh would make inquiries about Fitzgerald, and track the bastard down. Four men, Marsh, Chapman, More, and Dutton, decided to go along to give the party some strength; two were going for company money, and two were quitting the mountains.

They left on February 29, 1824. Having in mind to miss the worst weather and take a shorter route besides, they went south, up the Powder River to its headwaters, and crossed to the Platte River, instead of going northeast to the frozen Missouri and then southeast along the river; from there they could follow the river directly east to Fort Atkinson at Council Bluffs.

By the time they struck the Platte, spring was on its way and the ice was breaking up. Mountain men never walked where there was a river to carry them, so the five stopped and built a bullboat. The Platte was too shallow to float almost any kind of boat. Bullboats were the exception. They were generally saucer round, were made from buffalo skin stretched over limbs and caulked with buffalo fat, and had almost no draft. Glass and his comrades pushed off downstream close to the end of March. It looked like a lark to Hugh. He not only had companions, he was headed into the territory of his brothers, the Pawnees. Fat country to a mountain man, with plenty of buffalo, the sun warming the land with a gentle hand, the cottonwoods beginning to turn green, and Indians who would treat him like a long-lost brother.

Where the Laramie comes into the Platte, where Fort Laramie was to be later on, the travelers spotted a sizable cluster of Indian lodges. Some braves came down the bank and waved, gave the sign language for peace, and called out for their white brothers to put in. Hugh would have paddled by, except for one thing the Indians couldn't guess: He recognized their lingo. They were Pawnees. He explained to his friends and put straight to the bank.

Hugh clambered out of the bullboat addressing the Indians in their own language, and identified himself as their brother and the son of one of their great chiefs. They put their arms around him, one at a time, and greeted him solemnly and gladly. He told the others to get out of the boat and come into the village. They were going to get a good feed. Besides, Pawnee women were as willing and as much fun as any squaws, and white men were still a novelty among them. And leave your rifles, he said. You don't need them, and it's an insult for a friend to bring weapons into a Pawnee camp. You might rile them.

Glass and three of his companions went to the tipi of the highest-ranking Indian and settled down for a smoke and a feed. Dutton stayed near the boat, suspicious. As the squaws were bustling around to serve their guests, Glass heard something telling: The language of the Pawnees and Rees was almost identical, but the Rees pronounced certain words differently. That squaw was a Ree. He knew by that way of talking. He looked around quickly and carefully. Impossible that the Rees could be three hundred miles from their territory. But he was sure now, and he spoke low: "These are Rees. Let's cache."

One of the leaders understood English and replied,

"No, we're Pawnees." But Glass wasn't about to listen. The four cleared out and ran for the boat. The Rees came after them, screeching.

Dutton was already in mid-river in the bullboat when they reached the shore. Their rifles were gone, of course. They scattered.

Within five minutes Glass was crouched in a crevice in some rocks, hoping the Rees would miss him in the falling darkness. More was cut down in Glass's sight; then Chapman was killed close by. Glass huddled further down. While he waited for blackness, hearing nearby the awful cries of glee over the mutilated bodies, he figured out what had happened: The Rees had split up after the Arikara campaign. One band had gone to live with the Mandans; another band had disappeared westward, no one knew where. Well, they had come a long way to join their near-relatives the Pawnees, just where Glass would run into them. And they were mean as ever. Hell of a thing for a hoss to run in with the same band of Indians three times in nine months in three entirely different places and damn near get rubbed out three times. His luck was running bad.

Glass snuck out of the rocks and made some miles downriver before daylight. Then he cached in some rocks and took stock. Maybe his luck wasn't so bad after all. "Although I had lost my rifle and all my plunder," he said later, "I felt quite rich when I found my knife, flint, and steel in my shot pouch. These little fixens make a man feel right peart when he is three or four hundred miles from anybody or anyplace." Especially if the same man was left in the same fix eight months before without any fixens, and without able arms and legs. Wagh! He'd done it before and he could do it again. Besides, he still had Fitzgerald to even up with.

Hugh changed his aim from Fort Atkinson to Fort Kiowa. It was four hundred miles away, which was closer than Atkinson. He had no worry with food this time: The cows had recently dropped, and he could easily catch up with the calves only a few days old. He made meat as often as he felt inclined, and hit Fort Kiowa in May.

When he got on down to Fort Atkinson with the letter for Ashley, he got a couple of surprises and gave a couple. Dutton and Marsh had arrived before him, having joined up and come together down the Platte. They had reported him dead at last, and here he was again. The other surprise was mutual—with John Fitzgerald. Fitzgerald had heard that Glass was alive from Cayewa Brazeau up at Kiowa last December, and had been relieved to find out from Marsh and Dutton just a couple of weeks before that the old man had gone down. Yet here he was, not only alive, but murderous.

Hugh was right gratified to find Fitzgerald, until he found out one thing: Fitzgerald was now a member of the U. S. Army, and killing him would get a man executed. Hugh blustered into the office of Captain Riley, demanding fair play. The officer brought Fitzgerald in.

Finally. There Fitzgerald stood, hangdog as Hugh could want. Funny, though, he couldn't hate the niggur quite as much as he wanted to. Maybe he'd had too much good luck of late to keep all that hating cached up inside. "You ran out on me dyin'," he accused Fitzgerald. "You was paid well enough, and you said you'd stay till I was good or gone down. But you got scared and run off. And you stole what I might have lived by. Stole it so you could get some money that wasn't yourn and so nobody'd know what you done. Well, I count you got something to think on the rest of your string."

Riley dismissed Fitzgerald and made Glass an offer. If

Glass would clear out, Riley would give him back his rifle and other possibles, and stake him what he needed to get started again. Hugh took it.[2]

He decided though, to try his luck somewhere else. He set out with a band headed for Santa Fe. For four years he trapped the streams of the Southwest. In 1829 he came back to Yellowstone country as a free trapper. In 1833 he tried his luck against the Rees once more. It had played out. Rees killed and scalped him and his companion, Edward Rose.

Glass, though, had become a grizzled legend to the men he shared robes, campfires, and fat cow with. He went jauntily at death four times in a row in one year, and came away with the upper hand. He had mountain luck. He showed incredible skill, endurance, and courage. With those, he survived in fact, and has survived in legend.

SECOND INTERLUDE

The Trapper and Trapping

THE FIRST MISSIONARY WHO CAME WEST TO SERVE *the Indians (Jason Lee, in 1834) was put off by their savage demeanor. He was even more put off by the uncivilized style of the mountain men. For they looked like Indians and they acted like Indians. Maybe Indians couldn't help it. But for white men to carry on like that—repulsive.*

If Lee's judgment was questionable, his observation was accurate. The men who went up the river to trap beaver adopted Indian ways speedily. Within six months they wore an incongruous blend of white and Indian clothing. Their boots had given out and were replaced by moccasins. Moccasins went well in the mountains once a man learned to walk in a glide, putting his whole foot down at once instead of clomping the heel down first. And they could be replaced easily. You gave a squaw a little vermilion or a tiny mirror and she would get you shod. You tried to be careful, though, to get the moccasins made of skins that had been used for lodges and exposed to the constant smoke; if they weren't smoked, they would shrink when they got wet and send a man limping to the creek in the middle of the night to soak them again so he could sleep.

The cloth pants were gone too—ripped—and long since replaced with buckskin. Buckskin wore forever, eventually getting black and hard with grease, and you didn't have to pay a price jacked way up because someone had brought your pants by horseback from St. Louis. The fringes came in handy, too, for various repairs. Likewise you wore a buckskin capote, a loose affair that draped you from shoulders to knees, over a buckskin shirt. If the squaw who made them for you had decorated your clothes with beads and porcupine quills, and your face was well weathered, you might look Indian enough to fool a greenhorn.

Most mountain men went beyond dress in becoming Indian. They learned Indian skills. They learned Indian dances. They could be as terrifying as any Blackfoot when they let out their war whoops. Even Indian medicine made more sense than white religion to a lot of them, and some adopted Indian religion.

They sat cross-legged on the ground, first from necessity and then through preference. They lived in lodges made of animal skins, slept in buffalo robes and, worst of all, they lived with Indian squaws. Many a white woman starting on the Oregon Trail muttered "heathen" under her breath when she first saw the ex-trapper who was to be her guide.

The mountain man didn't outfit himself like a white man either. He had no possessions other than what he could carry on his back, because Indians might run off his horses at any time. He had a Hawken rifle (muzzle-loading), a pistol, a Green River (the brand name of his knife), some powder, some balls, traps, a horn of medicine to bait beaver, flint and steel, pipe and tobacco, and some odds and ends. Some of this gear he carried on his belt or slung over a shoulder, where he could get at it in a hurry. The rest of it he carried in his possible sack. The mountain man was a roving man, and all he carried were the fixings that kept a man alive.

His reason for being in the Rocky Mountain country—or at least the reason he gave people back in the settlements— was the beaver. The beaver streams were the original gold mines of the West. When no one knew about the gold and silver lying around like gravel for the taking, everyone knew about beaver. The beaver grew the one fur better than any other for making felt hats; that's why the fanciest and most expensive hats were called "beavers." Beaver pelts would bring five dollars a pound in St. Louis. That lure had drawn men across the continent when there were still plenty of unsettled areas east of the Mississippi. Five dollars a pound if a man could get them to St. Louis. And the Rockies running over with beaver! Just west of the mountains, the tale went, you didn't have to trap them. You could kill them with clubs.

After the white men stopped relying on the Indian trade for pelts, they took them by trapping. It was a skilled operation: The trapper watched the creek or river *for the slack water and the beaver dam that had created it. Then he walked downstream and waded back up toward a likely place, killing the man smell. He set the heavy trap—traps weighed five pounds each and cost upwards from ten dollars—in shallow water, and pinned the trap chain to the bottom in deeper water with a stick driven down. Otherwise, the beaver would drag the trap onto the bank and get loose by gnawing the clamped paw off. Then the essential touch: He dipped a stick into his horn of castoreum, and planted the stick near the trap, so that the beaver would stand up by the trap to sniff the stuff.*

The idea was to make the beaver come to medicine. Castoreum is a scrotal secretion of the beaver, probably used in mating and in defining territory. A trapper depended on it to draw the beaver to the trap. When caught, the beaver would usually head for deep water and, held down by the trap, it would drown. If the prey managed to pull the stick out of the creek bottom and go some distance with the trap, the stick would float and identify the spot. (There lies the origin of the expression "the way the stick floats," meaning "what it means," or "signifies.") All this done, the trapper waded back down and out of the creek, at a safe distance. Since these were all mountain streams, largely snow-fed, the bones of his legs ached by that time from the awful cold. He generally set a line of half a dozen traps; and checked them at sunset and sundown. When the catch fell off, he would move on to another area.

The trapper's movements were dictated by the beaver. Spring fur was the best, thick after the long winter. Summer fur was too thin to be worth his effort. Fall fur was good again. In winter, the weather kept the trappers holed up. So they traveled up and down streams in the

*spring and fall; they sat out the winter in lodges, often
enough making their camps with friendly Indians. And in
the summer they gathered from all over the West to one
selected spot, usually a comfortable valley, for a rendezvous. Here they met the packtrain sent up from the States
with supplies, and traded the year's plews for balls, powder,
traps, whisky, and doodads for presents for the Indians. As
it turned out, even a trapper who had an exceptional year
gave up his plews for only a little in the way of supplies.
The mark-up from St. Louis price to mountain price might
go as high as two thousand percent.*

III

Falstaff's Battalion

WHEN MAJOR ANDREW HENRY STARTED IN COMMAND
of a brigade for Fort Henry in September of 1823, he left
William Ashley, Jedediah Smith, and another brigade at
Fort Kiowa chafing at the bit. They didn't have enough
horses to get going west.

Ashley and Henry now had three groups of men engaged in an enterprise that was getting more desperate by
the day. In a year and a half they had managed to get their
men shot to pieces several times. They had taken no beaver to speak of, and had no particular prospects of getting
any. At the moment, twenty of their men were waiting for
Henry at the mouth of the Yellowstone; more than a
dozen, including Hugh Glass and Jim Bridger, were
marching west under Henry; another sixteen or so were
lying around uselessly at Fort Kiowa. General Ashley

was wondering whether his grand enterprise, intended to make him independently wealthy, might not turn him into a pauper.

Ashley and Henry had gotten the business started in the spring of 1822. Their concept was simple—to compete with the Missouri Fur Company for beaver along the Missouri River by pushing all the way to the river's sources in the Rocky Mountains. Missouri Fur had opened the business a decade and a half earlier, when Manuel Lisa and John Colter trapped and traded high on the river, but it had gone badly. Henry himself, as a brigade leader, was chased out of the area of the sources of the Missouri (called the Three Forks) by the Blackfeet and quit the fur trade. Lisa had had some success, but business had languished in the last ten years.

Ashley and Henry had started with just one new idea. Instead of hiring their trappers as employees, they would contract with them for half their furs and make them substantially free agents. Otherwise, the old procedures: ascend the Missouri by keelboat, a slow and ugly proposition; get the furs, called plews, by some trapping and a lot of trading with the Indians; operate out of forts for safety; and float the plews back down to market.

The plans had not gone well. In 1822, Henry got set with Fort Henry at the mouth of the Yellowstone, but the trappers he sent further up the Missouri lost some lives to the Blackfeet. In 1823, Ashley got another bunch of recruits headed upriver to join Henry and augment the trapping forces, but they ran into serious trouble at the Arikara villages. The Rees had attacked them, killed fifteen, and forced them to retreat. Ashley had shored up with reinforcements from Henry, brought downriver, and had solicited the help of the Missouri Fur Company and the U. S. Army. But the campaign against the Rees turned into a farce. Ashley backed down the river in a bad mood. He had lost men and money. The river was closed to him. He had no choice but to try to make the fur trade work by land. That had not been tried.

The General, assessing his position, had reason to be discouraged.

The balance would swing according to the caliber of the men he hired. They were an odd assortment. Some were hard-living, hard-drinking, hard-bragging voyageurs— rivermen; they were strong but unreliable; they were reported to be cowards. Others were young adventurers, out for a taste of the wild; they were unknown quantities. Or they were bound boys run away from their masters, or men on the lam from the law, or other kinds of outcasts.

Jim Clyman had helped Ashley round up the 1823 bunch. Ashley told him that willing hands would likely be found "in grog Shops and other sinks of degradation." Clyman obliged, and then summed up the crew succinctly: "A discription of our crew I cannt give but Fallstaf's Battalion was genteel in comparison."[1]

Falstaff's battalion had got the hell shot out of it at the Arikara villages. Henry had then taken half of it toward the fort on the Yellowstone. Ashley looked over the other half and wondered. His hope rested mainly with the young man he had chosen to lead this brigade, Jedediah Strong Smith.

Smith, though only twenty-four, had demonstrated his courage and expertise a number of times. He had gone up the previous year with Henry, and was chosen to go alone downriver to take a message to Ashley. In the Ree attack he was trapped on a beach under heavy fire, but distinguished himself in leading the return fire and then the retreat. When Ashley asked for a volunteer to carry a plea for help to Henry, about three hundred miles away through rugged country, Smith stepped forward, and had gotten through. Ashley responded by getting him designated captain in the Ree campaign and by putting him in charge of this outfit.

Jed Smith was clearly an unusual young man. He was well educated. He had a keen intelligence. He was deeply religious: At the burial of one of the men killed by the Rees, Jed had surprised everyone by offering a touching prayer. He was solemn, quiet, and ambitious. Ashley and everyone else could see that he would have prospered back in civilization. No one knew quite why, aside from his love of hunting, he had chosen to go to the Rocky Mountains with an assembly of outcasts and misfits. But Ashley saw in Smith one excellence which would make him a leader. In a land that meant constant danger and hardship, he had the one quality of character that mattered most: He never waited, doubted, dawdled, or hesitated in the face of events. Confident, capable, eager to act, he moved forward to meet them.

Ashley was lucky in some of his other recruits too. Here was Tom Fitzpatrick, also twenty-four, a slender Irishman full of drive and intelligence. Bill Sublette, a tall, thin, gaunt, strong-willed man. Jim Clyman, a lank, grave, slow spoken Virginian who fancied Shakespeare and turned a few verses himself. And Edward Rose, a mixture of white, black, and red blood who looked like a villain, fought savagely, and had an explosive temper.

When Ashley got together enough horses to carry the provisions but not the men, Smith marched them west. He intended to strike up the White River, across the Black Hills, and into the center of Crow country. There he would join an outfit sent up the Bighorn by Henry. The Crows had been unswervingly friendly to the white man, and their lands were full of plews. The route had never been tried, but that didn't matter to Smith. He had a borrowed guide for the first quarter of the journey, and his mountain sense for the rest.

They followed the guide up White Clay Creek, a small stream running thick with white sediment. It tasted pungently sweet. The guide warned the men that it would bind their bowels tight, but they drank it greedily. On the third day out, around noon, the guide advised them to carry all the water possible. They were going to cut across a large bend in the river, and the next water was twenty-four hours away. Scooping up what little they could, they trudged on through the dry, rolling hills. That night they camped in a spot bristling so with cactus that they could barely find room to spread their blankets. Before noon the next day they came on the water hole. It was baked dry, so dry that digging didn't make any sense. They rested and walked on. It was fifteen miles to the river.

That afternoon, the brigade straggled out all over the countryside. The men's eyes stung from the alkali dust. Their tongues swelled in their mouths until they couldn't speak. Their minds wandered into half-fantasy. The guide managed to goad his horse on faster than the others and moved out of sight. The men strayed off to the left and to the right in half-conscious hopes of finding water. The company spread out over a mile.

Jim Clyman found his packhorse more cooperative than the others. He pushed hard in the direction he had last seen the guide. Looking over his shoulder from time to time, he wondered whether the outfit would ever get back together again, or whether some of the men might not wander off into the sagebrush, sink down, and die.

He swung off to the right of the guide's path. And there—providential sight—he stumbled on a water hole.

Clyman fired his rifle as he charged into the water. He even outran his horse. Standing shoulder deep, he soaked it up with his body, gulped it down, dunked his head, wallowed in it. After a bit he clambered out and fired his rifle again. He saw another man and horse. This time the horse outsprinted the man and splashed in first. As soon as the man could wet his throat enough, he halloed. One by one they labored in, fired their rifles, dunked, and shouted. By dark all had gotten to the hole except for Captain Smith and two others. Captain Smith had been bringing up the rear to herd wanderers in the right direction.

The young, slender Smith walked in through the falling dusk. He waded into the water and took his ease for a moment. Then he said that the other two had given out and he had buried them up to their heads in the sand. Keep them from drying out, he said. He looked around and added that since he felt like he could still walk, he would go back after them. He took a kettle of water, a horse, and rode out as collectedly as he had walked in. He brought the exhausted men in during the night. The next morning they walked four or five miles on to the river. The guide was sitting calmly on the bank waiting for them.

Higher up the valley of White Clay Creek they came onto a band of Sioux and traded for enough horses to get the brigade mounted. The guide turned back with the horses borrowed at Fort Kiowa. They rode on to the Chienne River and came into its badlands. The soil was loose and grayish. In a misty rain it stuck to the horses' hooves in great globs. It was bad going—not a foot of level land in sight; a bewildering maze of ravines and canyons crisscrossing everywhere, and all of it moving toward the

Missouri River as fast as the rain could carry it. Finally they got into the Black Hills. They seemed delightfully alpine after the dusty plains, and the men found some hazelnuts and plums.

As they labored down the ravines and ridges on the west side of the Black Hills, the horses began to fail. Smith thought he must have reached the sources of the Powder River, the edge of Crow country, so he sent Rose on ahead to find the Crows and left three men behind to wait while five horses recuperated. Rose had lived with Crows and spoke their language.

In a brushy bottom, while the men were leading their horses in single file, a grizzly charged into the line and then lumbered toward the front. Smith challenged it. By the time they drove the bear off, Smith was sprawled on the ground and bleeding. Clyman checked him over. Old Ephraim had broken several ribs. He had also gotten Jed's head into his mouth. The left eye was gashed. The skull near the crown was stripped bare. The right ear was hanging by a thread. Everyone stood about wondering what someone else would do. Finally Clyman asked Smith what should be done. The captain said, "One or two go for water. Get a needle and thread and sew up the wounds around my head."

Clyman figured that if Smith, bleeding profusely, had enough gumption to give instructions, then Clyman had enough to stitch him up. He floundered and fretted, Smith coaching him all the way. Finally he managed to sew the edges of the wounds back together except for the severed ear. He said he couldn't do anything about it. "Stitch it together some way," said Smith. Clyman looked, hesitated, and began to poke the needle through the various edges and pull the thread tight enough that flesh would touch flesh.

Water was about a mile away. Smith lifted himself onto his horse, rode the mile, and then let the men install him in the only tent. In ten days he was ready to ride. The scarred ear, the missing eyebrow, and the scalp scars would clearly stay with him the rest of his life. The men looked at him with renewed respect. Each wondered if he would have that kind of poise and presence of mind.

Clyman used the recovery time to explore the area. He discovered that the Chienne or Shian River drained the west slope of the Black Hills as well as the east, so they were not to the Powder River yet. He also found a slate quarry where Moses must have received the stone tablets with the Ten Commandments, and a grove where the trees were turned to stone, for a fact.

When they did get to the Powder River, Rose brought in some sixteen Crows who offered to share winter camp with the white men. Jed drove his men on across the Big Horn Mountains, through mazes of hills handsomely supplied with game, across the Big Horn River, and up the valley of Wind River. By the time they found the Crow camp they were exhausted, and the season of the hard cold was on them.[2]

The Crow people and Crow country were remarkable. The Crow men were tall, handsome, and statuesque; the women were handsome rather than beautiful, but they made up for that with their passion for white men. Men and women alike had a keen, ribald sense of fun; Crows were the practical jokers of the mountains. Babies were strapped onto horses before they could walk, so all Crows were superb horsemen. Their women had such skill in making clothes and moccasins that even the tribes at war with the Crows would stop to trade for them. And Crows had proved peaceable with whites. From the time of John Colter forward they fought with most of the neighboring tribes, but never with the trappers. Their only vice as far as the trappers were concerned was that they loved to steal horses. They would talk candidly about their horse-stealing episodes even with the men they had stolen from. Neither the whites nor the Crows let a little pilfered horseflesh stand in the way of friendship, though. The Crows told the trappers frankly that they would never kill whites; if they did, the whites would stay away from Crow country and the Crows would not be able to make off with their horses.

The Crows called their land Absaroka, land of the Sparrow Hawk people. They held that it was the best country in the world. "The Great Spirit," claimed one chief, "has put it exactly in the right place; while you are in it you fare well; whenever you go out of it, whichever way you travel, you fare worse. . . . To the south, you have to wander over great barren plains; the water is warm and bad. . . . To the north it is cold; the winters are long and bitter, with no grass; you cannot keep horses there, but must travel with dogs. What is a country without horses? On the Columbia they are poor and dirty, paddle about in canoes, and eat fish. . . . They are always taking fish-bones out of their mouths. . . . To the east, they dwell in villages; they live well; but they drink the muddy water of the Missouri— that is bad. A Crow's dog would not drink such water. . . . The Crow country . . . has snowy mountains and sunny plains; all kinds of climates and good things for every season. When the summer heats scorch the prairies, you can draw up under the mountains, where the air is sweet and cool, the grass fresh, and the bright streams come tumbling out of the snow-banks. There you can hunt the elk, the deer, and the antelope, when their skins are fit for dressing. . . . In the autumn, when your horses are strong and fat from the mountain pastures, you can go down into the plains and hunt the buffalo. . . . And when winter comes on, you can take shelter in the woody bottoms along the rivers; there you will find buffalo meat for yourselves and cotton-wood bark for your horses: or you may winter in the Wind River valley, where there is salt weed in abundance. The Crow country is exactly in the right place. Everything good is to be found there. There is no country like the Crow country."[3]

The mountain men found it well supplied with water, wood, and game. Even better, they found it full of high-quality plews. Even in St. Louis, people knew that Crow beaver was better than Missouri River beaver. With good companionship, lessons in mountain craft from the reigning native experts, and plenty of sex, the trappers passed a happy winter on the Wind River.

But Jed Smith was eager to move on. The Crows had told him about the country just over the mountains. There the creeks were so jammed with beaver that a man didn't need to trap them. He could club them on the banks. Jed had to see that. Besides, he had a private project. He wanted to make a map of the West and have it published back in the States. He wanted to see what he hadn't yet seen.

So, in February, well before the snow started melting, he moved his brigade north along the foot of the Wind River Mountains and tried to force his way through a high pass. Too soon. Deep snow forced them back to the Crow camp. There he consulted with his friends about how to cross the mountains. They drew lines with their fingers on a buffalo robe heaped with sand piles representing mountains. The way was south along the Wind River range. There, not far from the head of a river called the Popo Agie, a wide gap opened. Beyond, was a river called the Siskadee, on the west side of the continental divide.

Around the first of March winter oppresses the high valley of the Popo Agie. The cold has driven the buffalo to lower elevations where they can paw through the thinner snow to the grass. The snow has drifted so that the shape of the land is deceptive, hollows and rises smoothed over. One color dominates, a white that stretches to the sky on either side and is fringed by the black of high ridges. Nothing here reminds the men of earth or of living things.

The company is hungry. It has had no fresh meat since it left Wind River. Jim Clyman and Bill Sublette push out ahead in the vague hope of finding game in a frozen waste.

The horses labor through snow, alternately deep and shallow, and struggle up the steep incline. The wind sweeps off the ridges like a personal enemy. Bill draws his capote tighter and turns his head away, but the wind whirls around and snaps back into his face, a demon amusing itself. His blanket is crusted with ice around his face. His breath has frozen on his whiskers. When he gets his blanket too near his eyes, the lashes freeze to it. He has not felt anything in his hands and feet for several hours. But they ride up, scanning the flats and slopes, until the sun disappears behind the mountains above them to the west, and throws the valley of the Popo Agie into cold, purple shadow.

Just then they spot three bulls standing in the open about a mile away. They look at each other and admit that the horses are not up to a chase. So they dismount, prime their rifles, and start crawling across the snow and the hard, patchy ice. They don't notice the cold much now, but the light powder spits up in their faces. They don't know whether they'll be able to get close enough for a shot before the bulls see them.

One of the bulls lifts his head, paws, fidgets, and looks about to break. He's seen them. Too long a shot for a sure kill. They both spring up, steady their Hawkens, and fire. The bulls thunder off. But one runs strangely. Maybe a broken shoulder. So Bill hurries back toward the horses and Jim follows on foot. The bulls are running up. Maybe he can pen the wounded one near the ridge a mile away. He trots as fast as he can go, sometimes sinking into the snow, sometimes crunching across ice until he breaks through. He cuts through some timber, and when he comes out, there stands the bull in easy range.

He raises his rifle, his shoulders heaving with his gasping breaths, points it almost carelessly, and lets fly again. Luck: The bull sways and pitches forward into a small gulley.

By dark they have stripped some of the meat off. They gnaw at it raw. They have struck small fires several times, burning sagebrush, but the north wind scatters the fire as fast as they build it. Finally, they give up and crawl into their blankets. The wind is still wilder now and whips snow at them from every angle. After a few minutes they begin to feel the real cold—seeping in through their blankets from the packed snow underneath. They wriggle all night in their blankets, unable to sleep, stirred by images of their arms and legs frozen into permanent crouches by morning, their eyelids frozen open, and their bodies cold as ice-covered stones.

At dawn, each discovers that the other is still alive. They mutter from blanket pile to blanket pile. After a few minutes, Jim agrees to get up and gather sagebrush for a fire while Bill tries to get his hands warm enough to grip flint and steel. But the steel is so cold that it grabs the skin and burns it. Neither can grip the flint and steel firmly enough to strike a spark. All right; they fire their rifles into the dry pile. Nothing. And nothing more to be done. Bill wraps back up in his robes and lies down to die.

Jim, though, isn't ready for that. He struggles with his saddle, hoping he can ride. When he cinches it on, he asks Bill whether he can ride if Jim saddles his horse. Bill says no. He doesn't even want to try. Jim tries again to strike fire. No luck. Finally he stands up, looks at Bill, and decides he has to leave. Bill will be dead before he can get back with the brigade. Jim just stands, staring down. Suddenly he gets an idea. He gropes in last night's little fire for a coal that might be warm. His finger is burned. He scrapes and sees a tiny coal, no bigger than a kernel of corn. Hoorah! He tosses it into the pile of sagebrush, and little flames spurt up. Hoorah again! In a minute he has a fine little blaze going.

They grin at each other and stick their hands and faces almost into the fire. The wind blows the smoke straight into their faces, but they pull it gladly into their lungs. After a few minutes, Jim saddles Bill's horse while Bill gathers sagebrush to keep the fire going. When they get started, Jim walks to stay warmer, but Bill crouches on his horse, half dead. In two hours, they make it to timber. Jim starts a fire while Bill sleeps, exhausted, on his robes. After half an hour Bill is gnawing broiled buffalo off a stick.[4]

The brigade rode across the ridge at the top of Popo Agie, down to the Sweetwater, and into the most violent wind they could remember. It had cleaned the south slopes of this gap in the mountains right down to the grass. It had also cleared the game out. For two nights and one day the men huddled sleepless in their blankets without a fire—the wind always kept sweeping it away. On the second morning Clyman and Branch, fed up with freezing and starving, walked down the Sweetwater into a little canyon and crawled behind some rocks out of the wind. Branch saw a mountain sheep on the rocks above and promptly shot it. The animal was kind enough to topple down at their feet. They packed the sheep back upstream and tried to broil it. But the wind still scattered the fire too fast. All crawled back into their blankets. In the middle of the night Clyman felt the wind lull, built a fire, and got the meat cooking. All the other trappers rose to the smell and spent the night chewing and yarning.

Finally, the brigade moved down to an aspen grove to wait out the weather a spell. Before the middle of March Jed Smith got them marching up again, toward Southern Pass.

The sky was brilliant with sunlight now, and cupped close overhead in the deep, intense blue peculiar to high mountains. Below, winter still toyed with them, jamming the hollows with soft, deep snow, and whisking the flats bare. The men's hats, shoulders, and faces glistened with caked ice as they rode upwards, single file. Occasionally, the wind would pounce on the snow and spew it up in small clouds, so that they rode in a snowstorm on a clear day. On the sixth day, Jed thought, they might have topped the pass. But the land looked level as the sea, and he could not be sure.

He sent Sublette and Clyman out again to hunt. The men had had nothing to eat for four days. When Jed brought the brigade up, Clyman and Sublette had just killed a buffalo. Everyone hacked at the steaming carcass and ate the flesh raw. Then they packed the meat and moved on, hoping to find wood for a fire. They failed. But Jed could look back, that twilight, to see that they were below the crest of the gap, and forward to see the slopes make a long incline. They had done it. They had found passage through the Rocky Mountains. Though they could see no water, and had to melt snow to drink, they now stood west of the continental divide, where all waters flowed to the Pacific.[5]

He told the men. They were too hungry, exhausted, and cold to cheer. They were not men to give serious voice to whatever the crossing meant to them. Neither was the lean, scarred, quiet young man who led them. He did not even form the words of satisfaction that were in his mind. But he looked solemnly over the ridges that let the earth down to the valley of the Siskadee, with a kind of reverence in his westering eyes.

On the third day beyond the pass, they got to the Siskadee. Jedediah took six men south along the river to trap and left Tom Fitzpatrick in charge of the other three to trap up to the sources of the river. (Some had stayed in the Crow camp and joined the outfit that came down from Fort Henry. Rose decided to live again with the Crows; he had made himself popular with them by handing out Jed's trading goods with a too free hand.) So now they had their first season in the West's most splendid beaver country.

They stood in the creeks, swollen with melting snow and right at the temperature of freezing, until their knees ached. They saw the aspens begin to go green while patches of snow flecked the quiet groves. They watched the Indian paintbrush come back into pink and then violent red, and the columbine rise, almost colorless, and then grow into delicate violet. They found prairie hens underfoot, birds so dumb you could sometimes kill them with a stick. They noted the game coming back to higher country, and made more than their share of meat.

They waded into creeks and thought that no man—at least no white man, which was what mattered—had ever stepped into that water before. They gave names to creeks, gulleys, ridges, peaks. Everything was new, fresh, and innocent as God had made it. They felt sometimes like Adam in the Garden of Eden—all the world newborn, ready to be looked at, touched, smelled, inhaled, known for the first time, and given a word for the first time. Spring was seeping into the mountains. The beaver were jamming the streams. They were in the Rocky Mountains, by God, with no lawmen to tell them what to do, no tax men to charge them for doing it, and no preachers or high-falutin' women to tell them that a man's pleasure wasn't right. It was a good time. Now they knew why they had come to the mountains.

In June, Tom Fitzpatrick turned his outfit downstream and then up Big Sandy Creek and through South Pass to the Sweetwater. There they had left a cache of provisions the previous March, and there Jed Smith was to meet them. Since Smith hadn't arrived yet, the little Irishman sent Clyman down the Sweetwater a ways. Filled to the brim with melting snow, the river might be navigable. It would be a way to get the fine spring catch back to Missouri, although Fitz couldn't figure whether it ran into the Platte or the Arkansas. After a while Jed came in with a lot more packs of plews. They were off to a bang-up start.

Tom and two others built bullboats to try to float the furs down. Jed followed the river looking for Clyman. When he got to a big river coming in from the south—Jed judged it to be the Platte—he found Jim's shelter and stack of firewood. He also found Indian sign; a war party of

maybe twenty braves, he could see, all over the area. He
didn't need any further sign to know that the slow-spoken
Virginian had gone under.

Jim Clyman, fishing in his possibles sack for flint and
steel, hears voices. Carefully still, he raises only his eyes
and studies the opposite bank of the Sweetwater. Indians,
mounted. Clyman makes less movement than the cotton-
wood branches that hide him. The Indians get off their
horses directly across from him and scoop up firewood.
He counts twenty-two of them, and maybe thirty horses.
He considers: Don't know the tribe. Maybe friendly,
maybe not. Lone white liable to be coup even for friendly
ones. Time to leave his accommodations. Thirty yards
ain't enough space between him and Indians.

He turns gently away from the little lodge he's built
and the firewood he's piled up. Ground in back of him
sandy, half a mile wide. Moon coming up full. Sand
will show prints as clear as snow. He picks up his sack
and rifle, fixes his eyes on the Indians, and starts backing
across the sand flats. Slowly and carefully, always watching, he backs until the ground lifts and turns to rock.

Safe now, for a while. He climbs along the rock ridge
till the river cuts it, swims the twenty yards of freezing
water, and climbs a bluff. Here he can keep an eye on the
critturs from a toluble distance. And wait for Fitzpatrick
and company in peace, if not in comfort.

Some of the Indians lie down and sleep, others keep
the fires going. Jim just sits and observes. Near midnight
they all get up and get the horses together. Suddenly two
of the animals bolt and start swimming across the river.
The Indians holler and go across after them. Damn—

right toward where Jim made his camp. He tenses, waiting to see whether they'll see his backward tracks. They ride all over the sand flats. No shouts, no cries for coup. Finally, with the two horses, they cross the river again and ride off to the north. Jim can relax now, and catch some sleep.

The next morning Jim does some exploring, and comes on a deep, swift place upstream where the river chops right through a ridge. The rocks stand four hundred feet on either side. Boats would spill there. We'll have to put 'em to float further down.

Movement on the bank. Indians file on foot to the river. About twenty of them. Jim watches from the top of the rocks. He was right there a while ago. They might see his sign. But they make a raft, ferry their belongings across, and walk on south.

Damn, this place is overpopulated. He goes back to his rock watchtower of the night before, where he can see his camp and spot his friends when they come, and waits.

But they don't come. Three days. Jim can't figure what's keeping them. Have Fitz and the other two gotten rubbed out? Have they gone looking for Jed Smith and his outfit? Have they turned around, for some reason he can't imagine, and gone back across South Pass? Eight, nine, ten days. Jim has no idea what might have happened. On the twelfth day he takes stock. He has plenty of powder, but only eleven balls left. He could go upstream looking for the brigade. But if he doesn't find it—because everyone is gone under, or because they have left the meeting place—he will lose time looking for them. Then he might not have enough balls to get him back to civilization.

He ponders the long, long walk to the settlements. If the Sweetwater is running into the Platte here, it will take him to Fort Atkinson on the Missouri. If it is running into the Arkansas, it will take him way south into country he has no knowledge of, hundreds of miles in the wrong direction. If he hunts for the other trappers, he might starve. If he starts for the settlements, he might get lost. And it is a great yaw of miles over the plains to Fort Atkinson—if he's lucky enough for this big river to be the Platte.

He starts walking downriver. It is the second or third day of July. His only notion of the distance or the terrain is from last autumn's march west with Jed Smith, made about a hundred miles north of here. Though Jim has no way of knowing it exactly, he has almost six hundred miles to trudge.

The days are scorching hot. He walks along the river to stay near water. Off to the right rises a low, dry range of mountains. Off to the left, baked plains as far as he can see. The river bends north for a couple of days, east for a couple, southeast for a couple. No Indians, not much game, almost no vegetation away from the river. The days are nothing but one sweating step after another, endlessly, in a country flat as a knife-blade. Here and there, fragments of hills, buttes, mesas, or chimney rocks thrust up, carelessly scattered in broken, random patterns that make no sense. Strange, illogical, disquieting landscape.

He has lost track of the days now. A week downriver, maybe, he comes across something odd—a bullboat drifted up onto a sand bar. Must be white men around—Indians never build bullboats. He scouts around for sign of whites, but the only sign he sees tells him that a large village of Indians camped there. He plods on downriver. One day he sees Indians running buffalo on the far side of the river, too far away to tell what tribe. He is acutely lonely, but decides to press on.

The days string by tediously. Tired of scraping for food, Jim takes time to shoot one of the hundreds of buffalo along the river. He makes a fire and builds a rack of thin, green twigs horizontally above it. Cutting the meat as thin as he can, he lays it across the rack to dry. For two days he repeats the process. Finally he admits that he is waiting mostly in the hope of seeing someone. Right now he would take a chance of losing his hair for a chance to talk to any human being, even a coup-hunting Indian. But no one appears.

Further downriver he comes into a large stand of cottonwoods and hears martins twittering. He sits down and takes his ease for several hours, listening to the birds because they remind him of civilization.

More days, divided only by the rhythm of his moccasined feet skimming past each other. He kills another buffalo and this time makes a halter of rawhide. He has seen wild horses around, and maybe he can get a ride back to Fort Atkinson. (This river seems too far north for the Arkansas.) Later, he stands perfectly still: A handsome black stallion is walking to the river to drink. Maybe he can stun the horse with a shot through the neck above the spinal cord. If he misses, he'll waste one of his last balls. He fires, and the animal clambers up the bank and falls. But its neck is broken.

He walks on and on, dejected and lonely. He has passed the butte and mesa terrain now. He is trudging over flat prairie stretching beyond flat prairie without a break to the horizon in every direction. And the horizon just keeps easing away in front of him. Could give a man a perverse idea of what the Bible means by eternity.

Sign—a lodge trail. A whole village crossed here recently. He has been walking, he figures, for maybe a month.

He is unbearably lonely. So he chooses to take a risk. He wades across the Platte, a ridiculously shallow river, and follows the trail.

An Indian sees him on the outskirts of the village. Clyman makes gestures of friendship and walks behind the brave to the center of the village. They are Pawnees—likely friendly, except that he is alone. They exclaim and debate about him. Finally they make a trade with him on their terms. He gives up all his possibles, everything he needs to survive. They hand him a little parched corn and send him on his way.

Away from the river, Clyman picks his way across broken country. The mosquitos are devilish. He is quickly on starving times. After a couple of days of hunger, he sees two badgers fighting. He grabs bones from the ground and kills both of them savagely. With no way to make a fire and no way to cut the meat, he rips it off with his teeth and eats it raw. And he trudges on, now through a steady rain.

At length he happens on a trail that seems to be going in the right direction. He fixes his mind on following it to the end, wherever it goes. Weak and exhausted now from starvation, he stumbles along the trail. He is dizzy from time to time. He is afraid that if he falls, he will sleep and never get up again. On the second day of walking the trail, he feels his nerves jump constantly. He is heavy with sleep. Several times he falls asleep walking, and tumbles to the ground. Then he bounds up with a nervous jerk and stumbles on.

After one fall, he gets up and walks, but notices after two or three hundred yards that he's going back the way he came. He turns around and labors in the other direction. He can barely push one foot in front of the other. His head hangs on his neck, eyes down. Finally he raises his eyes—and sees in the distance the Stars and Stripes flying over a fort.

He faints straight away. When he wakes up, he has no idea how long he's been unconscious. He looks again toward the flag and trembles with relief, feeling waves of weakness; he is on the verge of crying. He tries to stand up, falls down again, tries to stand, falls, and after several more attempts finally just lies back. As he waits, the tightness in his chest begins to ease. He can feel the air coming better. Finally he gets on his feet and strides easily to the fort. "Certainly no man ever enjoyed the sight of our flag better than I did," he will write later.[6]

At Fort Atkinson he gets a lot of surprising news. Three other Ashley-Henry men came in three or four months earlier on foot and in as sad a condition as he—Dutton, Marsh, and later, Hugh Glass. The bullboat he found was theirs, and the Indians in that village killed their two companions. Now Jim hears for the first time the story of Hugh Glass, the grizzly, and Glass's hunt for Fitzgerald. And after ten days of rest, more news walks in—Tom Fitzpatrick and two trappers from Jim's own outfit.

They have made exactly the same journey Jim made, also on foot. They overturned their bullboat, Tom explains, in that cut through the mountains Jim saw. And Jim finds out why his friends never joined him. Jed Smith rode down to find him, saw his lodge, noted the Indian sign all over the area, and concluded that they had killed him. Jim remembers that he was away from that spot only one day—when he went exploring the cut. Jed must have come by then.

Young Fitzpatrick promptly shows his spunk. He writes to Ashley about the fine year's catch and then turns straight around on borrowed horses and goes back to where they spilled the boat. He means to bring the furs down. If the

Platte route has seen a lot of disaster this year, Tom doesn't care. He leaves for the Sweetwater about the first of September and gets back to Fort Atkinson in the last week of October. By then Ashley has come up from St. Louis with more men and supplies. Fitz confirms, in person, two pieces of good news for him: The country beyond the divide is a trapper's Eden. And the Platte provides a natural, easy, overland route straight toward South Pass.

Jim Bridger had been listening to the other trappers argue for days. It was winter camp, 1824–25. Last summer, after Fitzpatrick left, Jed Smith had led his own trappers, and a lot of others from Fort Henry, which was now abandoned, back through South Pass to the new territory. Jed himself had then taken an outfit north and had not come in for wintering. The rest—maybe fifty men—pushed west and came onto what they called Bear River. They trapped it north, around a huge horseshoe turn, and back south. They settled in here to spend the winter, built lean-tos and crude versions of tipis for shelter, made plenty of wood and meat. Now there wasn't much to do, so they argued about what direction the river ran downstream, after it churned through the narrow, rapid-filled gorge just ahead. Or they spent their time playing cards, telling lies, and horsing around. They were just horsing around when they prodded Jim to settle the argument by going downriver. He was only twenty, a little gullible, and sensitive about his standing with the men: He still had the affair of Hugh Glass to live down.

So Jim reckoned he would. He started building himself a bullboat. He stuck thick willow branches in the ground and forced them into a bowl shape. He lashed small, limber twigs onto them, and stitched pieces of buffler hide together with gut string, lashing them to the framework with rawhide. Then he melted buffler fat and caulked the seams with it. No boat, not even a canoe, had less draught than a bullboat. It might look like a bowl, and steer like one, but it was buoyant with a vengeance. Ought to keep him from grounding and flipping in those rapids.

The men chuckled as he made it, and some of them tried to warn him off: The rapids would turn him over for sure; the river might disappear underground with him still on it; Indians would ambush him; and what if he couldn't walk back over the mountains? Jim fretted, but he didn't let them know. He just cut himself a long pole and pushed off.

He felt a slow force take hold of the bottom, and the banks began to slip by in a gentle blur. He tried to get the sense of the current under his feet. He felt the thousand energies brought down from the thousand rivulets that fed it, energies that somehow remained separate, pushing him this way and tugging him that way, with an odd, many-faceted urgency. It was forcing him along faster with each tug toward those rapids. He tried to figure how to steer it best before he got there. But the boat resisted. It seemed unstable as a teeter-totter, and he had to keep from shifting his weight too far to one side. He couldn't so much steer as make it careen across the water for a moment, before the current worked its will again. The current was the boss. He hoped that it shot for the deepest spots, and not over any falls. The boat was already leaking.

Quicker and quicker came the pace, the river taking him into its groove and easily shooting him forward with a power he couldn't control, and maybe didn't want to control. He felt himself begin to get excited.

The first white water looked like dozens of little spurts

and turnings of energy. The water would turn smoothly, with a glistening surface, into a small, wide V, dart between two rocks, and froth back on itself beyond them. It riffled, fluted, spun downward, tossed its head back up playfully. He could feel all these movements under his feet like muscles working in firm rhythms. Ahead he could see a long staircase of these, like steps down a gentle hillside. The water seemed quick and alert as it slipped through the rocks. He let the current do the steering and readied the pole to fend off rocks. This was fun.

Soon he saw the real white water. The churning sucked at his stomach before he got there. He let the current pull him into a long V and catapulted into the rapids. The boat bucked and banged about. It bounded over rocks at a rakish angle, righted itself in the foam beyond, and spun away in the grip of the current. When he splashed into the first foam, he fell hands down into the freezing water in the boat. The boat spun and rushed on backwards. It hit the next boulders hard, and he nearly sailed out. The cold spray slashed into his eyes and blinded him for a moment. When he could see, the boat had come through the rocks by itself, and caromed downstream like driftwood. All the power belonged to the river now.

A wild horse could not have done more to throw him out. The river reared, slipped out from under, ripped him sideways, and then shot him at boulders. He spun in every backwater for a split second, and then was shot forward. It wouldn't let up. It looked the same ahead.

Jim Bridger was terrified, exultant, and strangely clearheaded. He braced and went with the thrilling energy. Time after time he jammed the pole against rocks and flew over them where the water did. Time after time the boat miraculously landed bottom-side down and swept on. Time after time he thought he had been bucked off, but came down still in the boat.

Then he realized. The boat was about to split apart. Branches of the frame were broken, water was pouring through tears in the hides. He looked at the walls of the canyon and judged his chances for a swim. Not good. Then he looked ahead and saw the water flounce up white a last time and riffle out into green. He charged the last hundred yards and floated out onto slow water.

His feet planted on either side of the boat, knee-deep into icy water, Jim Bridger whooped at the top of his lungs.

He poled awkwardly to the bank. Then he made a fire, dried his clothes and possibles, and looked around. High point of rocks just downstream. He dressed, climbed it, and saw that the Bear River ran south. That settled that. But he could see, far to the south, what looked like a big lake. He considered. Then he thought he'd go have a look at it.

When he had emptied the boat and improvised a couple of repairs, he got back on the river. And the next day he floated gently onto the big lake. No sight of land to the south. He stuck his finger in the water and tasted it. Salty. Bitter with salt. He looked south and saw water all the way to the horizon. The ocean! By God, the Pacific Ocean! He'd found it!

He put in, explored the shoreline, and started walking back to camp. When he told the trappers what he'd discovered, they were skeptical. Then they began to see that the boy was telling what he'd really seen. Some of them said there would be big ships along here from time to time, with whisky and 'bacca and other fixens. But some of them said that the Pacific was much further west. Jim must have found an inland salt lake.

Not for a year and a half, though, would they be sure of
what he had found. For this was the Great Salt Lake.
Didn't matter to Jim just what he'd found. He'd showed
them something, anyways.[7]

The Hudson Bay Company had anticipated that American trappers would penetrate west of the mountains, and
they were worried about it. Oregon, meaning all the territory west of the Rocky Mountains and north of forty-two
degrees (the modern states of Oregon, Washington, Idaho,
and more) was disputed land. Pending an agreement between the governments of the United States and Britain,
it was occupied jointly. Hudson Bay knew that at least two-
thirds of it would eventually be ceded to the Americans,
so they intended to take all the beaver possible while the
taking was good. And they didn't want the Americans to
press all the way to the Columbia and Fort Vancouver. So
HBC set an aggressive plan: a scorched-earth policy. Skin
the land just west of the mountains clean of beaver. Create a beaver desert, and the Americans will not find it
worth while to push across it.

The plan went awry from the start. Jed Smith, after
crossing South Pass in the summer of 1824, came across
an HBC brigade and followed it north, in comradely fashion, all the way to Flathead Post. So the young partisan
had gotten a convenient guide to territory the British
were keeping to themselves, and he had filled in some
white space on his map.

He wintered there and followed another outfit, led by the
tough and wily Peter Skene Ogden, back south. Ogden
led him straight to the valley of the Bear River. And there,
much to Ogden's disenchantment, sat dozens on dozens
of American trappers—an Ashley brigade (with Bridger

as one member), a brigade out from Taos (led by Etienne Provost), and handfuls of free trappers—men who had come to the mountains with Missouri Fur or Ashley-Henry, detached, and trapped on their own hook because they liked it that way. Americans were underfoot everywhere, cleaning out the country ahead of him. His hopes for a big catch, he noted in his journal, were blasted.

The Americans didn't cotton to the sight of Ogden either. When they heard that he was flying a British flag and that he had crossed the mountains to take beaver in U. S. territory, they were ready to fight. They didn't want any Englishers spoiling their Eden.

They found their deadliest weapon before Ogden himself arrived. Fourteen of Ogden's trappers, separated from the main party, reached the Americans first. A little casual conversation established that Hudson Bay was paying less than four bits a pound for plews and charging scalpers' prices for goods. Ashley was paying $3.50 a pound. So a free trapper named Johnson Gardner made deserters of the fourteen and led them, with a couple dozen American trappers, to make a stand against John Bull.

The war party stopped a hundred yards from Ogden's camp. Gardner shouted to all the British trappers that they were now on free soil, and whether or not they were indebted or engaged to Hudson Bay, they should consider themselves free men. Proudly he bellowed out the American price for beaver.

The next day, Gardner strutted straight into Ogden's tent and told the partisan that he was trespassing on U. S. territory. Britain had given it up, Gardner lied baldly. Ogden was a little too clever for this maneuver, and answered that he would wait for instructions from his own government. Gardner hinted blatantly that Ogden was risking his skin, and went into the tent of one of the Iroquois *engagés* of HBC. When Ogden followed him, the Iroquois threw the truth in his face. All the Iroquois would have deserted before if they had met any Americans. Now they were leaving regardless of what Ogden said. Gardner added righteously that HBC had been treating these men like slaves.

They did leave, taking their plews with them. Ogden was barely able to keep the horses HBC had lent them. He decided to skip immediately, since he was afraid every man would leave him. Before he got completely away, he lost twenty-three trappers (half of his freemen) and seven hundred plews—more than $4,000 in fur by American mountain prices. A resounding defeat. He could not create a beaver desert without trappers.

Tom Fitzpatrick, meanwhile, guided General Ashley and a pack-train of provisions up the Platte to its forks, along the South Platte to the mountains, and finally across South Pass. It had been a rough journey. Since they had started about the first of November, it had been executed in the bitterness of the plain and mountain winter, a trek of men and horses exhausted and starving. Jim Clyman came back to the mountains with this train. Two newcomers were notable: Robert Campbell, a young Irishman of wealth who had come to the mountains in hope of saving himself from tuberculosis; and Jim Beckwourth, the son of a Missouri planter and a slave woman who, with Edward Rose, was one of the first blacks in the mountains.

When they got to the Siskadee, Seedskeeder, or Shetskedee, as the mountain men variously called it, Ashley divided his forces: Clyman would lead a trapping party north to the river's sources, Zacharias Ham would lead one directly west, and Tom Fitzpatrick would take one south along the river. Ashley himself would also go downriver—to explore, not to trap. The General, too, was curious about the geography of the West, and considered that a man of his stature would do well to report some of it to the American government and people. He left instructions that he would cache the goods forty or fifty miles downriver, at a place conspicuously marked, and that all his men were to make a rendezvous there about July 10.

The General bullboated down the river for some five weeks. The boats pleased him because they were able to buoy up an astonishing amount of weight. The river and countryside did not. The land proved almost barren of game, and he regularly went hungry. The river turned out to be a series of rapids and deep gorges, so he spent as much time making awkward portages as he did floating. Still, he got down as far as the mouth of the Duchesne River, ran into some trappers from the Provost party, learned that the Spaniards had named this stream the Green River, and heard for the first time about the doings of his trappers and their encounter with the British. Eager to check out the state of his business, he got some horses and rode back to the rendezvous spot on Henry's Fork of the Green.

He found his men gathered from far and wide, along with free trappers and HBC deserters. They all needed the goods that were manufactured back in the States. And, to his surprise, he discovered that they loved the mountains so much that they wanted to avoid the settlements permanently.

Here might be a business as big as the furs themselves. Let the men trap on their own; buy the beaver from them at a cost that would still permit a profit in St. Louis; and make money on the sale of goods besides. If trapping was an unpredictable business, the mountain market for powder, balls, knives, and other basics was not.

The logic of the midsummer rendezvous also struck Ashley and his men. Since summer beaver wasn't worth taking, and summer was also an ideal time to get supplies to the mountains, circumstances melded perfectly. If the men wanted to stay in the mountains year-round, why not supply them every summer at a rendezvous? So the General made scrupulous notes about what to bring—not only kettles, ammunition, traps, and tobacco for the men, but foofuraw for the Indian women—ribbons, cloth, bells, mirrors, needles, and other dainties and trinkets. They'd be perfect enticements for enchantable squaws. And most of all, he learned, bring whisky. The mountains gave a man a whopping thirst.

All this was fine with the General. He was not an adventurer but a solid citizen. Though he had failed in last year's bid for the governorship of Missouri, he was committed to being influential in the community. Now he might make a profit in the mountains while staying in the settlements. But he needed a field captain. Andrew Henry had returned from the Rockies last summer and quit. Dogged by bad luck, Henry would have no more of the mountains. So during this rendezvous Ashley took young Jed Smith aside and proposed a partnership. Smith had distinguished himself in every way: He had completed dangerous missions alone; he had proved a cool, eagerly competent leader of men; he had led the way across South Pass to a trapping paradise. He was a master of mountain craft, and he was acute enough to be a fine businessman. Jed accepted. In three years, he had risen from novice hunter to full partner.

So ended the first rendezvous. It had been calm. The men had held some riding and shooting contests, but they had nothing to drink and no squaws to dally with. When Ashley turned back toward St. Louis, with Jed Smith in tow and a fortune in fur on his horses, he wondered at this strange breed he was leaving behind. They preferred life in the wilderness to the blandishments of civilization. He had brought them out as employees, but many of them had become free agents. Most of them were unnervingly wild. All of them were expert at what they did—otherwise they'd have gone under.

Ashley had started to exploit the mountains by the traditional keelboat system with employees under military discipline. He had ended by disseminating independent trappers all over the Rockies and improvising the rendezvous system. Falstaff's Battalion had become the mountain men and their quintessential representatives, the free trappers.

THIRD INTERLUDE

Yarning

LISTEN TO BLACK HARRIS: ASKED BY A LADY WHETHER he hasn't traveled a good deal, he spins a tale for his answer:

"A sight, marm, this coon's gone over, if that's the way your 'stick floats.' I've trapped beaver on Platte and Arkansa', and away up on the Missoura' and Yaller Stone; I've trapped on Columbia, on Lewis Fork, and Green

River; I've trapped, marm, on Grand River and the Heely [Gila]. I've fout the 'Blackfoot' (and d–d bad Injuns they are); I've 'raised the hair' of more than one Apach', and made a Rapaho 'come' afore now; I've trapped in heav'n, in airth, and h—, and scalp my old head, marm, but I've seen a putrefied forest."

"La, Mister Harris, a what?"

"A putrefied forest, marm, as sure as my rifle's got hindsights, and she shoots center. I was out on the Black Hills, Bill Sublette knows the time—the year it rained fire—and everybody knows when that was. If thar wasn't cold doin's about that time, this child wouldn't say so. The snow was about fifty foot deep, and the bufler lay dead on the ground like bees after a beein'; not whar we was tho', for thar was no bufler, and no meat, and me and my band had been livin' on our mocassins (leastwise the parflesh), for six weeks; and poor doin's that feedin' is, marm, as you'll ever know. One day we crossed a 'canon' and over a 'divide,' and got into a periara [prairie], whar was green grass, and green trees, and green leaves on the trees, and birds singing in the green leaves, and this in Febrary; wagh! Our animals was like to die when they see the green grass, and we all sung out, 'hurraw for summer doin's.'

" 'Hyar goes for meat,' says I, and I jest ups old Ginger at one of them singing birds, and down come the crittur elegant; its damed head spinning away from the body, but never stops singing, and when I takes up the meat, I finds it stone, wagh!

" 'Hyar's damp powder and no fire to dry it,' " I says quite skeared.

" 'Fire be dogged,' says old Rube. 'Hyar's a hos as'll make fire wood. Schr-u-k—goes the axe agin' the tree, and out comes a bit of the blade as big as my hand. We looks at the animals, and thar they stood shaking over the grass, which I'm doggone if it wasn't stone, too. Young Sublette comes up, and he'd been clerking down to the fort on Platte, so he know'd something. He looks and looks, and scrapes the tree with his butcher knife, and snaps the grass like pipe stems, and breaks the leaves a snappin' like Californy shells.

" 'What's all this, boy?' I asks.

" 'Putrefactions,' says he, looking smart, 'putrefactions, or I'm a niggur.' "

"La, Mister Harris," says the lady; "putrefactions, why, did the leaves, and the trees, and the grass smell badly?"

"Smell badly, marm," says Black Harris, "would a skunk stink if he was froze to stone? No, marm, this child didn't know what putrefactions was, and young Sublette's varsion wouldn't 'shine' nohow, so I chips a piece out of a tree and puts it in my trap-sack, and carries it safe to Laramie. Well, old Captain Stewart (a clever man was that, though he was an Englishman), he comes along next spring, and a Dutch doctor chap was along too. I shows him the piece I chipped out of the tree, and he called it a putrefaction too; and so, marm, if that wasn't a putrefied peraira, what was it? For this hos doesn't know, and he knows 'fat cow' from 'poor bull,' anyhow."[1]

Black Harris was indulging in a favorite mountainman pastime—yarning. A St. Louis newspaper picked up his yarn and offered it, bowdlerized, to the public.

Yarning was partly mountain journalism. When mountain men would meet on the trail, or come into a fort, they would exchange news: who had raised hair, who had gone under, where good doings had been found,

*what new valleys, passes, lakes, and streams had been
learned, what strange and wondrous places had turned
up, and what deeds had been done. A grapevine for news.*

*On certain occasions yarning took on a special impor-
tance. In the winter a small brigade of men might hole up
in a sheltered spot on, say, the Salmon River that offered
enough game and enough wood. They would huddle in
their lodges, dip regularly into the pot that was always
simmering for a piece of meat, take a draw on a pipe,
and yarn the days away. In the summer, the mountain
men and the Indians would walk and ride from all over
the West to a single valley, maybe a spot high up on the
Green River, and have a huge jamboree. Aside from
boozing, fighting, gambling, and fornicating, they com-
peted to see who could tell the best stories.*

*At these annual rendezvous, and during the long win-
ters, the news grew into the yarn and the tall tale. What
was wanted here was not fact, but entertainment. The
mountain man exaggerated, embellished, added color,
and finally invented whole hog. Passing on a story just
as you heard it was sign of a poor imagination. The
mountain man learned to take pride in his skill at spinning a yarn. Somewhere in this process, as news passed
into entertainment and beyond, the yarn became a kind
of art.*

*Most yarns had some basis in fact. Black Harris might
not have seen a petrified forest, but his story grew from a
real germ. Likewise, stories circulated for years that
John Colter had wandered into hell itself, where the water came out of the ground boiling and a man could smell
the sulphur and see the flames flickering out of the ground.
Colter told his accounts of Yellowstone and of Colter's
Hell accurately; but a little stretching turned him into the
discoverer of hell on earth. And the stories that sprang*

up later about some mountain man's meeting with the devil were only another small stretch away. Jim Bridger told a story about having shot at an elk close by; when the elk didn't move, Bridger checked it out. He found out that the elk had been twenty-five miles away, and he had been looking at it through a glass mountain, which acted as a magnifying glass. Bridger was adding a lot of curlicues, but there is an obsidian mountain in Yellowstone.

So yarns transformed reports into fiction. The fiction may not have been hard to believe, considering that this country was full of things a man couldn't believe and that Easterners didn't believe, and considering that the mountain men were superstitious anyway. Along the way, through version after version, the yarns were transfigured into myth. They became a kind of figurative truth: The mountain men saw themselves, their country, and their deeds in Bunyanesque proportion, so they made their experience into Bunyanesque tales. Later, when the mountain country was overrun by greenhorns who didn't know any better, the yarn stretched further and became a deliberate put-on to dupe the innocent. Mark Twain, arriving a generation after the heyday of the mountain man, heard the grandchildren of these yarns and dubbed them tall tales.

Some of the best grew up around Bridger, who became a legend. The guide of a wagon train, a mountain man who had known this country when his clients were toddlers, might while away the time by telling them about the winter it snowed for 70 days and 70 nights without stopping. The snow come 70 foot deep on the ground. In the Great Basin, where Bridger's brigade was holed up, herds upon herds of buffler froze solid standing up. Come the thaw, the Bridger boys skinned 'em, rolled 'em into

*the Salt Lake, and pickled 'em. Made meat for themselves
and the whole Shoshone nation for ten years, they did.
Bridger, in his last years, used to tell one to children about
himself: The Blackfeet had run him into a box canyon.
His rifle and pistol were empty, his knife was lost, there
was no way out, and the Blackfeet were almost on top
of him. Bridger would pause to let tension mount.
What happened? Well, those Injuns killed him. Scalped
him, too.*

*Lewis Garrard, who lived with trappers and recorded
his experiences in a book,* Wah-to-Yah and the Taos
Trail,[2] *heard a classic of the genre:*

*Challenged by a fellow trapper, Louy, to recall the
time he "seed the old gentleman," Long Hatcher draws
on his pipe to keep the fire in, frowns with a look of
concentration on time past, and spins his yarn in quintessential trapper language:*

*He went up to Purgatoire Creek, he recollects, because
he had heard about lots of beaver there. But some Arapahoes ambushed him. He had to cache and they got his
animals, except for Blue, his mule. He was hungry as a
wolf, and was thinking about making meat when he remembered something: He'd been to this spot once before, and had cached some Taos Lightning—Touse, or
arwerdenty, as he calls the whisky.*

I looked round fur sign, and hurraw fur the mountains,
if I didn't find the cache. An' now, if this hos hasn't
kissed the rocks as was pecked with his butcherknife
to mark the place, he's ongrateful. Maybe the gravel
wasn't scratched up from that cache *some!* an' *me,* as
would have given my traps fur *"old bull,"* rolled in the
arwerdenty—wagh!

I was weaker an' a goat in the spring; but when the

Touse was opened, I fell back, an' let it run in. In four swallers I 'cluded to pull up stakes fur the head waters of Purgatoire for meat. I roped old Blue, tied on my traps, an' left.

It used to be the best place in the mountains fur meat—me an' Bill Williams *has* made it *come*—but nothin' was in sight. Things looked mity strange, an' I wanted to make back track; "but," sez I, "hyar I ar, an' doesn't turn, surely."

The bushes was scorched an' curled, an' the cedar was like fire had been put to it. The big brown rocks was covered with black smoke, an' the little drink in the bottom of the kanyon was dried up. We was now most under the old twin peaks of Wah-to-yah; the cold snow on top looked mity cool an' refreshin'.

Somethin' was wrong; I must be shovin' backards, an' that afore long, or I'll go under; an' I jerked the rein, but I'll be doggone—an' it's true as there's meat a runnin'—Blue kept goin' forrad. I laid back, an' cussed an' kicked till I *saw* blood, sartain; an' I put out my hand fur my knife to kill the beast, but the Green River wouldn't come. I tellee some onvisible sperit had a paw thar, an' it's me as says it—bad "medicine" it was that trappin' time.

Loosin' my pistol—the one traded at Big Horn, from Suckeree Tomblow, time I lost my Yute squaw—an' primin' my rifle, I swore to keep rite on; fur, after stayin' ten year, that's past, in these mountains, to be fooled this way wasn't the game fur me, no how.

Well, we—I say "we," fur Blue was some—good as a man any day; I could talk to her, an' she'd turn her head as if she onderstood me. Mules are knowin' critters— next thing to human. At a sharp corner, Blue snorted, an' turned her head, but couldn't go back. Thar, in front, was a level kanyon, with walls of black an' brown an' gray stone, an' stumps of burnt pinyon hung down ready to fall onter us; an', as we passed, the rocks and trees shook an' grated an' creaked. All at oncet Blue tucked tail, backed her ears, bowed her neck, an' hinnied rite out, a raring onto her hind legs, a pawin' an' snickerin'. This hos doesn't see the cute of them notions; he's fur examinin', so I goes to jump off, to lam the fool; but I was stuck tight as ef tar was to the saddle. I took my gun—that ar iron (pointing to his rifle, leaning against a tree), an' pops Blue over the head, but she squealed an' dodged, all the time pawin'; but 'twasn't no use, an' I says, "You didn't cost moren two blankets when you was traded from the Yutes, an' two blankets ain't worth moren six plews at Fort William, which comes to *dos pesos* a pair, you consarned ugly picter—darn you, anyhow!" Jest then I heerd a laffin'. I looks up, an' two black critters—they wasn't human, sure, fur they had tails an' red coats (Injun cloth, like that traded to the Navyhoes), edged with shiny white stuff, an' brass buttons.

They kem forrad an' made two low bows. I felt fur my scalpknive (fur I thought they was 'proachin' to take me), but I couldn't use it—they were so *darned* polite.

One of the devils said, with a grin an' bow, "Good mornin', Mr. Hatcher?"

"H—!" sez I, "how do you know me? I swar *this* hos never saw you afore."

"Oh! we've expected you a long time," said the other, "and we are quite happy to see you—we've known you ever since your arrival in the mountains."

I was gittin' sorter scared. I wanted a drop of arwerdenty mity bad, but the bottle was gone, an' I looked at them in astonishment, an' said—"the devil!"

"Hush!" screamed one, "you must not say that here—keep still, you will see him presently."

I felt streaked, an' cold sweat broke out all over me. I tried to say my prayers, as I used to at home when they made me turn in at night—

> Now I lay me down to sleep—
> Lan'lord fill the flowin' bowl.

P'shaw! I'm off agin, I can't say it; but if this child could have got off his animal, he'd tuk "har," and gone the trail fur Purgatoire.

All this time the long-tailed devils was leadin' my animal (an' me on top of her, the biggest fool dug out) up the same kanyon. The rocks on the sides was pecked as smooth as a beaverplew, rubbed with the grain, an' the ground was covered with bits of cedar, like a cavyard of mules had been nippin' an' scatterin' 'em about. Overhead it was roofed; leastwise it was dark in thar, an only a little light come through holes in the rock. I thought I knew whar we was, an' eeched awfully to talk, but I sot still an' didn't ax questions.

Presently we were stopped by a dead wall—no opening anywhar. When the devils turned from me, I jerked my head around quick, but thar was no place to get out—the wall had growed up ahind us too. I was mad, an' I wasn't mad nuther; fur I expected the time had come fur this child to go under. So I let my head fall onter my breast, an' I pulled the old wool hat over my eyes, an' thought for the last, of the beaver I had trapped, an' the buffler as had took my G'lena pills in thar livers, an' the "poker" an' "euker" I'd played to rendevoo an' Fort William. I felt cumfortable as eatin' "fat cow" to think I hadn't cheated any one.

All at once the Kanyon got bright as day. I looked up, an' thar was a room with lights, an' people talkin' and laffin', an' fiddles a screechin'. Dad, an' the preacher to Wapakonnetta, told me the fiddle was the Devil's invention; I believe it now.

The little feller as had hold of my animal, squeaked out—"Get off your mule, Mr. Hatcher!"

"Get off!" sez I, for I was mad as a bull pecked with Camanche lances, fur his disturbin' me, "get off? I have been trying to, ever sence I came in this infernal hole."

"You can do so now. Be quick, for the company is waitin'," sez he, piert-like.

They all stopped talkin' an' were lookin' rite at me. I felt riled. "Darn your company. I've got to lose my scalp anyhow, an' no difference to me how soon—but to obleege ye—" so I slid off as easy as if I'd never been stuck.

A hunchback boy, with little gray eyes way in his head, took old Blue away. I might never see her agin, an' I shouted—"poor Blue! goodbye Blue!"

The young devil snickered; I turned about mity starn—"stop your laffin' you hellcat—ef I am alone, I can take you," an' I grabs fur my knife to wade into his liver; but it was gone—gun, bullet-pouch, an' pistol—like mules in a stampede.

I stepped forrad with a big feller, with har frizzled out like an old buffler's just afore sheddin' time; an' the people jawin' worse 'an a cavyard of parokeets, stopped, while Frizzly shouted—

"Mr. Hatcher, formerly of Wapakonnetta, latterly of the Rocky Mountains!"

Well, thar I stood. Things was mity strange, an' every darned niggur on 'em looked so pleased like. To show 'em manners, I said—"How are ye!" an' I went to bow, but chaw my last 'bacca ef I could, my breeches was so tight—the heat way back in the kanyon had shrunk them. They were too polite to notice it, an' I felt fur my knife to rip the doggone things, but recollecting the scalptaker was stolen, I straightens up, an' bows my head. A kind-lookin' smallish old gentleman, with a black coat and briches, an' a bright, cute face, an' gold spectacles, walks up an' pressed my hand softly—

"How do you do, my dear friend? I have long expected you. You cannot imagine the pleasure it gives me to meet you at home. I have watched your peregrinations in the busy, tiresome world, with much interest. Sit down, sit down; take a chair," an' he handed me one.

I squared myself on it, but a ten-pronged buck wasn't done sucking, when I last sot on a cheer, an' I squirmed a while, oneasy as a gut-shot coyote. I jumps up, an' tells the old gentleman them sort of "state fixins," didn't suit this beaver, an' he prefers the floor. I sets cross-legged like in camp as easy as eatin' *boudin*. I reached for my pipe—a feller's so used to it—but the devils in the kanyon had cached it too."

"You wish to smoke, Mr. Hatcher?—we will have cigars. Here!" he called to an imp near him, "some cigars."

They was brought on a waiter, size of my bulletbag. I empties 'em in my hat, for good cigars ain't to be picked up on the peraira every day, but lookin' at the old man, I saw somethin' was wrong. To be polite, I ought to have taken but one.

"I beg pardon," says I, scratchin' my old scalp, "this hos didn't think—he's been so long in the mountains, he forgets civilized doins," an' I shoves the hat to him.

"Never mind," says he, wavin' his hand, an' smilin' faintly, "get others," speakin' to the boy aside him.

The old gentleman took one, and touched his finger to the end of my cigar—it smoked as ef fire had been sot to it.

"Wagh! the devil!" screams I, drawin' back.

"The same!" chimed in he, biting off the little end of his'n, an' bowin' an' and spittin' it out—"the same, sir."

"The same! what?"

"Why—the Devil."

"H—! this ain't the holler tree for this coon—I'll be makin' 'medicin';" so I offers my cigar to the sky, an' to the earth, like Injun.

"You must not do that here—out upon such superstition," says he, sharplike.

"Why?"

"Don't ask so many questions—come with me," risin' to his feet, an' walkin' off slow, a blowin' his cigar smoke, over his shoulder in a long line, an' I gets alongside of him, "I want to show you my establishment—you did not expect to find this down here, eh?"

My britches was stiff with the all-fired heat in the kanon, an' my friend seein' it, said, "Your breeches are tight; allow me to place my hand on them."

He rubbed his fingers up an' down once, an' by beaver, they got as soft as when I traded them from the Pi Yutes on the Heely (you mind, Louy, my Yute squaw; old Cutlips, her bos, come with us far as Sangry Christy goldmine. She's the squaw that dressed them skins).

I now felt as brave as a buffler in spring. The old man was so clever, an' I walked 'longside like a 'quaintance. We stopped afore a stone door, an' it opened without touchin'.

"Hyar's damp powder, an' no fire to dry it," shouts I, stoppin'.

"What's the matter—do you not wish to perambulate through my possessions?"

"This hos doesn't savy what the 'human' for prerambulate is; but I'll walk plum to the hottest fire in your settlement, if that's all you mean."

The place was hot, an' smelt bad of brimstone; but the darned screechin' *took* me. I walks up t'other eend of the "lodge," an' steal my mule, if thar wasn't Jake Beloo, as trapped with me to Brown's Hole! A lot of hellcats was a pullin' at his ears, an' a jumpin' on his shoulders, a swingin' themselves to the ground by his long har. Some was runnin' hot irons in him, but when we came up, they went off in a corner a laffin' and talkin' like wildcats' gibberish on a cold night.

Poor Jake! he came to the bar, lookin' like a sick buffler in the eye. The bones stuck through the skin, an' his har was matted an' long—all over jest like a blind bull, an' white blisters spotted him, with water runnin' out of 'em. "Hatch, old feller! *you* here, too?—how are ye?" says he, in a faintlike voice, staggerin' an' catchin' on to the bar fur support—"I'm sorry to see you *here*, what did you"—he raised his eyes to the old man standin' ahind me, who gave him *such* a look: he went howlin' an' foamin' at the mouth to the fur end of the den, an' fell down, rollin' over the damp stones. The devils, who was chucklin' by a furnis, whar was irons a heatin', approached easy, an' run one into his back. I jumped at 'em and hollered, "You owdacious little hellpups, let him alone; ef my sculptaker was hyar, I'd make buzzard feed of your meat, an' *parfleche* of your dogskins," but they squeaked out to "go to the devil."

"Wagh!" says I, "ef I *ain't* pretty close to his lodge, I'm a niggur!"

The old gentleman speaks up, "take care of yourself, Mr. Hatcher," in a mity soft, kind voice; an' he smiled so calm an' devilish—it nigh on froze me. I thought ef the ground would open with a yairthquake, an' take me in, I'd be much obleeged any how. Think's I—you saint-forsaken, infernal hell-chief, how I'd like to stick my knife in your withered old breadbasket.

"Ah! my dear fellow, no use in tryin'—that is a decided impossibility"—I jumped ten feet. I swar, a "medicine" man couldn't a heerd me, for my lips didn't move; an' how he knew is moren this hos kin tell.

"Evil communications corrupt good manners. But I see your nervous equilibrium is destroyed—come with me."

At t'other side, the old gentlemen told me to reach down for a brass knob. I thought a trick was goin' to be played on me, an' I dodged.

"Do not be afraid; turn it when you pull—steady there—that's it"—it came, an' a door, too. He walked in. I followed while the door shut of itself.

"Mity good hinges!" sez I, "don't make no noise, an' go shut without slammin' an' cussen' 'em."

"Yes—yes! some of my own importation; no! they were made here."

It was dark at first, but when the other door opened, thar was *too* much light. In another room was a table in the middle, with two bottles, an' little glasses like them to the Saint Louy drink houses, only prettier. A soft, thick carpet was on the floor—an' a square glass lamp hung from the ceiling. I sat cross-legged on the floor, an' he on a sofy, his feet cocked on a cheer, an' his tail quoiled under him, cumfortable as traders in a

lodge. He hollered somethin' I couldn't make out, an'
in comes two black, crooked-shank devils, with a round
bench on one leg, an' a glass with cigars in it. They
vamosed, an' the old coon inviting me to take a cigar,
helps himself, an' rared his head back, while I sorter
lays on the floor, an' we smoked an' talked.

We was speakin' of the size of the apple Eve ate, an'
I said thar were none but crabapples until we grafted
them, but he replied, thar was good fruit until the flood.
Then Noah was so hurried to git the yelaphants, pinchin'
bugs, an' sich varment aboard, he furgot good apple-
seed, until the water got knee-deep; so he jumps out,
gathers a lot of sour crabs, crams 'em in his pockets, an'
Shem pulled him with a rope in the ark agin.

I got ahead of him several times, an' he sez—"Do you
really believe the preachers, with their smooth faces,
upturned eyes, and whining cant?"

"Sartainly I do! cause they're mity kind and good to
the poor."

"Why I had no idea you were so ignorant—I assur-
edly expected more from so sensible a man as you?"

"Now, look'ee hyar, this child isn't used to be abused
to his own face—I—I tell 'ee, it's mity hard to choke
down—ef it ain't, sculp me!"

"Keep quiet, my young friend, suffer not your temper
to gain the mastery; let patience have its perfect work. I
beg your pardon sincerely—and so you believe the Bible, and permit the benighted preachers to gull you un-
sparingly. Come now! what is the reason you imagine
faith in the Bible is the work to take you to Heaven?"

"Well, don't *crowd* me an' I'll think a little—why,
it's the oldest history anyhow: so they told me at home.
I used to read it myself, old hos—this child did. It tells
how the first man an' his squaw got hyar, an' the buffler,

an' antelope, an' beaver, an' hosses too. An' when I see it on the table, somethin' ahind my ribs thumps out: 'look, John, that's book you must be mighty respectful to,' an' somehow, I believe it's moren human, an' tell 'ee, it's agin natur to believe otherwise, wagh!"

Another thing, the old gentleman mentioned, I thought was pretty much the fact. When he said he fooled Eve, an' *walked* about, I said it was a *snake* what deceived the ole 'oman.

"Nonsense! snake indeed! I can satisfactorily account for that—but why think you so?"

"Because the big Bibles, with picters, has a snake quoiled in an appletree, pokin' out his tongue at Adam's squaw."

"P'shaw! the early inhabitants were so angry to think that Satan could deceive their first mother, and entail so much misery on them, that, at a meeting to which the principal men attended, they agreed to call me a serpent, because a serpent can insinuate himself so easily. When Moses compiled the different narratives of the earlier times, in his five books, he wrote it so too. It is typical, merely, of the wiles of the devil—my humble self"—an' the old coon bowed, "and an error, it seems, into which the whole world, since Moses, have irretrievably fallen. But have we not been sitting long enough? Take a fresh cigar, an' we will walk. That's Purgatory where your quondam friend, Jake Beloo, is. He will remain there a while longer, and, if you desire it, can go, though it cost much exertion to entice him here, and then only, after he drank hard."

"I wish you would, sir. Jake's as good a companyero as ever trapped beaver, or gnawed poor bull in spring, an' he treated his squaw as ef she was a white woman."

"For your sake, I will; we may see others of your

acquaintance before leaving this," sez he, sorter queer-like, as if to say—"no doubt of it."

The door of the room we had been talkin' in, shut of its own accord. We stopped, an' he touchin' a spring in the wall, a trapdoor flew open, showin' a flight of steps. He went first, cautioning me not to slip on the dark sta'ars; but I shouted "not to mind me, but thankee for tellin' it though."

We went down, an' down, an' down, till I 'gan to think the old cuss was goin' to get me safe, too, so I sung out—"Hello! which way; we must be mity nigh under Wah-To-Yah, we've been goin' on so long?"

"Yes!" sez he, much astonished, "we're just under the twins. Why, turn and twist you ever so much, you loose not your reckoning."

"Not by a long chalk! this child had his bringin' up to Wapakonnetta, an' that's a fact."

From the bottom we went on in a dampish, dark sort of a passage, gloomily lit up, with one candle. The grease was runnin' down the block as had an augerhole bored in it for a candlestick, an' the long snuff to the end was red, an' the blaze clung to it, as if it hated to part company, an' turned black, an' smoked at the p'int in mournin'. The cold chills shook me, an' the old gentleman kept so still, the echo of my feet rolled back so hollow an' solemn. I wanted liquor mity bad—mity bad.

Thar was noise smothered-like, an' some poor feller would cry out worse 'an Camanches chargin'. A door opened, and the old gentleman touchin' me on the back, I went in, an' he followed. It flew to, an' though I turned rite round, to look fur "sign" to 'scape, ef the place got too hot, I couldn't find it.

"Wa-agh!" sez I.

"What now, are you dissatisfied?"

"Oh, no! I was just lookin' to see what sort of a lodge you have."

"I understand you perfectly, sir—be not afraid."

My eyes were blinded in the light, but rubbin' 'em, I saw two big snakes comin' 'at me, thar yaller an' blood-shot eyes shinin' awfully, an' thar big red tongue dartin' back an' forad, like a painter's paw, when he slaps it on a deer, an' thar wide jaws open, showin' long, slim, white fangs. On my right, four ugly animals jumped at me, an' rattled ther chains—I swar, ther heads were bigger an' a buffler's in summer. The snakes hissed an' showed thar teeth, an' lashed thar tails, an' the dogs howled, an' growled, an' charged, an' the light from the furnis flashed out brighter an' brighter; an' above me, an' around me, a hundred devils yelled, an' laffed, an' swore, an' spit, an' snapped their bony fingers in my face, an' leaped up to the ceiling into the black, long spiderwebs, an' rode on the spiders bigger an' a pow-derhorn, an' jumped off onter my head. Then they all formed in line, an' marched, an' hooted, an' yelled: an' when the snakes jined the percession, the devils leaped on thar backs an' rode. Then some smaller ones rocked up an' down on springin' boards, an' when the snakes kem opposite, darted way up in the room an' dived down in their mouths, screechin' like so many Paw-nees for sculps. When the snakes was in front of us, the little devils came to the eend of the snakes' tongues, laffin', an' dancin', an' singin' like eediuts. Then the big dogs jumped clean over us, growlin' louder 'an a cavyard of grisly b'ar, an' the devils holdin' on to thar tails, flopped over my head, screamin'—"we've got you—we've got you at last!"

I couldn't stand it no longer, an' shuttin' my eyes, I yelled rite out, an 'groaned.

"Be not alarmed," and my friend drew his fingers along my head an' back, an' pulled a little narrow, black flask from his pocket with—"take some of this."

I swallered a few drops. It tasted sweetish an' bitterish—I don't exactly savy how, but soon as it was down, I jumped up five times an' yelled—"out of the way, you little ones, an' let me ride," an' after runnin' long side, and climbin' up his slimy scales, I got straddle of a big snake, who turned his head around, blowin' his hot, sickenin' breath in my face. I waved my old wool hat, an' kickin' him in a fast run, sung out to the little devils to get up behind, an' off we all started, screechin' "Hooraw fur Hell!" The old gentleman rolled over an' bent himself double with laffin', till he putty nigh choked. We kept goin' faster an' faster till I got on to my feet (though the scales were mity slippery) an' danced Injun, an' whooped louder than 'em all.

All at once, the old gentleman stopped laffin', pulled his spectacles down on his nose an' said—"Mr. Hatcher, we had better go now," an' then he spoke somethin' I couldn't make out, an' the animals all stood still; I slid off, an' the little hellcats a pinchin' my ears, an' pullin' my beard, went off squeakin'. Then they all formed in a halfmoon afore us—the snakes on ther tails, with heads way up to the black cobwebby roof; the dogs rared on thar hindfeet, an' the little devils hangin' every whar. Then they all roared, an' hissed, an' screeched seven times, an' wheelin' off, disappeared, just as the light went out, leaving us in the dark.

"Mr. Hatcher," sez the old gentleman agin, movin' off, "you will please amuse yourself until I return"; but seein' me look wild, "you have seen too much of me to feel alarmed for your own safety. Take this imp fur a guide, an' if he is impertinent, *put him through*;

and, for fear the exhibitions may overcome your nerves, imbibe a portion of this cordial," which I did, an' everything danced afore my eyes, an' I wasn't a bit scairt.

I started fur a red light as came through the crack of a door, a stumblin' over a three-legged stool, an' pitchin' my last cigar stump to one of the dogs, chained to the wall, who ketched it in his mouth. When the door was opened by my guide, I saw a big blaze like a peraira on fire—red and gloomy; an' big black smoke was curlin', an' twistin', an' shootin', an' spreadin', and the flames a licking the walls, goin' up to a pint, and breakin' into a wide blaze, with white an' green ends. Thar was bells a tollin', an' chains a clinkin', an' mad howls an' screams; but the old gentleman's "medicine" made me feel as independent as a trapper with his animals feedin' round him, two pack of beaver in camp, with traps sot fur more.

Close to the hot place was a lot of merry devils laffin' an' shoutin' with an old pack of greasy cards—it minded me of them we played with to rendezvoo—shufflin' 'em to "Devil's Dream," an' "Money Musk"; then they 'ud deal in slow time, with "Dead March in Saul," whistlin' as solemn as medicine men. Then they broke out of a suddent with "Paddy O'Rafferty," which made this hos move about in his moccasins so lively, one of them was playin', looked up an' sed—"Mr. Hatcher, won't you take a hand—make way, boys, fur the gentleman."

Down I sot amongst 'em, but stepped on the little feller's tail, who had been leadin' the Irish jig. He hollered till I got off it—"Owch! but it's on my tail ye are!"

"Pardon," sez I, "but you're an Irishman!"

"No, indeed! I'm a hellimp, he! he! who-oop! I'm a hell-imp," an' he laffed, and pulled my beard, an' screeched till the rest threatened to choke him ef he didn't stop.

"What's trumps?" sez I, "an' whose deal?"

"Here is my place," sez one, "I'm tired playin', take a horn," handlin' me a black bottle, "the game's poker, an' it's your deal next—there's a bigger game of poker on hand," an' pickin' up an iron rod heatin' in the fire, he pinched a miserable burnin' feller ahind the bars, who cussed him, an' run way in the blaze outen reach.

I thought I was great at poker by the way I took the plews an' traps from the boys to rendezvoo, but hyar the slick devils beat me without half tryin'. When they slapped down a bully paid, they'ud screech an' laff worse 'an fellers on a spree. Sez one—"Mr. Hatcher, I reckon you're a hos at poker away to your country, but you can't shine down here—you are nowhar. That feller lookin' at us through the bars, was a preacher up to the world. When we first got him, he was *all-fired* hot and thirsty. We would dip our fingers in water, an' let it run in his mouth, to get him to teach us the best tricks—he's a trump—he would stand an' stamp the hot coals, and dance up and down, while he told us his experience. Whoopee! how we would laugh! He has delivered two long sermons of a Sunday, and played poker at night on fip antes, with the deacons, for the money bagged that day; and, when he was in debt, he exhorted the congregation to give more fur the poor heathen in a foreign land, a dying and losing their souls for the want of a little money to send 'em a gospel preacher—that the poor heathen 'ud be damned to eternal fire ef they *didn't* make up the dough. The gentleman as showed you around—Old Sate, we call him—had his eye on the preacher for a long time. When we got him, we had a barrel of liquor, and carried him around on our shoulders, until tired of the fun, and then threw him in the furnace yonder. We call him "Poke," for that was his favorite game. "Oh, Poke!" shouted my friend, "come here; thar's a gentleman wishes you—we'll give you five drops of water, an' that's more than your old skin's worth."

He came close, an' though his face was poor, an' all scratched, an' his har swinged mity nigh off, "make meat" of this child if it wasn't old Cormon as used to preach to the Wapakonnetta settlement! Many a time this coon's har's stood on eend, when he preached about t' other world. He came close, an' I could see the chains tied on his wrists, what they had worn to the bone, showin' the raw meat, an' dryed and runnin' blood. He looked a darned sight worse an' ef Camanches had skulped him.

"Hello! old coon," sez I, "we're both in that awful place you talked so much about, but I ain't so bad off as you, yet. This young gentleman," pointin' to the devil who told me of his doin's—"this young gentleman has been tellin' me how you took the money you made us throw in on Sunday."

"Yes," sez he, "ef I had only acted as I told others to do, I would not have been here scorching for ever and ever—water! water! John, my son, fur my sake, a little water."

Just then a little rascal stuck a hot iron in him, an' off he ran in the flames, caching on the cool side of a big chunk of fire, a lookin' at us fur water; but I cared no more fur him than the Pawnee, whose topknot was stuck in my belt, fur stealin' my cavyard to the Coon Creeks; an' I sez—

"This hos doesn't give a *cuss* fur you; you're a sneakin' hypercrite; you deserve all you've got an' more too—an', lookee hyar, old boy, it's me as says so."

I strayed off a piece, pretendin' to get cool; but this coon 'gan to git *scairt*, an' that's a fact, fur the devils carried Cormon till they got tired of *him*; "an'," sez I to myself, "an' *haint* they been doin' me the same way? I'll *cache*—I will—fur I'm not overly good, specially since I came to the mountains. Wagh! but this beaver must be movin' fur deep water, if that's the way your stick floats."

Well now, this child felt sorter queer, so he santers 'long slowly, till he saw an open place in the rock; not mindin' the imps who was drinkin' away like trappers on a bust. It was so dark thar, I felt my way mity still (fur I was afraid they'ud be after me); I got almost to a streak of light, when thar was sich a rumpus back in the cave as give me the trimbles. Doors was slammin', dogs growlin' an' rattlin' thar chains, an' the devils a screamin'. They come a chargin'. The snakes was hissin' sharp an' wiry; the beasts howled out long an' mournful; an' thunder rolled up overhead, an' the imps was yellin' an' screechin' like mad.

"It's time to break fur timber, sure," and I ran as ef a wounded buffler was raisin' my shirt with his horns. The place was damp, an' in the narrow rock, lizards an' vipers an' copperheads jumped out at me, an' clum on my legs, but I stompt an' shook 'em off. Owls, too, flopped thar wings in my face, an' hooted at me, an' fire blazed out, an' lit the place up, an' brimstone smoke came nigh on chokin' me. Lookin' back, the whole cav-yard of hell was comin', an' devils on devils, nothin' but devils, filled the hole.

I threw down my hat to run faster, an' then jerked off my old blanket, but still they was gainin'. I made one jump clean out of my moccasins. The big snake in front was closer an' closer, with his head drawed back to strike; then a helldog raked up nearly long side, pantin' an' blowin' with the slobber runnin' outen his mouth, an' a lot of devils hangin' on to him, was cussin' me an ' screechin'. I strained every jint, but no use, they still gained—not fast—but gainin' they was. I jumped an' swore, an' leaned down, an' flung out my hands, but the dogs was nearer every time, an' the horrid yellin' an' hissin' way back, grew louder an' louder. At last, a prayer mother used to make me say, I hadn't thought of fur twenty year or more, came rite afore me clear as a powderhorn. I kept runnin' an' sayin' it, an' the niggurs held back a little. I gained some on them—Wagh! I stopped repeatin', to get breath, an' the foremost dog made such a lunge at me, I forgot it. Turnin' up my eyes, thar was the old gentleman lookin' at me, an' keepin' alongside, without walkin'. His face warn't more than two feet off, an' his eyes was fixed steady, an' calm an' devilish. I screamed rite out. I shut my eyes but he was thar too. I howled an' spit an' hit at it, but couldn't get the darned face away. A dog ketched hold of my shirt with his fangs, an' two devils, jumpin' on me, caught me by the throat, a tryin' to choke me. While I was pullin' 'em off, I fell down, with about thirty-five of the infernal things, an' the dogs, an' the slimy snakes a top of me, a mashin' an' taren' me. I bit big pieces out of them, an' bit an' bit agin, an' scratched an' gouged. When I was most give out, I heerd the Pawnee skulp yell, an' use my rifle fur a pokin' stick, ef in didn't charge a part of the best boys in the mountains. *They* slayed the devils right an' left, an' sot 'em runnin' like goats, but this hos was so weak fightin', he fainted away. When I come to, we was on the Purgatoire, just whar I found the liquor, an' my companyeros was slappin' thar wet hats in my face, to bring me to. Round what I was layin', the grass was pulled up an' the ground dug with my knife, and the bottle, cached when I traded with the Yutes, was smashed to flinders 'gainst a tree.

"Why, what on airth, Hatcher, have ye bin doin' hyar? You was a kickin' an' taren' up the grass, an' yellin' as ef yer 'har' was taken. Why, old hos, this coon don't savy them hifelutin' notions, he doesn't!"

"The devils from hell was after me," sez I mity gruff, "this hos has seen more'n ever he wants to agin."

They tried to git me outen the notion, but I swar, an' I'll stick to it, this child saw a heap more of the all-fired place than he wants to agin; an' ef it ain't fact, he doesn't know "fat cow" from "poor bull"—Wagh!

IV

Quest For Buenaventura

THE TALK OF THE RENDEZVOUS OF JULY, 1826, WAS new country. A couple of hundred trappers, half of them working for Ashley and Smith and half of them free trappers, had come to Cache Valley from Snake River country, Green River territory, and even from Santa Fe. Etienne Provost led the bunch from Santa Fe, with reports of beaver on the Southwestern rivers, the Rio Grande, the Heely (Gila), and the Colorado. The Blanket Chief, Jim Bridger, who had just begun to get a reputation for Indian fighting, had come back from Snake country. Broken Hand Fitzpatrick showed up. So did Cut-Face (Bill) Sublette and David Jackson, the discoverer of Jackson Hole. Jim Beckwourth came in bragging about a battle where a handful of men had held off 500 Blackfeet and probably killed 100, if Beckwourth knew fat cow from poor bull. (Since he could outlie any child in the mountains, his listeners may have been skeptical.) Jed Smith had taken a brigade due west of the Great Salt Lake, into unknown country, looking for the Buenaventura River; he found no sweet water, no beaver, and no game until he turned north toward the Snake, as his men told it.

Beckwourth told a story about when the time they were wintering in the valley of the Salt Lake and some Bannocks ran off with eighty of their horses. Fitzpatrick led one party for five days through the snow on the Bannock's trail before they caught up. Then he split the band in two. Fitzpatrick led the one that attacked the Bannocks to distract them, and the Blanket Chief himself captained the other. (Bridger flushed a little when Beckwourth told this part; at twenty-one, he was becoming a leader of the roughest men in the hull land.) Beckwourth went with Bridger and stampeded the herd. When the two parties joined up and Fitzgerald got around to having the horses counted, the whites had come out forty head to the good.

Several hundred Shoshone Indians came down from Snake country for this rendezvous. Some of the men called them Snakes because of the sinuousness of their finger movements when they talked sign language. They were good Indians, Bridger reckoned, mebbe the best. A man could trust the critturs.

Ashley came with the year's supplies, and the drinking began. Arthur Black and several others guzzled enough that they wanted to dance, and promptly took up a version of the Shoshone war dance. The Indians thought they were a little crazy, and joined in. One man started bragging that he could lick any niggur in the mountains, be he man, painter, or Old Ephraim. The man next to him, without a word, blind-sided him with a fist and knocked him groggy. Buffalo-witted as he was, the first got up and launched into the brawl. Within five minutes they were both sprawled unconscious on the ground. Bridger opined that whisky should be declared champeen, as it had knocked them cold as a mountain crick. When they got up, the men embraced and swore that they loved each other, and would be glad to toe it out again, whenever the other was ready.

That night several of the men who had wintered in Snake country located their favorites and bedded down. One brave grinned at his brothers and marveled at the stupidity of a white man who would give such a wonder as a shiny mirror for the mere loan of a squaw for the night. Other braves, with a great show of everlasting friendship, lent their women and refused any pay from their lifelong comrades, the Longknives. The teenage girls flirted audaciously with the trappers by the outrageous maneuver of not looking to the ground in the presence of men. It had never occurred to the Shoshones that anyone would consider chastity a virtue, so the girls took their pleasure that night.

A few trappers were unlucky—the ones who had taken Shoshone squaws as lodge-mates last winter. Now each discovered that his wife's every relative was tied to him as an eternal blood brother, and that every blood brother was to get a present as a token of devotion. One Shoshone woman could turn out to be related to an astonishing percentage of the Shoshone nation. That much in beads, cloth, vermilion, and tobacco could blow a year's wages. Some of these married men relieved their troubles by trying out a fresh woman in the cottonwoods; others found it convenient to return the bride to her people permanently, with no hard feelings. After all, her father could now trade her to another white for another horse or two.

The next morning the Shoshones raised an alarm: Blackfeet. Three Snake men and two women who had gone out to gather roots had been killed and scalped by the Shoshone's long-time enemies. Omogua, a Snake leader with a reputation for prophesy, challenged Sublette: "Cut-Face," said the old man, "you say that your warriors can fight—that they are great braves. Now let me see them fight, that I may know your words are true."

Cut-Face called out the trappers, taking the precaution to add that any who were cowards should stay in camp. Then they and the Snake braves attacked. The Blackfeet retreated several miles and dug in at a hollow beside a lake. The pitched battle went on for six hours before the mountain men and Snakes considered themselves avenged. Sublette and Beckwourth scrambled almost into the Blackfoot stronghold to rescue a man injured in the battle. Beckwourth, the mulatto who later became a Crow chief and earned a reputation as the biggest scoundrel and braggart in the mountains, later inflated the battle into a huge victory for his forces: 173 Blackfeet killed and scalped against eleven Snakes killed, but none scalped, and no trappers killed.[1]

Indian and white alike celebrated that night, with dancing, drinking, singing, and fornicating. The Cache Valley had provided meat in abundance, and they feasted on buffalo hump, ribs, liver, and kidney, plus roasts from deer and elk, all browned on a spit over an open fire. The willows and cottonwoods sheltered them along the banks of the Bear River, in a country that was bare and treeless a hundred yards from the river. The trappers told their tall tales, and the Indians came out buckskin fancy for the whoop-it-up. Sublette, who had just returned from St. Louis with Ashley, was standing to one side, watching. He lifted his tin cup and said quietly, "Hurrah for mountain doin's."

The next morning they turned out at sunrise, checked the horses, looked at their gear to make sure no Shoshone had slipped a gift away from his white brother in the dark, and got the fires started under the deer, elk, and buffalo meat again. Talk turned back to the new country they had mapped out in their minds—which held every creek and ridge of the whole mountain and plain country in their particulars—and speculated on the roaming of the coming year.

One question stood out: Where was the Buenaventura River? Lewis and Clark, twenty years before, had followed the Clearwater, Snake, and Columbia Rivers from the continental divide to the ocean. They had judged that two rivers ran parallel to their route farther south—the Multnomah, of which they found the western end in Willamette Valley, and the Buenaventura. Persistent tales had it that a huge lake, called the Salado, existed in the Great Basin, and that a river flowed out of it due west, reaching the ocean at San Francisco Bay or at Monterey. The trappers now knew that the lake was Salt Lake, so the Buenaventura must flow west out of it. That would be the route to Californy, the country where the sun shone gently all year, the land stayed green and abundantly fertile always, game was so plentiful a man scarcely had to shoot center to live easy, and lusty señoritas waited ripe and willing. Why, there might even be beaver westward, and sartinly in Californy. That place would shine.

The search for beaver was important, though maybe not urgent. The men knew that they could make good hunts still in Siskadee country and up on Lewis's River, the Snake. But the Hudson Bay Company was competing for the Snake territory and would try to stir the Indians up against the Americans. Crow country ran plentiful with beaver, but they'd been there, to a man. They hadn't been to Californy. Plenty of land westwards a white man hadn't even seen.

General Ashley called for the men to assemble after breakfast. They liked him well enough. Though he did seem to think he was above them, and had sat out yesterday's squabble with the Blackfeet, he took chances like a genuine mountain man, and knew a Blackfoot's moccasin sign from a Crow's. Since he was an officer of the Missouri militia, and an influential politician besides, he spoke to them now with a decorum suiting his station:

Mountaineers and friends! When I first came to the mountains, I came a poor man. You, by your indefatigable exertions, toils, and privations, have procured me an independent fortune. For this, my friends, I feel myself under great obligations to you. Many of you have served with me personally, and I shall always be proud to testify to the fidelity with which you have stood by me through all danger, and the friendly and brotherly feeling which you have ever, one and all, evinced toward me. For these faithful and devoted services I wish you to accept my thanks.

My friends! I am now about to leave you, to take up my abode in St. Louis. Whenever any of you return thither, your first duty must be to call at my house, to talk over the scenes of peril we have encountered, and partake of the best cheer my table can afford you.

I now wash my hands of the toils of the Rocky Mountains. Farewell, mountaineers and friends! May God bless you all![2]

It was well done. Even if the General had used some words they didn't know, they cottoned what he meant. He probably had fine fixens in that home, which might do nicely if a man wanted to set on a chair again.

What he said wasn't news. Every child had heard the tale that the General had got what he wanted and was getting out of it. The real news pleasured every man there: The new proprietors of the Company, succeeding Ashley-Smith, were Jed Smith, Bill Sublette, and David Jackson, fine niggurs all. Most of the men had followed at least one of the three as his booshway, had set in camp and yarned with all of them, and had got shot at with them. All three of them could read and write and keep track of what the men had coming. The main thing was, each of them had the ha'r of the b'ar in him.

Smith, who didn't put out many words, was the most respected man in the mountains. Every man knew that he had found the land route to Crow country, had found South Pass, and had led out west of Salt Lake looking for the Buenaventura just last spring. He was some distant from the run of the men: Aside from not saying much, he carried a Bible which he read pretty often. A lot of them had heard him pray when a man was buried. Most of the men figured that God wasn't much use out here—He stayed on His own side of the Missouri River—but they reckoned that 'Diah was doing the right thing.

He was even making a map, the tale had it—a map to show the whole of the West to the government of the United States, which also stayed mostly on its own side of the Missouri. That was why he had followed the Englishers clear to Flathead Post, and why he had hunted for the Buenaventura this last spring. That was why all the men believed the rumor that Jed Smith intended to strike out southwest from rendezvous. The maps back in the States said that the Buenaventura showed the way to Californy. If it didn't flow straight west or northwest from Salt Lake, why, then, it must go out southwest. Old Jed would find it. Maybe he'd find beaver too, or maybe he wouldn't. But every man of them was sure that he would follow the Buenaventura to Californy. And most of them wanted to go along.

Daniel Potts sent a letter back with General Ashley to his parents, and he promised that his next letter would come from the mouth of the Columbia itself, brought by ship clear around Cape Horn. If Smith didn't say it, Potts knew blame well that that's where Smith was headed. It just made sense.

Though Smith didn't say it in so many words, his new partners knew it too. They sat in a spacious tipi to talk about business prospects. A fire burned in the center, its smoke wafting out through the hole at the top. The hides along the sides were rolled up a couple of feet to let in the evening breeze. A pot sat on the fire, boiled meat simmering in its water. The three agreed that they had to take a lot of packs of plews this first year. They had bought the company from Ashley by signing a note for $11,000, to be paid in beaver at three dollars a pound in St. Louis. Or, if they gave him notice by special dispatch to St. Louis in the spring, Ashley would bring supplies to next summer's rendezvous and take the plews back with him, deducting the cost of transportation from the price of sale. The three suspected that Ashley had gotten the most profitable part of the business in supplying them. In any case, they would have to make good hunts in the coming fall, and Sublette would make the winter journey to St. Louis if things were going well.

Sitting cross-legged around the fire, they hashed out

their plans. Jackson and Sublette would take their brigades into Snake country. The beaver was some there, and they had established good relations with the Shoshone nation. But Bill and Dave would have to get the bulk of the beaver this year, for 'Diah had in mind to gamble. He would set out southwest of Salt Lake and find the Buenaventura, if it was there. He would explore that country and go as far as he had to go to find beaver. If the gamble paid off, he would open up a rich new country for hunting. But he might come back empty-handed, so Bill and Dave would have to make sure of their hunts and decide about the express to Ashley on their own.

If Jackson and Sublette reckoned that what their senior partner really had in mind was to be the first man to see new country and to fill in the area carefully lettered UN-EXPLORED on his map, they didn't say so.

Smith went about getting ready.[3] He chose seventeen men to go with him: Harrison Rogers was to be his clerk and second-in-command; Rogers, a Missourian and a Calvinist, would distribute supplies and keep a daily journal of the expedition. He added to his list Arthur Black, who had been along since 1823; Manuel Eustavan; Robert Evans; Daniel Ferguson; John Gaiter; Silas Gobel, a blacksmith; John Hanna; Abraham Laplant; Manuel Lazarus; Martin McCoy; Peter Ranne, a negro; James Reed, another blacksmith; John Reubascan; John Wilson; and a Nipissing Indian from Canada whom they called simply Neppasang. Despite his letter home, Daniel Potts was disappointed and left behind along with a lot of others who wanted in. Those would be some doin's, out westward.

Smith stocked in powder, balls, traps, and jerked meat for his men. He took a large quantity of trade goods for the Indians he would meet—combs, bells, lead, rings, knives,

ribbon, cloth, mirrors, tobacco, and various doodads—
presents that were the price of admission to each tribe's
territory. Smith wanted to make friends with the Indians,
not fight them. He was securing a business future.

The night before the expedition, Jed had whisky issued
to each of his men for a big blow-out. It was a time for
celebration. The mountain men had grown to love the
Cache Valley with its gentle weather, summer and winter, good water from the Bear River, and bountiful game;
the meadowlark, the hermit thrush and wood thrush, the
oriole, and the mountain jay lightened the air with their
chirpings. The place made a man seem, somehow, welcome.
After this first rendezvous there, the mountain men learned
to think of Cache Valley as their home in the Stony Mountains. They decided to have another rendezvous the following summer. The small one of 1825 had been useful; this
one had turned into a county fair and been helpful, besides.
They would come to Bear Lake next July.

"Levé, Levé," shouted Rogers at first light of the morning of August 16, and stirred himself toward being ready
to get gone. *"Leche lego, leche lego,"* he cried in bastard-
ized mountain lingo at the stragglers two or three minutes later. The men wolfed down their breakfasts. They
got the mules loaded, saddled their horses, made a last
check of their possible sacks, and mounted up. They came to
eighteen mounted men and about fifty horses and mules,
all told. Smith sat his horse in front, Rogers in back. The
Shoshones stared at the line as it started moving. Ranne,
the black, clucked at a pubescent girl, a girl he had had,
who took a few steps out from her family lodge and looked
ready to bolt back. Omogua raised a hand as Smith
passed. The only sound was creaking leather until Evans stuck his pistol straight up and fired. Dan Potts, in

the Shoshone encampment early to trade or still there from last night, looked quietly at the line. Black shouted out to him, "I'll eye ye at rendezvous, Old Coon, if ye hold onto you ha'r."

They moved down the Bear River that day, and the next day into the valley of the Salt Lake, then due south along the lake's eastern edge. Though they were still on home ground, Smith took the usual nighttime precautions. The horses and mules were first let out to graze and then, at bedtime, hobbled within the circle of the sleeping men. He set a guard. Even the friendliest Indian would sneak a horse away, for sport or for honor.

They tramped on, across the Weber River and along the Jordan. The Wasatch Mountains thrust up to 12,000 feet on their left. On the sixth day, they moved up Eutaw Valley to Eutaw Lake and ceremoniously greeted the Yutes.

These Indians knew the white man. The tale was that half a century earlier, two Spanish friars had passed through their country. Since then, occasional parties had made their way to Eutaw Lake from Santa Fe, including those led by Provost. Smith smoked the pipe gravely with the Yutes, gave them his compliments, proclaimed his friendly intentions, and handed out presents—three yards of red ribbon, ten awls, a razor, a dirk knife, a brass-handled knife, forty balls, some arrow points, and half a pound of tobacco. Then he asked about the country west and south of there, because Eutaw Lake was the real kicking-off point. No trapper had ever gone west or south of the lake.

The Yutes couldn't tell him much, they said. The tribe had lived, since before the memory of the oldest men, around this lake and in Eutaw Valley. Of the other land they knew little. Of beaver they knew nothing, of rivers only rumors. A man might have to travel many sleeps without water, they suggested. And he might have to eat the parfleche soles of his moccasins, because little game would go to such a place, animals being wise. One brave seemed to be saying, through signs, that if a man went ten sleeps in that direction, and then ten or twenty more, he could come to the end of the world. But the Yutes did not know.

Jed Smith, moving his men out the next morning, was glad that he had brought seven hundred pounds of dried buffalo meat. They rode south, keeping the Wasatch range to their left, the country drying up all around them. The hills were burnt sienna now. The buffalo sign had disappeared. They saw only an occasional antelope or mountain sheep, and a lot of black-tailed hares. Because they had nothing else, Jed or Rogers shot the rabbits and roasted them. Jed wondered when the country would get better.

After three days, they struck a fine river, a dozen yards wide and deep to a man's chest. But it was not the Buenaventura, because it was flowing back north. Jed figured it must empty into Eutaw Lake. He pushed up the valley of Ashley's River, as he named it. The valley was entirely barren of trees; they found grass only in the dry beds of side streams that flooded during the spring runoff. The animals' hooves kicked up clouds of gritty dust that got in the men's eyes and noses. No game.

On the second day they ran into some Indians, the Sampatch; there were only a couple of handfuls of them, and they were friendly. Jed passed out gifts to these proprietors of a pitiful land. They trekked on seventy miles more, and the valley simply closed up. No sense in trying the steep, narrow, forbidding cut of rock the river poured out of. Jed turned right up Clear Creek, labored to the top of the ridge, and looked west and south.

A calm ocean of sagebrush, gray-green nearby and gray-blue in the distance. The September heat was searing—the sunlight glare so intense that it seemed that a man might touch it. Taking a breath hurt because the air was as dry as it was hot. Jed knew that he could not be sure of finding water as far as he could see. In the distance, to the west, hills as barren as a grindstone floated above the horizon, half-connected to the earth. He looked at the half-green of junipers nearby; these at least were real. He expected to find no game. He touched his horse and moved south, down the sterile valley.

The men began to grumble now. This was no beaver country, they muttered. Water might have made this place, they could see from the strange formations, but it had high-tailed out for good and left the country to the baking sunlight. Nobody could live here; they spotted an occasional Indian in the distance, elusive as the mountain sheep. Even as they spoke, their tongues began to thicken and their lips cracked in the dryness.

The buffler meat was gone, and they had nothing left to eat. Why, it was madness, setting out into such a hell without a thing to fill your belly and no hope of finding it. The first night they had a dry camp. Each man sat, dazed by his own misery, thinking about water. That night they dreamed tantalizingly of Cache Valley, the sweet water of the Bear, and of buffler hump or buffler liver eaten raw.

A horse sank down in his steps the next morning and gave out. Some of the men cut him open and drank his blood. Jed kept them from cutting him up for meat; he thought he saw a likely spot for water ahead, and they couldn't lose any time getting to it. Hell of a thing. Further on, he stopped the line while he searched. He didn't say much, but he seemed sure of what he had to do and what he could do. An hour later he led them to a tiny spring with a few tufts of grass. That night they killed one of the weaker horses for meat—it didn't make much difference which one, Black remarked, unless one of your moccasin soles was fatter than the other. The next day was the same, except that the camp was dry again, and the next the same again, until they found another piddling spring. The following morning three horses were dead, and they stayed to jerk the meat. About a week after they set out across this useless plain—the men weren't keeping track of time—they came to a sort of river. Jed named it the Lost River because it kept getting lost from its bed, popping out only here and there in small holes. The animals ran headlong for the water, which was brackish; they pawed and brayed and whinnied when there wasn't enough. The men grumbled, dug holes, and let the water seep in with irksome slowness.

The next morning they struck south again. Now the country was changing, and probably for the worse. The mountains and the flat-topped hills glowed red. As they went on, the landscape converted into lurid red walls, pinnacles, battlements, buttresses, and cathedrals of stone. One man muttered that they were about to descend into hell and, sure as water runs downhill, would meet up with the Old Gentleman himself. Reed, Wilson, and Ferguson grouched that they were going to hell all right, thanks to Mr. Smith. Black recollected that Moses and his people had spent forty days and forty nights wandering in the desert, and they were going to go the old boy one better. Smith and Rogers, both devout, said nothing at all, but they noticed that it was some better that the men were talking, better than riding in a sullen or hopeless silence.

It was maddening. Every one of these men, who had seen the Godforsaken places of the West before, knew that water had made this strange country that was more like a fantasy than anything they had ever seen. Running water. Running water had shaped this place and left it dry as a piece of paper that has got soaked and dried up, shriveled and parched. Water had been everywhere. And now not a god-damn drop to drink.

Why did Smith force on? Sure as a prairie hen is a fool and a Crow will steal horses, there was no beaver here. He led them on like it was some damned mission to push forward. But they wanted to live. So had the horses and the one mule that had folded up. Rogers himself wondered what it would come to. And he noticed, when they camped, that the fading sun glowed red on the red rock and red in the west, and after a while a man couldn't tell which was the airy sky and which the solid earth.

They walked slowly through the furnace dryness and the ember-red rock for several days, eating nothing but the flesh of the dying horses and drinking nothing but blood. The animals had been too wobbly to ride for days. Then, running among a few thorny bushes, armored against the savage desert, they found a dry wash and followed it downward. Soon they came on a small, swift river cutting through the barren rock.

The animals tripped over each other as they went pell-mell for water. The men jumped in and let their bodies soak it up. The water was brackish again, but Jedediah called it the Adams, in compliment to the President of the United States. He didn't care that the Spaniards thought it was their territory. The braying of the mules and the whinnying of the horses and the shouting of the men, after their swollen tongues had gone back to normal, made a kind of poor man's celebration. That night they feasted on horse-meat. Too much water had killed as surely as too little.

Jedediah sat apart from the meek good-timing; for the first time in quite a while, he had the leisure to work on his map and his journal. He also thumbed his Bible, its cover worn as a boot sole.

They rested there beside the Adams for a couple of days, letting the ponies rest and jerking the meat of the ones that had died. They expected no game ahead; the river made its little groove through stone, and the color it brought to the land was not green, but rust. The rock held no more sign than did a squaw's heart, one said. The finest they could do would be a measly rabbit or so, to feed eighteen men. And they'd see no human faces.

Riding on, they wound through the red-walled canyon, snaking into stranger and still stranger land. The men could ponder on something other than their next drink now, and could gape at the country that is now Zion National Park. Several of them thought it some; others thought it hellish; others just felt the swaying motion of the horse, heard the clap of hoof on stone, and closed into a half-stupor in the heat. When they woke up the next morning, Manuel Eustavan had disappeared. They wondered whether he could make it back to good country.

The second day downriver, they came on a creek running in from the north, and saw some crude huts of long cottonwood and willow branches on the bank. And, by God, some scrawny little patches of cornstalks, standing up stunted but thick with corn, and some crawling vines with pumpkins sitting underneath. "Hurrah," they cried, "don't that shine!" And an Indian woman, just hearing, stood up among the corn, looked across, and ran.

Jed took some foofuraw and went toward the huts alone. The Indians were naked except for a spot of rabbit fur, and shy as antelopes. He sat for a while, spreading his marvels on the earth and sometimes holding one out, as a man woos a frightened dog. Finally a bold one came out of the brush, and eventually the rest followed. Then he led them to the men and horses. They had never seen a white man before, nor a horse. A naked boy crept up, touched Ranne's black hand, and scooted off, giggling. They still acted skittish. But Jed found out that they called themselves Pa-Utches or Paiutes. When a couple of the men shot their pistols, the poor Paiutes cringed, and bolted. All of them were scrawny and scraggly, poor specimens even for Indians, the men thought. Jed treated them just like people. They traded him some corn and pumpkins, plus a marble pipe and a flint knife that Jed had saved for William Clark, way back in Missouri. Jed called the stream Corn Creek and moved on.

A little further on Jed saw a cave and crossed the river to inspect. Behind the entrance the cave widened out into a large room—filled with rock salt. Jed got some specimens for General Clark. As they rode now, the canyon deepened into a narrow gorge. The walls fell so sheer to the river that the party had to move into the river bed to keep going. Gradually the gorge narrowed so that even the sun didn't reach to the bottom except at mid-day, and they traveled in half-twilight the bulk of the time. They had to walk most of the way now, and a horse died nearly every day. This place looked like it might steepen just a little more and plunge straight into the earth. Wagh! They'd have to walk into hell, and they judged that their scrawny mules wouldn't get even that far.

And then they came out of the gorge into a beige waste-land. Even the red faded now, as though the land were too poor to afford any color. White sand stretched away from them, and the bony ribs of mountain were dust-colored and, sometimes, black. Jedediah pushed on without a word.

The only foliage was sagebrush, and a cactus Jed named "cabbage pear," a sort of prickly pear that looked like an egg standing on its small end. In this blighted country, Neppasang deserted. No one troubled to wonder what chance he had.

A couple of days later they came to a huge, surging river of a muddy, reddish brown. Jed knew it for the Siskadee. And now he understood why it was called the Colorado. It was about October 1. This river would take him, he had heard, to the Gulf of California. He was within reach of the Spanish country, Californy. The river quickly turned south. To his right yawned the Mojave Desert. But the men looked east across the river and saw another miserable patch of corn and a small hut.

They spent half a day getting across the deep, strong Colorado. The Pa-Utche farmer on the east side, living alone with his family there in his spot of desert, traded them garden sass for the white man's goods. And he mentioned an Indian village down the river maybe fifteen sleeps. Many Indians. Much to eat.

Greasewood and some stunted trees lined the river valley. They moved south slowly, finding the going ornery along the bank, but they weren't fool enough to go far from the only water. It was a bad journey. So many horses had died, and the ones left were so miserable, that all the men had to walk all the time. The horses got so emaciated that their backbones stood up in ridges and the skin made gullies between their ribs. For twenty-one days they staggered downriver, supported only by the thought, the dream, the shimmering fantasy of the Indian gardens ahead. Before long they were thin as cornstalks, gaunt, and a little tetched by the blistering heat.

They stumbled into the Mojave villages in the last week of October. Half the animals were dead now, the rest about to be, and the men near enough. But this place was a positive settlement, a small paradise after the furnace-rock purgatory. The mountains had drawn back here and left a broad valley. Green had come from somewhere—willow and mesquite along the river. Though it was (and is) the hottest place that folks were to try to live in, in the entire Southwest, it seemed a garden. The Ammuchaba Indians, or Mojaves, grew corn, beans, and pumpkins, and, besides that, watermelons and muskmelons, and, besides that, a little wheat corn. By God! This was civilization! Down toward the south end of the valley a strange rock formation stuck its points up into the sky, narrow and spiky like the leaves of the agave bush, as a reminder of what surrounded them.

These Ammuchabas knew the white man. Spanish friars had been through this way several times. One of the Indians even spoke Spanish lingo pretty good, and they knew where the missions of California lay to the west. They knew because some of them had slipped over there and stolen horses from the mission herds; they also sometimes went to the ocean over there to gather sea shells for trading.

After coming over unknown country and marching toward possible starvation, all the way from Eutaw Lake, Jed had found known territory. The Ammuchabas were friendly and glad to trade their garden goods for manufactured mysteries. They would even trade their horses for Jed's withered animals and some more presents. Most crucial, they knew the way to California across a desert that looked worse than anything he had passed.

If California had been only a notion Jed half-entertained before, he had to commit himself to the Spanish settlements now. He might not be able to get his men and horses over the trail they had just come by; or, if he could, it would be unprofitable: There wasn't a beaver between there and Salt Lake. He had lost the fall hunt completely. Maybe he could make it up in California; the tales had it that California was warm the year round, so he could even trap during the approaching winter. He would strike toward the southern end and move his men north toward San Francisco and make excuses to the Mexican authorities for being there without passports. From San Francisco he could turn east to rendezvous. He could even move up the Buenaventura from its western end and follow it to Salt Lake, if it went to Salt Lake. Then he would have found two routes to California.

He would have explored in a southwesterly direction, and then directly from west to east. He would have filled in the blank space of that map. If he could also get some plews, he would feel better about a bad expedition. Meantime, he let his men rest for two weeks. They lazed, ate all they wanted, drank freely, dazzled the Ammuchabas with glittery things, and had their first women in too long a time. The Ammuchaba men were tall and powerfully built, and wore either nothing or a loincloth. The women were roundish and friendly; they wore nothing but a fringe of bark around their waists. They were bubblingly curious about the black white man, Ranne. Some of the girls were pretty enough to catch the fancy even of the austere Jed. Jed and Laplant, who spoke crude Spanish, spent time talking with the Spanish-speaking Indians to learn what they could of California.

On November 10, they set out with two guides, both runaways from the forced christianizing of the missions, on the Mojave Trail. They followed their guides west and sometimes a little north through one of the earth's most severely desolate regions. They rode on a dry, crumbly soil that would support nothing but the woody yucca and an occasional cabbage pear, both plants that survived by absorbing moisture from the dry air and not from the earth. They rode across sandy washes cut by water at some time or other. They rode across the flat beds of dry lakes crusted with a light soil as fine as grains of salt. They wound in-between mountains that were absolutely barren; some of them were bleached white as the bones of a dead buffalo; others were lava black; some were lumpy, like the droppings of some gargantuan beast, a macabre joke of God.

This desert didn't make sense. God had made the earth to give life, every kind of life, and one kind springing from another, as they well knew. This land was not only barren of life, it repelled life. It was a land of cinder cones; it had been burned to death. Those mountains, alone in God's creation, nurtured no living thing. They were heaps of rubble.

The march was from water hole to water hole. On the first evening, they rode to a dry wash coming off a mountain, and their guides swung off their horses for no reason a man could see. The Indians just started scraping in the sand. After a couple of feet the sand got moist. A foot more, and salty water began to seep in. It was foul but drinkable. The horses were jumpy, like they might bolt, so the men spread and dug their holes. The water came, but stingily, with a maddening slowness.

If the desert sun fried them all day, the moon froze them at night. They huddled in their robes and barely dozed, restless to move on. The next day was the same, and they found a seep that made an excuse for a spring that night. From then on they tried to travel nearer dawn and twilight, and to rest during the oven of the day and the bitter cold of the night. They plugged their way painfully through this hostility which prospectors were to name the Devil's Playground.

About the sixth day out, they walked their horses onto a huge flat expanse that gleamed white in the sun. The sheer whiteness was blinding. One of the men reckoned that the pearly gates couldn't shine brighter. Several of them remembered that it was like walking into the biggest snowfield in Absaroka on a sunny day, when a man could go snowblind as fast as he could blink. Except that there was more sun and glare here, and it was hotter than snow is cold. It was the bed of Soda Lake, dried into a salt flat.

They turned left along the bed, which was easy going, followed the edge of the sink, and finally camped on its surface. That night Jed recorded the location of the sink on his map, and noted in his journal that it had "a crust of beautiful white salt, quite thin. Under this surface there is a layer of salt from a half to one and a half inches in depth; between this and the upper layer there is about four inches of yellowish sand."[4] Practical Jedediah always noted where salt was to be found. Digging was useless that night, in the lake that wasn't wet. The moon turned its surface into a pale, white ghostland, and keened the chill.

At first light, they found the river that didn't run. Not far up its dry bed stood a couple of pools of water, surrounded by a few hardy willows and cottonwoods. Men and horses alike waded in to their chests. Plodding west and a little south along this river, they discovered pools capriciously swelling to the surface. Jedediah named it the Inconstant River. Luckily, the pools kept cropping up.

Day after day they wound along the Inconstant. The desert around stayed barren. They saw the spiny cactus, yucca, some greasewood, and an occasional Joshua tree, its strange arms undulating skyward. Rogers said those trees looked like they might be praying. Someone added drily that they had good cause. God must be testing them like He did Job, because He sure as hell wasn't answering their prayers.

The same bleak mountains spotted the landscape. The only hope for change lay due west, where a solid range rose up, running north and south. Just left of west, they could even see snow on the tops of peaks that topped ten thousand feet. There would be water, and wood, and game. Beyond those mountains, Jed figured, must be the mission and the Pacific Ocean.

The pools of standing water got more regular as they snaked along the Inconstant toward the eastern slopes of the San Bernardino Mountains. The river even developed a trickle. Where the river forked, they went right, west, and started up the brushy slopes. In time they fought their way up to a fair-sized lake. The men began to smile occasionally. From the top of a pass, they looked down into the San Bernardino Valley.

They saw meadows, orchards, vineyards in the distance, and far beyond a thin bluish strip below the horizon, more a light than a color really, that must be the Pacific. Most amazing of all, they saw a pale flickering, like green fire, in the meadows. It was the first grass of the California winter, brought by the new rains. In the last week of November, after fifteen days in the desert, they had journeyed from a torrid summer into a gentle spring.

And into the Promised Land. Among the live oaks, arching their branches over the ground in a stately benediction, they could see herds of animals—thousands of cattle, horses, and some sheep. They traveled on down to

the lower slopes, westward, passing several Indian herds-
men. When they camped, an old Indian came to them
and, in good Spanish, invited them to the mission farmhouse nearby, a pair of long, barrackslike buildings. The
Indians gave them plenty of cornmeal, killed a fat young
cow for them, and set the men to feasting. A couple of emissaries arrived from the mission proper and politely invited Jedediah to join them at the main establishment. He
went. The men had their first real blow-out since the rendezvous. Well, it had been mean country, but the thing
had come out shinin', hadn't it? They didn't even need to
lay eyes on them señoritas just yet.

To Jedediah, two things mattered most: that he had pioneered a route to California, and that his brigade was in
a desperate situation. They had no provisions left, almost
no plews, and no right to be in this foreign country.

He surrendered his arms and sat down to write the
governor of Upper California. He described his situation
and asked permission to pass northward through Spanish
territory to the Bay of San Francisco. From there, he said, he
would follow the Buenaventura east, cross the mountains,
and proceed to Salt Lake.

The next morning Rogers got a note from Smith in-
structing him to bring the company in to the San Gabriel
Mission. When they arrived, the men were disarmed.
Smith and Rogers were treated to a splendid dinner, with
whisky, plenty of wine, and cigars, in the company of two
of the priests. Rogers noted in his journal that they now
expected to stay at the mission for some days, waiting for
word from the governor. He didn't have to add that he relished the prospect.

The men didn't particularly take to having their weapons removed. Were they prisoners? Wal, if they were, they
reckoned it would shine for a spell anyways. Black pro-

posed to Gobel, with a grin, that they size up the Spanyard women. They liked what they found out—that the señoritas considered it a positive honor to sleep with a white man. Or a black white man. They were downright brazen.

One came straight up to Rogers, who spoke no Spanish, asked him to make her a *blanca pickanina*. After repeating herself several times and making some gestures to indicate what she wanted, she got through to Rogers. But she had gone against the grain of his Calvinist background and his sense of propriety for a white man. "I must say," he recorded in his day-book, "for the first time I was ashamed, and did not gratify her or comply with her request, seeing her so forward, I had no propensity to tech her." The good man was much provoked, to have written it down. He says nothing about the times before, when he was not ashamed, and did "comply." "The women here are very unchaste," he noted. "All that I have seen and heard speak and appear very vulgar in their conversation and manners."[5] What Rogers found vulgar other men found a fantasy come alive. They had all the fun they could want.

After awhile, though, they began to get bored and restless. After a few days, Smith rode to the Pueblo of Los Angeles, nine miles distant, to inquire about getting horses and mules. He could get as many as he wanted, he was told, when the governor gave him permission to move on. But the days dragged on with no response from the governor, José Maria Echeandia, and all got impatient. Smith put Gobel and Reed, the blacksmiths, on a small project, making a bear trap for the mission. The mission, in return, gave Smith cloth, and his nearly naked men made themselves shirts. Wilson was insolent, and Jed had him flogged; that quieted him down. Rogers handed out rings to the men, who, in turn, distributed them among the ladies.

The Mission of San Gabriel ran, at this time, a prosperous and benevolent tyranny. A few friars and some soldiers ruled several thousand Indians, teaching them at once the benefits of Christianity and the virtues of agriculture. They were more or less at war with the "savage" Indians of the interior, and their own Indians lived in a kind of gentle slavery. They produced hides and tallows for trading to the ships that ranged the coast, and their own whisky and blankets. The benevolent rulers had their claws as well: Jed's two guides, runaways from the mission, were imprisoned; one died in prison, and the other had to be saved from execution by a priest.

Almost two weeks after they arrived. Jed was summoned to San Diego to see the governor. This gentleman proved to be suspicious. He knew nothing about beaver or beaver trapping, but he knew that Smith had brought an American party across the desert and into Spanish territory. That was unprecedented. Why should he not believe that they were on a military expedition, spying on Spanish territory? That they were an advance guard of many more Americans to come into Upper California? That there were more than the sixteen men this Smith admitted to? That the government of the United States did not covet his province as a new territorial acquisition? The government of Mexico did not like the idea of these Americans tramping all over Mexican land, which extended all the way to Texas and on to the Salt Lake.

To convince the governor that "I was only a hunter and that dire necessity had driven me here"[6]—which was mostly but not completely true—Jedediah gave him the journal he had kept on the way, gave him eight fine pelts, and showed him the use of beaver. But the governor, Smith wrote the American embassy, seemed inclined to require

Smith to go to Mexico City to settle the matter. That would involve months of delay, and Jed would lose the spring hunt.

Fortunately, some shipmasters in San Diego harbor vouched for Jed's intentions, and the governor gave him permission to move on—with one crippling condition. The brigade was not to go north through California, but back across the desert by the way they came.

Content enough, Jed sailed to San Pedro, rode to the mission, and made preparations for moving on. On January 10 they started riding, without Daniel Ferguson, who hid from them and got to stay in California.

The fifteen men left also stayed in California, because Jed had his own interpretation of the governor's order. He moved the brigade back east and across the San Bernardino Mountains. But then, instead of going east across the desert, he followed the eastern slopes of the mountains north, through Antelope Valley, and over the Tehachapi Mountains into the huge San Joaquin Valley. This wasn't California, Jed reasoned, this was the interior. California was the strip along the coast controlled by the missions; this was free country. Besides, he had heard vague reports at the mission of lakes and beaver in the north of this great valley. Almost all he had to show for the fall hunt were marks on his map and notes in his journal. It was time to get something accomplished for Smith, Jackson and Sublette in terms of good, merchantable beaver fur.

At first the country was discouragingly desolate, but as he pushed farther north, Jed saw a huge range of mountains rise on the east. Clear, swift mountain streams roiled down, and gave the country the green of trees and grass, which in turn gave it deer, elk, antelope—and beaver. He trapped his way up the San Joaquin Valley, now in shinin' times. This was living that the mountain men took to: mild weather, even springlike weather, game in abundance, and beaver galore. They met a few Indians, naked creatures, virtually unarmed, who foraged on acorns and roots and caught occasional fish. They were friendly, but the men marveled at critturs who would live so poor on a land so rich.

As Jed moved north, he began to wonder where this mountain, as he called ranges of mountains, would break and let him through. The wall of rock and snow had looked solid for over 300 miles. He would have to start back toward rendezvous soon. In the first week of May he decided to give it a go. He was camped on a middling-sized river northwest of San Francisco. He would march along it into the mountains, force a way across, and strike east across the desert. Mount Joseph, as he had named the Sierra Nevada in honor of the friar who had treated him so graciously at the San Gabriel Mission, might not prove so formidable.

He trekked up the rough canyon of what was later named the American River. Soon the patches of snow on the north-facing slopes and in the shade developed into half a dozen inches of ground cover. The foliage dropped back, the pine disappeared, and the junipers were thinning. Jed noticed a solitary alpine lily poking its blossom through the snow, the first sign of spring at this elevation. But as the way steepened, the snow got deeper and deeper. The horses began to flounder. The men got off and led them, only to blunder into drifts and plunge in to the crotch. They were sweating heavily even in the snow: It was hard work. They were sinking in to the knees and walking sharply up besides. They were far beyond any possible food now; the game had been forced to lower elevations. The mules bore dried meat along with the plews of a good hunt; the weight made them more helpless against the snow.

They camped in deep snow on the fourth night. The men squatted in the snow around a small fire; firewood was sparse now. Everyone was miserable—worn to a frazzle, discouraged, frustrated. As they picked at their meals, Jed thought it over. Probably there was a way through here (and there was—Donner Pass). But all he could see was reach after reach of snowy wasteland, spreading on for no telling how many days' travel. They had had flutters of snow. A serious storm might make them unable to go on or go back. The animals were too burdened to struggle through. Two had died of cold, fatigue, and starvation the night before, and several looked like they would be dead before morning. He made up his mind to turn back. At this point, getting out would seem achievement enough.

Back down the creek, through the canyon, and into the valley. Five horses had gone under. Jedediah moved several days back along his own trail and made camp on the Appelaminy River.

Meanwhile the administrators of the mission system had heard that the Americans were still in California. The president of all the missions accused Smith of being responsible for a massive defection from the San José Mission. Jedediah, hearing the various rumors, wrote to the president explaining that he had tried to cross the mountains and failed; he was eager to move back to home territory as the Mexican authorities were to have him gone. The governor, though, decided that firmer measures were necessary: He instructed the military commander in San Francisco that Smith had overstayed his welcome; pending a decision from Mexico City, Smith was to be disarmed and held in San José.

Soldiers arrived at Jed's camp in late May. But the American captain was gone. Leaving the bulk of his men, he had taken two companions and started back up into the Sierra Nevada.

FOURTH INTERLUDE

Rendezvous

AFTER THE TRAPPERS ABANDONED THE SYSTEM OF *fixed posts, they needed a new way to get their furs to market and to buy supplies for the coming year. The answer was improvised in 1825, when they gathered from all over the country west of the divide to meet General Ashley on Henry's Fort of the Green River. This first rendezvous was a modest affair—Ashley had not yet learned that he would sell more whisky than anything else—but it did the job. The men got their provisions, and Ashley got the fur started toward St. Louis. The logic of the rendezvous system struck everyone: Summer was no good for trapping, and it was the best time to move a packtrain to the mountains. So it became an annual event, and never again was it a modest affair. It lasted until the early 1840s, when beaver was scarcely worth taking any longer, and it was the shinin' time of a mountain man's year.*

A new hand at rendezvous would wonder what he had gotten into. Take a man, for instance, who had come out from the States in 1826 with Ashley's packtrain to deliver supplies to the trappers and to take the furs back to St. Louis. He was greeted by a band of riders, white and In-

*dian together, shooting into the sky as though powder
and ball were as common as sagebrush. This strange
band provided escort to the wide, flat wooded spot in the
Cache Valley where hundreds of mountain men had spread
their robes, and hundreds—my God! thousands!—of
Indians had erected their lodges.*

*What he saw was Saturnalia. He had heard the tales,
on the way out, of the willingness of Indian women. Now
he could see an age-old adage in action: When different
races of men meet for the first time, they fight and then
they fornicate. His immediate interest was in seeing
whether he could really get something in the cottonwoods for the two or three doodads he had saved up. He
could.*

*The immediate interest of the veteran mountain men,
though, was the medicine water, the same whisky that
our rookie had seen General Ashley water down to half-
and-half with liquid from the Green River some miles
back, with ginger and red peppers for spicing. Some of
them drank until they vomited and, scarcely missing a
swig, went on guzzling. Others drank until they passed
out. Others drank until they got belligerent, roused a fist-
fight, and got knocked out. Drinking, for men who had
done without since the last rendezvous, a year earlier,
was the first order of the day. If Ashley was marking it up
from maybe twenty cents a gallon to five dollars a pint—
and watering it down besides—nobody really gave a damn.
It was a sight better than alkali water.*

*Besides, a man needed a little stupor to forget some
things. That a number of good hosses hadn't come to
rendezvous this year—must have gone under. That he
himself had had a couple of brushes with Blackfeet he'd
rather forget. That he was beginning to show signs of the*

clap again. That prices were so ridiculous that his fortune in plews would turn into just enough fixens for another year. That he was never going to make the fortune he boasted of in his annual letter home.

The rookie had nothing to forget and everything to wonder at. Here came a village of Indians to rendezvous putting on a show that would shame anything. The braves were making their horses gallop and prance and curvet, a maneuver in which the horse leapt into the air with both front legs at once, making little half circles from leap to landing. Men and women alike were dressed in their best buckskins and brightly painted. The squaws wore their jewelry—porcupine quills, or bear claws; they shined their buckskins with white clay, and they trimmed them in vermilion.

When they got their lodges set up, the village was a bazaar. White men dangled gadgets in front of the squaws' eyes and made a quick deal. Braves traded plews or robes for the white man's goods. Squaws offered mountain men buckskin leggings and shirts in return for beads or mirrors.

And they started into their long sessions with the hand game. They lined up in teams and bet on which hand held the magic emblem. This was a piece of carved bone. The gambler would put his fists together so that the bone could come away in either hand. The bettor would guess which hand it was in, and win or lose all on this fifty-fifty chance. Whites loved it as well as Indians, in spite of the magical incantations that the Indians would always use to bring luck.

Then the other contests would get rolling—riding, shooting, foot-racing, horse-racing, fighting, and whatever else one man might beat another in. The trapper had his pride to live up to. He would have to have women until he panted with fatigue, drink until he fell down, fight until he was knocked down, and then rouse his buddies from the sagebrush and force everyone to do it all again.

After a couple of days, it would simmer down. The debauch would turn to soberer sports like exchanging news, regreeting old friends, and telling yarns. Time to enjoy life.

Now a trapper might have the leisure to notice things— the peculiar feel of sunlight just before evening in high places, and warm rose of alpenglow, the sound of the creek and the sound of cottonwoods rustling beside it, the smell of meat, and the glint from an eye of a coyote skulking just beyond the fire, drawn to the smell. This was the time of fulfillment. And this was the time a trapper would spin his yarns, his stories bigger than the flapjack a cowhand once ate, or the spruce a lumberjack once felled bigger even than the whirlpool a Mississippi riverman once avoided with only a teaspoon of water to spare. Stories worthy of men like Paul Bunyan.

The mountain men stretched themselves out, in these stories and maybe in their lives, to the size of Paul Bunyan. This annual rendezvous was their carnival, their county fair, their Mardi Gras, their homecoming celebration, their harvest feast. Washington Irving describes one:

It was a rich treat . . . to see the "chivalry" of the various encampments engaged in contests of skill at running, jumping, wrestling, shooting with the rifle, and running horses. And then their rough hunters' feasts and carousals. They drank together, they sang, they laughed, they whooped, they tried to outbrag and outlie each other in stories of their adventure and achievements.

Here the free trappers were in all their glory; they considered themselves the "cocks of the walk" and always carried the highest crests. Now and then familiarity was pushed too far and would effervesce into a brawl and a "rough and tumble" fight but it all ended in cordial reconciliation and maudlin endearment.[1]

After the brawling, there was serious business to be done. The employees of the company had to keep back enough of their year's wages to set themselves up for next year; the free trappers had to trade their plews for fixens. Powder and lead were first considerations. Then they had to have geegaws to trade or make presents of to the Indians, maybe pants, shirt, or a capote, maybe even another horse or so. If they had lost traps last year, they would have to replace them. And certainly some tobacco.

The buying and trading could be rough. A man might have spent most of what he had on whisky in the first day or two. Then he had to face prices that were marked up as much as two thousand percent. A man who chose to live in the wilds had to pay dearly for the transportation of goods from civilization.

After a couple of weeks he would have had all the fun he could take at once. He would have chawed with the men he wanted to. He would have found out who was president of the United States, what wars had been won or lost, and whether the U.S. had got Oregon from the British yet. So he would clear out for his fall trapping. Hired hands followed their leaders, called partisans or bourgeois, to the chosen ground. Free trappers joined up with a company brigade or set out on their own, as they liked. "This child'll look on yuh next rendezvous," each would say to his friends, "if he's still got his ha'r."

V

Starvin' Times

BILL SUBLETTE AND DAVEY JACKSON HAD BEAVER TO
take. After Smith left Cache Valley for his speculative
expedition southwest in August of 1826, they got their
brigades ready to bring in the plews that would support
the company and pay off the debt to General Ashley. Jackson took his men north and west, to the proven Snake River
country. Sublette moved north and east toward the Grand
Tetons, Blackfoot country, taking with him Bridger, Potts,
Tom Fitzpatrick, and Beckwourth.

He crossed the Blackfoot River, the Portneuf, moved
up Henry's Fork of the Snake River (not the Green River,
which also has a fork named for Major Henry), turned
southeast through Pierre's Hole, struck the Snake again,
and followed it to Jackson Lake. He took his time. It was
still summer, plews were too thin to be worth the trouble of taking, and the men spent their days lazing and
hunting.

They would have been sizably more comfortable, though,
if Blackfeet had not been around. Minor skirmish followed minor skirmish. The whites lost some horses, but
no men. It was still disgruntling. They lost no men because
of the Indian notions about strategy. War, for the Indians,
was fundamentally a matter of honor, a trying-ground in
which a man could prove himself to have stature. If a
brave could steal a horse, he could boast back in the village;
if he could take a scalp, he could boast more struttingly; if
he could count coup, he could boast himself hoarse.
You counted coup on the enemy not by killing him, but

by showing the courage to ride straight up to him and striking him on the head with your coup stick. This idea saved
some trappers' lives.

More important, the Indian and Blackfoot notion of
war was not a battle in which you engaged an equal enemy, accepted some casualties for yourself, and wiped
him out or drove him from his position. A battle in which
a band on the warpath lost a single brave was a cause for
grieving. So the Indians preferred never to match strength
with any sizable group of trappers or other Indians. A
group of twenty trappers could make five hundred Blackfeet back off, simply because the Blackfeet knew that
the trappers were deadly shots and would take at least
twenty braves before they died. The usual Indian strategy, then, was to lie back, keep an eye out, and wait their
chance to catch the trappers singly or in pairs. A brigade
like Sublette's, made of perhaps three dozen men including free trappers, was reasonably safe; you were in danger
only if you wandered or straggled.

A yarn of Jim Beckwourth's, on the scale that made
him known as the Paul Bunyan of liars, is typical: Beckwourth and a Swiss trapper named Alexander went looking for half a dozen horses they had lost, and blundered
into two or three hundred Blackfeet, Beckwourth claimed.
The Indians chased them on foot. Alexander said he
couldn't run fast enough, so Beckwourth told him to hide
in a creek while Beckwourth lured the Indians away.
Somehow, when next they saw him, he had a two-mile
lead. Off he loped, with the divils screaming behind him.
He ran all the way to the Blackfoot Buttes, where his
brigade was supposed to be camped. It had moved on.
Beckwourth tells the rest of the story, in his autobiography, like this:

My feelings at this disappointment transcended expression. A thousand ideas peopled my feverish brain at once. Home, friends, and my loved one presented themselves with one lightning-flash. The Indians were close at my heels; their bullets were whizzing past me; their yells sounded painfully in my ears; and I could almost feel the knife making a circuit round my skull. On I bounded, however, following the road which our whole company had made. I was scorching with thirst, having tasted neither sup nor bit since we commenced the race. Still on I went with the speed of an antelope. I kept safely in advance of the range of their bullets, when suddenly the glorious sight of the camp-smoke caught my eye. My companions perceived me at a mile from the camp, as well as my pursurers; and mounting their horses to meet me, soon turned the tables on my pursuers. It was now the Indians' turn to be chased. They must have suffered as badly with thirst as I did, and our men cut them off from the river. Night had begun to close in, under the protection of which the Indians escaped; our men returned with only five scalps. According to the closest calculation, I ran that day ninety-five miles.[1]

Some eighty-nine miles farther than John Colter had sprinted in his tiff with the Blackfeet, as Beckwourth surely was aware. In his yarns, he one-upped every man in the West.

The mountain men did not treat Blackfeet like folks. They generally made a scrupulous effort to establish good terms with the tribes whose lands they hunted. They made gifts to compensate for trespassing, and they gave the cherished manufactured goods, medicine water, and tobacco in return for plews or clothing or supplies. But the Blackfeet, alone among all the Indians of the plains and mountains, were consistently hostile. Soon every chance meeting was an automatic battle: One side or the other, or both, had a score to settle. And the mountain men learned to take a grim pleasure in killing Blackfeet. Immediately before the yarn above, Beckwourth tells with great relish about burning some horse-thieving Blackfeet to death— forty-four of them. But the mountain men were not alone: Every tribe that lived near the Blackfeet fought with them continuously. The trappers became the enemies of the Blackfeet partly because they were the friends of the Crows, Shoshones, and Flatheads.

Around Jackson Hole, the brigade began to concentrate on beaver, and they worked their way slowly through an area of spectacular and awesome beauty. The range of the Grand Tetons—"big breasts," in the French that the trappers dropped casually into their English and Spanish—lifted from the sage flats to more than 13,000 feet in huge, jutting points. The Grand Teton itself rose slender as a lodge-pole pine, leaning to the east in a purple that made it seem not quite real. One party had been here before, but the place still seemed new and fresh. It made a man marvel and feel things he couldn't put a tongue to, things that were real, but went away if you poked at them with words. Why, it was easy enough to spend a whole day wandering around the edge of the lake, looking at the mountain flowers, the columbine, the aster, Indian paintbrush, pentstemon, and mountain laurel, not like any flowers people thought special on the flatlands. Or to be quiet and watch the trout lying still, then suddenly darting in the water that was clear as the air itself. Or to gather fruits and berries that clustered thick, just waiting for a man's hand, and spread them on biscuits around the fire that night. Or to stand amazed at the brilliant gold of the aspen in autumn. A man somehow wanted to raise his hand in a kind of salute and speak a psalm, except that words would be too light and easy.

Around mid-October they moved on, because the beaver, which the Indians held as the wisest of all animals, were getting trap-wary. They pushed on north toward the headwaters of the Snake River, over a divide, and came onto a timbered plateau. After all they had seen, this made them gape. Here lay a huge lake, "as clear as crystal," according to Dan Potts, and along its edge simmered boiling springs. Some of these springs looked fathomless. Others were boilings of clay, pink or white, like a mush-pot. And they threw globs of hot clay high into the air. The men could smell burning sulphur, and in some places sulphur spewed into the air. They dismounted and looked around, eagerly and cautiously. One of the men was loafing when the ground under him started shaking. Thinking that the earth might open up and swallow him straight into hell, he hightailed it. The roar behind him was so thunderous he thought it would knock him down. Water erupted into the air, "thick as a man's body and high as a flagpole," Jim Bridger said later. The men guffawed at the trapper, running for his life and afraid to look back.

They had wandered into Yellowstone. John Colter had described some bilin's. Might these be the ones? They didn't know. An official expedition would discover this wonderland more than four decades after Sublette's vagabonds camped there.

They decided to stay a spell. Old Ephraim made his presence felt a bit, but so did the deer and elk. After some days they realized that they had seen no redskin and no sign of the red man. Sublette wondered if the superstitious divils were afraid of the place. His own men were a little jittery about it, in fact. When they got back to

rendezvous, Bridger boasted that they had been to hell
and back. The trappers laughed at the tent-revival preach-
ments about hell, but when they looked around Yellowstone, they weren't so cocksure.

Here, in Yellowstone, Bridger got one of his tallest
tales: He saw a whole mountain made out of nothing but
glass. Couldn't see the top of the mountain, Bridger remembered seriously, nor the bottom neither, 'cause it was a
glass mountain. One day, when he was out hunting around
there, he spied an elk within shooting range. Shot him
plumb center and the crittur didn't fall—didn't even run
from the sound. Just stood while Bridger reloaded and
let fly again. Still nothing. Another shot or two and still
nothing. Bridger was hopping up and down, he was so
mad. He made up his mind to club the damn thing with his
rifle, since it wouldn't move. He started running and pretty
soon ran into something that knocked him flat on his
haunches. An entire mountain of glass. And that glass was
a telescope made by God. The elk he shot at was actual
twenty-five miles off.

Eventually they moved out of the second spectacular
area they had roamed within a month. They turned west,
crossed the continental divide, and trapped their way due
south to Cache Valley.

They arrived just as winter set in for sure, and Jackson
had already set up his winter camp along with a number
of Shoshones. He had plews aplenty. Sublette had had a
shinin' season, too. They decided to send an express to
Ashley, the promised word, asking him to fulfill his contract to bring supplies to rendezvous in the summer of 1827.
Sublette would go himself—across the Siskadee, through
South Pass, down the Sweetwater to the north fork of the
Platte, down the Platte across the Great Plains to Missouri,
and then into St. Louis. The mountain men stayed put dur-

ing the winter in their skin lodges, venturing out only to hunt and gather wood, because the mountain winters could easily swallow a man up. But this journey would have to be made in the dead of winter across rugged country.

Sublette chose one man to go with him: Moses (Black) Harris, the smithy of the yarn about the putrefied forest, and one of Beckwourth's two leading challengers for the title of champeen liar of the whole damn West. Alfred Miller, a painter among the mountain men, described him: "He was of wiry form, made up of bone and muscle, with a face apparently composed of tan leather and whip cord, finished off with a peculiar blue-black tint, as if gunpowder had been burned into his face."[2]

They set out on January 1, 1827—on foot. They had to get to St. Louis by March 1. Horses would have no chance against the deep drifts, and would be able to find nothing to eat anyway. They carried snowshoes and dried buffalo meat on their backs. A pack dog, a common beast of burden for the Indians, carried their other provisions lashed onto his back. He would have the easiest trip; he had the least weight and the most feet to distribute it on, so he would trot lightly on the snow while his human companions sank into it on the clumsy oddities they wore on their feet.

They wound up and back down along the big horseshoe bend of the Bear River, then east over a series of ridges and creeks to the valley of the Green River. They checked for sign and found it—not buffler sign, but Blackfoot sign. They knew the moccasin track. Damn. The Blackfeet should have been a couple of hundred miles north, and here they were on the move during the Moon of the Strong Cold. "If they's Blackfeet in these hyar parts," said Harris, "we'd best be south." So instead of following the Sandy northeast to South Pass, they circled south and approached the pass along the plains. They had no water, but they could melt snow in their kettle to a fare-thee-well. The west side of South Pass gave them God's plenty of snow, drifted deep enough to fall into like a well. And if your partner made too much commotion getting you out, the snow would cave in and bury you. The snowshoes did it fine, except that a man's groin muscles ached after a day of walking peculiar in 'em.

On January 15 they reached Independence Rock on the Sweetwater River and made camp away from the wind. They were two weeks out and due in St. Louis by March 1. Sublette wondered if they would make it. The going would be more level now, and their packs were lighter. But Sublette wondered about the bitter winter on those flat plains. If they were late, there might be no 1827 rendezvous, and no Smith, Jackson & Sublette.

It got worse as they moved down the Platte. The mountain winter was mild compared to the plains winter, with its howling winds, ferocious blizzards, and sub-zero temperatures. They couldn't find firewood, so they had freezing camps. They scooped out deep holes in the snow with their axes and crawled into them to sleep; the wind was colder than the snow. They chipped and gnawed at the frozen meat. Their food wouldn't last much longer. And they didn't see any buffalo at all, or anything else a man could shoot and eat. Finally they just kept walking when night came; it was warmer that way. They didn't sleep until they dropped. They learned to be glad for the nights that brought the thick, swirling snow. On clear nights the temperature drop was even more deadly.

Near Ash Hollow on the Platte they came across Pawnee sign. By this time they were staggering from weakness. "They's eatin's," spoke up Harris. "But we might be makin' the meat," They swung away from the river for three days and scooped handfuls of snow for water. They remembered what had happened to Jim Clyman when he met Pawnees.

A little later they came onto the trail of some Omahas—a sizable band that had been through there recently. By now they were starving and dizzy from hunger and fatigue. They followed the trail. Chief Big Elk received them warmly enough, but he couldn't help. In a winter like this, the Omahas were starving too. They plugged on. Soon they came across another band and, by this time, Sublette was desperate. He traded his butcher knife for a dried buffler tongue. He and Harris gulped it down instantly.

Near Grand Island they shot a raven. The two wolfed it down so fast that Sublette didn't remember whether raven tasted good or bad. They were not walking toward St. Louis, they were stumbling. They scarcely looked where they were going because they were looking inside their heads at hump ribs, boudins, and raw livers. On the blank white surface danced imaginary meals, sumptuous and maddening. They crowded the March 1 deadline out of Sublette's mind.

The dog lagged behind every day now and straggled into camp hours late. It had a bad leg and was even more starved than they were. They stood two hundred miles from civilization. One night, Sublette fell into camp exhausted, scraped the snow away for his blanket, and collapsed onto it. Harris broke some branches off some elms and made a little fire. Then he spoke his idea. They ought to kill that dog and eat him. Sublette wrangled with him, but finally gave in. Both men were so weak that they could hardly move, and lived in a half-fantasy land. Harris whacked at the dog's skull with his axe. The beast fell but got up. Harris whacked again and missed. He whacked a

third time, and the head flew off the axe. The dog, whining, got away into the dark. Harris and Sublette fumbled
around until they found the whining animal. Sublette
grabbed it and Harris stabbed it. Then they threw it onto
the fire to singe it. But the damned crittur wouldn't quit;
it kicked off the fire. Sublette grabbed his axe and smashed
its head in.

Then Sublette collapsed into sleep. Harris roasted the
flesh and ate. He saved some for Sublette in the morning.

Further downriver, they left the Platte and made southeast for the Kaw, to save some distance. It was bad going,
for the soft snow let them sink in. They shot a rabbit and
devoured it. Then they got to make some better time: They
happened on a Kaw trail which had packed the snow down
enough to support them. In a bottom they hit a shining
moment. They killed four wild turkeys and had a feast.
When they caught up with the Kaws, they were given
food. But they had to press toward St. Louis. Since Harris
had been gimping along on a sprained ankle, Sublette
traded his pistol for a horse. Two days later they reached
the Missouri, and they rode into St. Louis only three days
late.[3]

It had been a terrible journey. They were cold and miserable for two months; they almost died of starvation; they
had run constant danger from unpredictable Indians.
Black Harris liked it so much that he became a specialist
in the midwinter express, and developed a fine name as a
man of great leg. Sublette didn't enjoy the journey as
much. But he had saved Smith, Jackson & Sublette, at
least for a while.

In Cache Valley the Smith-Jackson-Sublette men had
passed an easy winter, their wherewithal being supplied

handsomely by their home in the mountains. Come spring, they split up again to trap. Jackson went back to the lower reaches of the Snake River and did well. Some other trappers made their way down to Eutaw Lake for beaver.

One of the few bad moments came when they were breaking up winter camp. One of the trappers strode out to make some meat, saw an antelope, and shot it in the head. When he went to skin the animal, he found the body of a Shoshone brave wearing an antelope head. Fitzpatrick, the booshway of the moment, decided the less said the better. He gave orders to break camp in a hurry. The Snakes were their friends, but you never knew how an Indian might take a thing like that. A chief, though, came over to ask why his friends the whites were leaving so soon. Finally Fitzgerald, against his better judgment, told him about the accident. The chief brushed it away and invited them to stay as friends. The brave was a fool to use that decoy, he explained. He knew that antelope wandered around in the sage, and that the white men shot at everything they saw. And then he made the peace with his people.

Jed Smith had got himself into a deep hole. When he came down from his attempt to cross the Sierra Nevada, he was left without time to get to the 1827 rendezvous. He would end up without supplies, with no idea of how his business was going, with no certainty even that his business still existed. And he had heard from Indians that the Spanish were on their way to arrest him. He thought on that and decided to gamble: He left his brigade in the hands of Harrison Rogers, took Silas Gobel and Robert Evans with him, and set out to cross the Sierra with only three men, cross the Great Salt Plain he would probably find on the other side, find food and water somehow, and make the rendezvous. Taking seven horses and two mules loaded with provisions, including hay for the animals in the land of eternal snows just ahead, he left on May 20. He had one day less than six weeks to get there.

He thought he might get across Mount Joseph with better route-finding and fewer, less burdened animals. So he rode up the Appelaminy River and into the rising foothills. The first night they camped on a creek where there was grass aplenty, and even flowers. The second, they camped in half a foot of snow, and the animals had to feed on the hay they carried. On the third, they followed washes that led them up, basin after basin, into high country. Now the snow was drifted deep. The three men, floundering in the deep snow to their hips, led their horses, lifting one leg straight up out of its hole, thrusting it a little forward, and sinking in again. The going was ugly. The trees were stunted now, but the three broke some branches for a small fire.

The next morning Jedediah walked into a deep, soft drift that looked like it might swallow him. He spread his body on the surface of the snow and crawled across it. Then he decided they would have to get out of the draw onto a little ridge. It would be worse in one way because of the wind, but the wind would also have swept most of the snow off the ridge.

Jed led the horses and mules while Gobel and Evans scrambled behind them, whacked them on the rumps, yelled at them, and tried to force them up the steep, slippery grade. After nearly an hour of tugging, prodding, beating, cajoling, and screaming, they made the ridge. Now the wind hurt. It buffeted them from odd angles, and it felt so cold a man didn't want to take it into his lungs. The horses were nervous and fidgety. Jed focused on a juniper ahead, warped by the wind, and made up his mind to get them that far. The tree rose from the rock, where its roots clung to the cracks, and three feet off the ground it bent down-hill. It had given to the wind for years, and had learned to turn its back, like a bowed woman with her hair blown forward by the gale. After the tree, he picked an outcrop-ping of rock for a goal and, above that, a pinnacle that might block their way, and after that another tree. He didn't know but what this route would dead end some-where above. That night they camped on the lee side of a boulder, and shivered all night long.

After an hour of laboring upward the next morning, Jed saw that the ridge ended in a headwall. They would have to get down the slope to the wash. They started con-touring to the right and angling gently downward. Jed led the mules ahead, because they weren't as skittish in bad places as the horses. Halfway down, one of the horses slipped, landed heavily on his left side, and started slid-ing down with his feet pawing the air. His whinnied scream went straight through the men. He slid down headfirst and hit the rocks at the bottom. They forced the other animals along the contour and into the gulley. When Jed went back to see about the horse, he found its head crushed. He shot it and took the equipment.

The next morning it was snowing large, moist flakes, like flapjacks spinning in the air. The wind had quieted; the cold had eased. They labored quietly up the draw, each man deep in his own mental wanderings. When they topped the main crossing ridge, Jed saw that the first slope down was steep and covered with a grainy snow. He began to crisscross downward, moving gingerly on the loose rocks underneath. One of the mules lost her footing, sat down, and started sliding faster on her rump, her tail spread behind like a broom. A hundred feet down she slid sideways, turned over, and went pack first into a drift, her hooves waving.

After a tense moment, she stood up, brayed, and shook herself like a wet dog. Evans and Gobel grinned at each other.

Jed looked at the mountain barrier ahead. They had to cross a wide valley, doubtless drifted deep and infuriating to struggle through, and then somehow, find a pass. He couldn't see a break in the high wall from here.

When they started climbing again, following a little canyon, Jed wondered if everything ahead was cliff. And he wondered whether, if it was, the horses and mules could get back to California before they starved. They would eat the last of the hay that night. Late that afternoon, just before dusk, on a narrow ridge, one of the horses suddenly jumped, lost its footing, and dropped over the side. The horse behind reared, whinnied its fear, staggered, and fell backward over the edge. Both of them tumbled a couple of hundred feet before they stopped. They didn't get up. Gobel and Evans stared down at the bodies. Jed decided to move on. If they tried to get their provisions, they'd likely lose a man.

The morning rose in half-light. The sky brightened, but they couldn't see the sun. The wind was down; the air glowed with the odd clarity of high mountains; the day seemed gentle.

Jed picked the way up the canyon, hoping that it would wind up to a saddle and not end in a wall. At noon, they saw that the way was clear: They had found a pass. From the top, in the bottom of a V between two sharp ridges, they looked east to where they had to go. The mountains fell sharply to a level plain; that stretched flat to another range of mountains, parched dry as a skull—but not as high as these.

They moved faster now. Gobel and Evans cussed at the

mules and horses as they scrambled from basin to basin, slipping and sliding in their hurry. They walked an hour into darkness and camped in a glen full of trees. For the first time since Californy, they built a huge fire and slept warm. The horses nibbled grass where it came through the patchy snow. The next day, they walked into the warmth of May, the Moon when the Ponies Shed. In eight days they had licked Mount Joseph.

More unknown country in front of them. Jed knew they had to strike northeast for the Salt Lake. He had come out from Salt Lake, just a year ago, heading due west and found a salt desert; he had been forced north to the Snake River to find game and water. And he had crossed the country south of here, through the desert around the Mojave villages; no game or water there. He wondered what was ahead.

He made east, riding across the broad, sandy valley, up over the dry mountains, and down the other side to a lake. All went well so far. The next morning they rode up a low ridge. When they reached the top, they could see a long way east. A flat and baked desert stretched almost to the horizon. A sawtooth ridge of bony hills ended it; since the sun had not yet risen above the hills, they lined the horizon black. Jed could only hope there was water out there, somewhere.

This time the desert was in its spring, and the cactus were blooming. It seemed strange to see little pink and orange flowers on the thorny plants, and oddly attractive. The five horses and single mule could feed off greasewood and creosote.

They rode on a huge, sandy plain. The wind blew steady and hard and dried them out. The sun narrowed their eyes to invisible slits. They regularly had to travel a day or two without any water at all. And soon they were walking across the sandy plain. The horses were as weak as they were themselves.

Sticking near the low mountains when they could, they occasionally found a spring. And there they would find Indians, naked and completely shy. They always ran from the pale men. Once Jedediah found out what they ate: He found a rock where they'd been pounding grasshoppers into mush.

After a week, a horse went lame. Gobel quietly took out his Green River and with his blacksmith's arm drove it in to the hilt. They drank the blood, roasted some meat, and set the rest to dry. Wouldn't take long in that sun. On the rest of the animals, the skin had begun to sag between the ribs like the meat laid across green twigs to be smoked.

One noon, when they were walking along with their eyes nearly closed against the glaring sun as the heat shimmered on the sand, they heard thunder. All six eyes shot toward the mountains: Rain. By God, rain! The horses and the mule heard it too, and jostled about. They moved fast toward where the ground began to rise, and soon they found a thick, muddy stream of water running down a wash. The ground, brick-hard underneath, scarcely absorbed it. They scooped it with their cups, drank it mud and all, and poured it over their heads. Evans, who had been suffering miserably, packed wet mud on top of his head and pulled his hat down over it. Then they moved on.

Before long they got more horsemeat. They were used to dying animals by now.

But the desert yawned in front of them as though it had no intention of ever letting up. At night they dreamed of water—of the Bear River wandering through the cottonwoods, of the Wind River, clear and cold, of the tiny creeks that ran through the pastures back in Missouri and

Ohio and Virginia, of the streams that turned the mills back home—and woke up dry.

They killed the third horse before it gave out on its own. Might they even run out of horsemeat? Except for an occasional rabbit, this place had no game. It was hard and dry and useless. No men who could be called men had ever lived here, or ever would. It had no place for life: It was pitiless.

A little over three weeks after they walked off the slopes of Mount Joseph, Smith, Gobel, and Evans were wondering whether they had a chance to live. They were reeling across the desert, staggering with weakness, desperately hungry and thirsty most of the time. Each man retreated into a personal blend of memory, delusion, and half-alertness to the bleak landscape. They said nothing to each other; there would be no point. Often they walked half the night. That meant miles without the heat, and there was no reason to stop until they collapsed.

Evans was the most miserable; Gobel, stronger, was badly discouraged. Smith had his doubts about their prospects, but he encouraged his companions with a forced optimism. Their only hope lay in the mountains. There, lifting above the blazing desert in lofty detachment, stood the land of eternal snow. Water must trickle down from those mountains somewhere. They had to find it before it was swallowed by the sand.

They turned north, walking east along the Deep Creek Mountains near the present Nevada-Utah border. Occasionally, they would see an antelope on the slopes, but never close enough to warrant a shot. Still, there must be water and grass for those antelopes, somewhere. After twenty-five miles of slogging northward, they found a creek and camped. When he had drunk and looked around, Jed ventured a cheerful opinion: "I think we must be near Salt Lake. Country sure looks like it." That night they talked about their friends, the tales they would tell of their trek, whisky, and buffler feasting.

The next morning they followed the creek until it ran into a small lake and didn't run out again. They filled their horns with water; the country ahead might be bone dry. After two dozen or more miles, they stumbled on a spring with drinkable water. Jed said they might find more palatable water further along, so they pushed on. They camped dry that night.

Not long after daybreak the next morning, Jed angled off to the top of a small hill to try to spot water. He saw nothing but sand flats and dry, spiny hills. The nearest hope of water was a snow-topped range fifty or sixty miles away. He caught up with Gobel and Evans and told them that he wasn't sure, but they'd probably find water near something black he had seen at a distance. He also confessed that he knew now they were not near Salt Lake. Evans and Gobel just stared at the sand.

Since one of the horses had given out while Jed was on the hill, he sent Evans and Gobel back for its meat and pushed on to search for water. He found nothing. When they came up, he saw that Evans and Gobel were even more discouraged. This country looked hopeless to them. Jed tried to cheer them up, but he knew the outlook was bleak. He wondered if they might give up.

They walked on, tiring in the soft sand that dragged them back. About four o'clock they stopped to rest by a small cedar, dug holes, and lay down in the cool sand to slake the agony of their bodies. An hour later they forced themselves on. All of life, all their minds, their muscles, their eyes, their dwindling energies were now focused on the need for water. Just after sundown, they saw some turtledoves. Since Jed was sure that doves never strayed far from water, he spent an hour hunting for it. He found nothing. Evans and Gobel ached too much to give a damn. When Jed told them, Evans gave an odd smile.

They lay down about ten o'clock, but slept fitfully. They dreamed of water—"of murmuring brooks, of cooling Cascades," Jed logged in his journal.[4] Half asleep, they could hear the murmur of tumbling water clearly, but they awoke to find themselves still in a parched desert. After an hour or two they gave up trying to rest and marched on. They made forty miles that day and found not a drop of water. They would die, they thought, with no one to care, or even know. This desolate wasteland certainly wouldn't know or care, aloof from them and from all living things.

The morning light showed only more desolation, and the sun made it less bearable than it had been at night. About ten that morning, Robert Evans quit. He lay down in the shade of a cedar and croaked that he couldn't go another step. He couldn't stay on his feet. If he crawled, he would only die a few yards away in the blazing sun. He knew he would die. He didn't care any more. He couldn't make it.

Smith and Gobel stayed with him a few minutes. They knew what they had to do—go on. They felt an overwhelming sympathy for Evans and agony at leaving him. But they had to try to save their lives. "The mountain isn't far," Smith told the dying man. "If we can find water, we'll bring it back to you." But they knew that they would probably die with him.

They stumbled on toward the mountain range. They could hardly grasp more than the motion of their legs. All that they were went into pushing one foot in front of the other. The mountain looked close, but even a couple of miles might be more than they could make. Soon they saw two Indians skirting them and heading in Evans's direction.

Not long after that they heard two gunshots. Evans was probably gone under.

Three miles from Evans, at the foot of the range, they came onto a spring. They were too exhausted to shout about it. Gobel jumped into it headlong, ducked his head, and started trying to gulp the whole pool. Smith poured it over his head. Minutes later he realized that he might have drunk enough to kill a man. Then he looked back toward where Evans had given out and saw a small waft of smoke. He wondered. He knew he had to give it a try.

After a few minutes of cooling off, Jed took his kettle, which held six or seven quarts, and filled it with spring water and dried meat. He was surprised at how easy the three miles seemed now. Before he could see Evans, he heard a cracking voice crying, "You got any water?"

"Plenty," Jed shouted. Evans was alive. He strode up and there Evans lay. He grabbed at the kettle and started glugging it down. After a moment he took it away from his mouth, shot Smith an impatient look, and said, "Damn! How come you brought meat?" Then he finished the kettle in one draught; he had gulped four or five quarts of water. "Why in hell didn't you bring more?" he managed, and then grinned a little. His voice was nearly gone.

Evans rested a few minutes and then moved on to the spring. They lounged beside it, occasionally taking a full dunk, for the rest of the day.

Jed caught up on his journal entries. "I have at different times suffered the extremes of hunger and thirst," he noted in his neat, slanted hand. "Hard as it is to bear for successive days the knawings of hunger, yet it is light in comparison to the agony of burning thirst and, on the other hand. I have observed that a man reduced by hunger is some days in recovering his strength. A man equally reduced by thirst seems renovated almost instantaneously. Hunger can be endured more than twice as long as thirst. To some it may appear surprising that a man who has been for several days without eating has a most incessant desire to drink, and although he can drink but little at a time, yet he wants it much more oftener than in ordinary circumstances."[5]

Jed intended to publish a book. If he was going to suffer, at least he could turn it to men's advantage with his observations.

As they rested, they saw Indians from time to time on the crests of the hills around. But the Indians disappeared as silently as they came to stare. They had never seen pale men before, nor horses, nor such strange possessions.

The next day they moved ten miles north through what came to be called Skull Valley. During the day they passed several salt springs and found, unbelievably, a lodge of two braves, a squaw, and two children. At first the Indians were scared, but when Smith made signs of being hungry, they gave the whites some antelope meat. They spoke a little like the Shoshones, and knew of that tribe, but they knew nothing about the Salt Lake. After a few days going northeast, they said, the whites would find buffalo. That night, when he camped by some brackish water, Jed climbed a hill and spotted what just might be a big body of water to the northeast.

Ten miles again the next morning. At the end of the valley they climbed a ridge and saw a huge expanse of water spreading northeast. They stared for a long moment and then grinned nervously. Could they let themselves believe that it was the Salt Lake? Maybe they could. Might we be, asked Evans and Gobel, so near the end of our trouble? Maybe we are. Because the Salt Lake would mean game and water in abundance. Like they figured heaven to be, it was a Kentuck of a place. Smith, not a man given to speak of his feelings, noted that night that the lake was "a joyful sight." He went on, "Those who may chance to read this at a distance from the scene may perhaps be surprised that the sight of this lake surrounded by a wilderness of More than 2000 Miles diameter excited in me those feelings known to the traveler, who, after long and perilous journeying comes again in view of his home. But so it was with me for I had traveled so much in the vicinity of the Salt Lake that it had become my home in the wilderness."[6] Gobel and Evans, not being men of learning, didn't know those fancy words for it, but they felt the same way. They relaxed by the fire and talked lightly of the fun of rendezvous while Jed wrote. There was a freshwater spring nearby—they had moved on twenty-five miles along the south edge of the lake—and they had seen several antelope. They hadn't got a shot at one, but maybe they would tomorrow. That night they ate the meat of their next-to-last horse.

Time still pressed them. According to Jed's daily log, the next day was June 28. They were due in the Cache Valley on July 1. They walked twenty miles along the edge of the lake until they came to the river that emptied Eutaw Lake into Salt Lake. Water was up: A mile from the river they started squishing through the marsh of cane grass and bulrushes. By the time they reached the river they were crotch-deep in overflow.

The river was deep, swift, and about sixty yards wide. They made a raft by tying bundles of cane grass together, and put their guns, possibles, and provisions on it. First Jed swam across, leading the horse and mule. Then he came back and floated the raft into the river. Jed swam

ahead with a rope in his mouth that was tied to the raft;
Evans and Gobel held on and pushed from behind. But Evans and Gobel were not particularly strong swimmers. The
current swept them downstream, and the rope got wrapped
around Jed's neck. Before it strangled him, they flailed their
way to shore.

When Jed got back to his animals and loaded them up,
they turned out to be mired down in the muck. He left the
beasts and their loads, struggled to dry land, and made
camp around a fire of sedge. Relatively speaking, they
could laugh about this bad luck.

Early in the morning they got the animals and dried
their things. They were surprised to realize how exhausted
they were, even yet. They walked north fifteen miles. Just
at dusk Jed got a shot at a bear and wounded him badly,
but he got away. They camped and ate the last of their
horse flesh. Exhaustion kept them from talking much, but
they said that tomorrow they would feed on fitten meat.

Jed went a little ahead to try and find a deer. About
eight o'clock he shot one that ran off. Finding a lot of
blood, he trailed it to a thicket. The deer was nearly dead,
so Jed took hold of its horns. The deer promptly upped
and ran off. Damn. Jed was annoyed with himself for not
making sure of it, and the men were downhearted. Jed
trailed the deer a while longer, found it, and this time began by cutting its hamstrings.

Immediately they struck a fire and got to feeding on
fine roasts. The buck was a fat one. They gorged themselves.
The feast, Jed wrote, was eaten "with relish unknown to a
palace."[7] After they ate, they cut the meat, dried it over the
fire, and spent the day luxuriating, with full stomachs.

On July 1 they walked north twenty-five miles, uneventfully. On July 2, they wound their way into the lower
end of Cache Valley. They saw a band of Indians and, for

once, Jed wasn't even careful. He walked straight into their camp and asked them where the whites were. These Indians turned out to be Snakes on their way to rendezvous, about two hundred of them. The whites, they said, were camped at the little lake, Bear Lake. Jed stayed the night with the Snakes. Come morning, he hired a horse and guide and rode into rendezvous, 1827.

Fitzpatrick and Jackson had come in earlier with their trappers, free trappers had arrived in abundance, and the Snakes had journeyed there in large numbers. Ashley's supply train had made the lake without Ashley but with Bill Sublette before July 1, bringing the first wheeled vehicle over to cross the Rockies—a small two-wheeled cannon. Sublette and Jackson had considered: Jed didn't show up, and he was not a man to fail his word. Neither had he sent an express to give news of the party. They suspected that he and most or all of his men had gone under.

So Jed Smith, Silas Gobel, and Robert Evans became heroes when they straggled in to rendezvous on July 3. Men clapped each other on the back and drank another tin cup of whisky diluted by the Green River. Jed had to tell at least the main part of his story to a crowd of trappers: How he had worked his way southwest and crossed the Mojave Desert into Californy; how the Spanyards hadn't been any too glad to see him; how they had trapped and lived good in Californy; how he had crossed Mount Joseph and the Great Salt Plain again; and how a dozen men were loafing back there in Spanish territory, waiting for Jed to come get them.

Several of the men had an idea. That cannon was no good against the Indians, except for show. Here was a reason to fire it: A salute to Jed Smith. Hadn't he found the way to Californy—a way some thousands of miles shorter than around Cape Horn? Hadn't he crossed the salt desert twice, the first to go that way each time? Hadn't he been the first to cross the high Mount Joseph? Hadn't he risked his ha'r, and near died of thirst, and come back alive? By God, he was some. The cannon blasted, and rolled back a few feet on its wheels. Hurrah for Jed Smith!

Jed took it quiet and glad.

FIFTH INTERLUDE

The Buffalo—Cuisine Première

THE MOUNTAIN MAN AND INDIAN ALIKE ATE ALMOST nothing *but buffalo meat. He took it fresh when he could, taking only his favorite cuts from the huge beast and leaving the rest for the wolves. When he couldn't make fresh meat, he kept himself alive on dried meat or pemmican provided by the last buffalo he killed. Necessity and taste worked together here: He stuck to buffalo partly because it was plentiful, but mostly because mountain gourmets agreed that it was the finest eating anywhere. Beaver tail, fat dog or "panther" were pleasant as a change; plants and roots were handy in lean times; but buffalo was the staple.*

The buffalo was an imposing animal. A full-grown bull stood higher than a man from hoof to hump, and maybe ten feet long from nose to tail. He would weigh out at close to a ton. Usually his coarse fur darkened from front to back, blending from yellow to brown to black. He had a skull so thick that no rifle of the time could penetrate it.

In the spring, dropping time, the buffalo moved in small bunches. A trapper would try to kill a bull then, because the cows, just light, would be poor. Any other time he would intend to get a cow because they were fatter and less tough. Thus the expression "to know poor bull from fat cow." The most fun in hunting buffalo came at mating season, from late summer, when the animals ran in huge herds and blackened entire prairies as far as the eye could see.

The trappers had two methods of hunting: One was to creep close to the buffalo from downwind, using a gully or some bushes for cover. If a trapper managed to get close enough, and if the buffalo did not catch the scent of him, he might kill several before the beasts figured out what was going on. (The trapper talk for "dimwitted" was "buffler-witted.") Indians often stalked carefully enough to get within killing range for a bow.

But if the hunter was out for sport, or if the buffalo noticed him before he got close enough for a shot, the chase started. His horse was what counted here, so good buffalo horses brought a handsome price in the mountains. The buffalo would stampede for wooded or gullied ground. The horse might have to go at full speed for four or five miles to catch them. The ground was booby-trapped with burrows, holes, ravines that could spill horse and rider at any moment, and often did, breaking the bones of animal and man. When he caught up, it was bedlam. Dust billowed everywhere. The hunter was choked and blinded. Clods of dirt hit him. Buffalo charged and tried to gore the horse, but it was trained to respond to the rider's knees alone. A fall meant being trampled to death. Through the clouds of dust, the hunter tried to pick out a young cow as a target.

He brought his horse alongside on the cow's right and

tried to throw her, in her tracks. If he missed, he had to reload on the dead run, pouring powder all over, spitting a bullet into the muzzle, banging the rifle butt on the saddle to seat it. But to almost every hunter this bedlam was a sheer delirium of excitement and exhilaration.

The buffalo was a hard animal to bring down. Frederick Ruxton tells how it was done:

Unless shot through the lungs or spine they invariably escape; and even when thus mortally wounded, or even struck through the very heart, they will frequently run a considerable distance before falling to the ground. . . . It is a most painful sight to witness the dying struggles of the huge beast. The buffalo invariably evinces the greatest repugnance to lie down when mortally wounded, apparently conscious that, when once touching mother earth, there is no hope left him. A bull, shot through the heart or lungs, with blood streaming from his mouth, and protruding tongue, his eyes rolling, bloodshot, and glazed with death, braces himself on his legs, swaying from side to side, stamps impatiently at his growing weakness, or lifts his rugged and matted head and helplessly bellows out his conscious impotence. To the last, however, he endeavors to stand upright and plants his limbs farther apart, but to no purpose. As the body rolls like a ship at sea, his head slowly turns from side to side, looking about, as it were, for the unseen and treacherous enemy who has brought him, the lord of the plains, to such a pass. Gouts of purple blood spurt from his mouth and nostrils, and gradually the failing limbs refuse longer to support the ponderous carcass; more heavily rolls the body from side to side until suddenly, for a brief instant, it becomes rigid and still; a convulsive tremor seizes it and, with a low, sobbing gasp, the huge animal falls over on his side, the limbs extended stark and stiff, and the mountain of flesh without life or motion.

The first attempts of a 'greenhorn' to kill a buffalo are invariably unsuccessful. He sees before him a mass of flesh, nearly five feet in depth from the top of the hump to the brisket, and consequently imagines that by planting his ball midway between these points, it must surely reach the vitals. Nothing, however, is more erroneous than the impression; for to "throw a buffalo in his tracks," which is the phrase for making a clean shot, he must be struck but a few inches above the brisket, behind the shoulder, where alone, unless the spine be divided, a death-shot will reach the vitals. I once shot a bull, the ball passing directly through the very center of the heart and tearing a hole sufficiently large to insert the finger, which ran upwards of half a mile before it fell, and yet the ball had passed completely through the animal, cutting its heart almost in two.[1]

After the unsuccessful attempt of a greenhorn to throw a buffler in his tracks, he might be introduced to the arcane mysteries of butchering by the men who had known where to aim. The difficulty was that you could neither hang the buffalo up nor turn him on his back. So you rolled him onto his belly and braced the legs outward. Then you made the first cut crosswise at the nape of the neck, and the second cut the length of the spine. Pulling the skin out from the body and spreading it as a ground cloth, you proceeded to take the cuts you wanted.

No mountain gourmet would pass up the boss, the hump and hump ribs, the fleece, the boudins, the liver and the tongue. Usually bones would be taken too, for marrow, along with the side ribs and belly fat. And the testicles, for the first Rocky Mountains oysters. Many moun-

tain men would take the liver immediately, dip it into the bile, and eat it raw as they were butchering. The feast that came later would consist of boiled hump and most of the other cuts slowly roasted on a spit (often the trapper's wiping stick), consumed alternately with marrow and melted fat. The crowning glory, at the end, would be the·tongue, dug out of the coals where it had been baking, "so soft, so sweet," says Ruxton, "and of such exquisite flavor, that a veil is drawn over the . . . raptures . . . excited in the bosom" of the greenhorn trapper.[2]

The boudins—guts—were a special treat. They were seared over the flames (although the Indians ate them raw and still warm). Ruxton describes the gusto applied to boudins: "I once saw two Canadians commence at either end of such a coil of grease, the mass lying between them on a dirty apishemore like the coil of a huge snake. As yard after yard glided glibly down their throats, and the serpent on the saddle-cloth was dwindling from an anaconda to a moderate-sized rattlesnake, it became a great point with each of the feasters to hurry the operation, so as to gain a march upon his neighbor and improve the opportunity by swallowing more than his just portion; each at the same time exhorting the other, whatever he did, to feed fair and every now and then, overcome by the unblushing attempts of his partner to bolt a vigorous mouthful, would suddenly jerk back his head, drawing out at the same moment, by the retreating movement, several yards of boudin from his neighbor's stomach (for the greasy viand required no mastication and was bolted whole) and, snapping up the ravished portions, greedily swallowed them."[3]

The mountain men consumed Bunyanesque amounts of meat at these feasts. Six, eight, and ten pounds of meat were the rule. One of the unusual properties of the rich,

*gamey buffalo meat was that no one stomach's objected
to any quantity. And it was a good diet. The mountain
men and the plains tribes subsisted on nothing else for
long periods. They never had scurvy; it became a commonplace that illness was unknown in the mountains.*

   *"Shinin' times" might mean splendid trapping or a splen-
did rendezvous to a mountain man, but most of all that
phrase meant buffalo feasting. It meant roasted hump
ribs, boudins, marrow, and fat, eaten with only a butcher
knife, grease and blood dripping onto buckskin. It meant
a long, digestive pipe and some good yarning over the
fire. And then the tongue, brought out as a last delicacy.
And the coyotes, all the while lingering at the edge of the
light, hoping for a tidbit. The trappers would throw a
small piece at a coyote as a prank. Before he got ten yards,
a wolf would growl at him, the coyote would meekly drop
the meat and, in a matter of seconds, he would be back at
the fire waiting for more. For hours they would toss the
little hunks to him and make him errand-boy for the wolf,
and laugh and laugh.*

VI

Rescue In Californy

IF THE MOUNTAIN MEN THOUGHT JEDEDIAH STRONG
Smith was some, they didn't stretch that to cover the
firm of Smith, Jackson & Sublette. The price their plews
brought stayed the same, three dollars a pound, but the
mountain price of goods was higher by half again what
they had paid two years before. A man could scarcely

afford blankets or cloth any more, except that he couldn't do without them. This year it took a little more whisky to forget.

Smith, Jackson & Sublette was in a squeeze. They were selling Ashley the beaver for roughly what they paid for it; he took the responsibility for getting it to St. Louis, where he might sell it, in a variable market, for five dollars a pound. They had done handsomely, turning over $22,000 in plews to the general, mountain price. But their profit had to come entirely from the provisions they sold to the trappers. So they opted for a healthy mark-up.

The men grumbled, but they bought, and they stayed in the mountains. What did money mean in the mountains anyway? If a beaver had any, it was stashed in a bank in St. Louis, doing him no good. A man didn't need it in the mountains. The going currency there was plews, or beads, or vermilion. And a niggur didn't need those to live. All he needed was his Hawken, a pistol, a Green River, some powder, lead, and ball, and some baccy. Plus his wits about him. Out here, the land offered up all that a crittur wanted—buffler, antelope and deer, sweet water, a touch of excitement, and the splendidest country on God's good earth.

It was God's country. Except that God stayed on his own side of the Missouri River. No churches here to cramp a man, nor preachers to tell him what to do, nor stern-eyed, strict women to look at him mean when he did what was natural. Nary a policeman to clap him in jail. Nary a law to push him around. Nary a lawyer to fool him fancy, nor a revenuer to steal his money for the government. Not a man to answer to. And God's finest sculpturin's to roam in. And if God had made the livin' a mite dangerous, wasn't that part of the fun?

So, if the things of civilization had got a bit expensive,

what did that count? If a child could trap for half his life and go back to the settlements broke, what did that count? They might have told their families that they were heading west to get their share of a fortune that would make the mines of Peru seem puny. They might even get Jed Smith to write a letter home for them declaring that they would come back rich. But most of them didn't have a mind to go back, rich or otherwise. Money was something for the settlements, and they didn't want the settlements. They were learning that whatever they had come to the Stony Mountains for, it wasn't beaver.

The partners made their plans for the coming year—and daring plans they were. Jed was to take a party back to California to rejoin his men on the Appelaminy River; then he would lead the combined parties north into Oregon, going however far he thought he was in United States territory. They would trap the entire Northwest and make their way back to the mountains via the Columbia River. If he could make it by next summer, fine; if not, he would join his partners in two years. And with a lot of plews—he was moving into rich, new country.

Jackson would trap Eutaw country and winter at Bear Lake. Sublette would be nearly as ambitious as Jed: He would head a brigade to trade far north with the Flatheads, the Nez Percé—and the Blackfeet. These marauders, the perennial bad boys of the mountains, seemed to have declared a temporary truce with their neighbors, and they sent an emissary to rendezvous to say that they wanted to trade with the whites. Sublette would give them a try.

This was a gamble. The Blackfeet had shot hell out of the Ashley-Henry men on the upper Missouri back in 1822–1823, and had massacred Missouri Fur Company men so relentlessly that that company had abandoned the mountains and gone back to its river trade. But Blackfoot lands had plentiful beaver. If their peaceableness was temporary, SJ&S would make hay while the sun shone.

The three smiled quietly about these plans of attack. They were carrying the fight to the British. All the SJ&S men would be working the joint-occupancy land that America shared with the British—Jackson securing territory well established for SJ&S, Smith and Sublette making new inroads into country that the British considered their own, territory that they trapped regularly, territory where the British had cultivated the Indians and the Americans had not. If they got in Peter Ogden's hair and got him riled, fine. Oregon was going to be American.

Sublette launched his attack with some forty men, including Jim Beckwourth, Jim Bridger, and probably Tom Fitzpatrick. (Jim Clyman, figuring he'd made what money he was going to make in the mountains, went back to St. Louis with the packtrain, bought a farm, and settled down temporarily. Later he got restless and came back to the mountains.) When Sublette got into Blackfoot country, the Indians suggested that he send some men to be the brothers of the Blackfeet, live as guests in their lodges, and trade with them. Sublette asked for volunteers and offered a handsome bonus. It was a risky proposition. Jim Beckwourth's high opinion of himself pushed him forward. Old Pierre Tontavantogan, a deserter from the British, volunteered as well. Jim Bridger, just twenty-three, but an old hand at mountain ways, something of a daredevil, cocksure, allowed as how he'd go too.

Beckwourth and Bridger came back with great tales of hairbreadth 'scapes. Of these two men who later came to be admired and scorned as the biggest liars in the West, Beckwourth deserved his reputation fully, and other trappers held him in no particular esteem. Bridger, though, either stretched his stories into transparent tall-tale entertainment or told the utter truth, and the trappers knew that if Jim said it happened, it did.

Beckwourth seems to have had his fantasy in working order here: The Blackfeet greeted him with open arms, he says, and he became a great man among them, able to dispense magical butcher knives and the like for plews. The band's chief, As-as-to (Heavy Shield), respected him so much that he asked Beckwourth to take his own daughter to wife. Thinking of prudence and influence as much as sex, Beckwourth recalls, he took the girl. After a few days of "hymeneal enjoyments," he hit a spot of trouble.

Some braves came back to camp with three white scalps. Beckwourth was furious; the Blackfeet were ecstatic. The tribe began its blood celebration, and Beckwourth forbade his wife to join in. He sat apart, but Old Pierre and Bridger decided to watch the savage fun. Before long they came back to Beckwourth and told him that his wife was the most splendid of all the dancers. Beckwourth's blood boiled. He strode right into the celebration and clubbed the girl in the head with his axe. She dropped like a duck with its head blown off. He walked straight back to his lodge and calmly warned Pierre and Bridger to get ready to fight for their own scalps. As for himself, he claims, he was collected: He knew they could only kill him once.

The tribe quickly whipped itself into a murderous fever, screaming for Beckwourth's blood. Suddenly, As-as-to stopped them. Remember, he said, that you kill your own wives if they have no ears for your words. This woman had no ears for her husband, and he had the right to kill her. Remember also, he went on, that we must have the powder and ball which the white man trades us. How can we fight our enemies, who have the white man's guns, if we cannot trade with the white man? Kill this man when next you see him, if you wish. But we have given our word to return him unharmed. That we must do.

Then he came into the lodge and declared to Beckwourth that he had done right, because the girl's ears were stopped up. So he offered Jim his other daughter, one with better sense and better ears, and more beautiful besides.

Beckwourth considered. It did seem a bit premature to remarry. But if he refused, the chief would judge that Beckwourth was disdainful of his generosity. And that would be fatal. So he thanked As-as-to, and the girl was presented. It turned out that she was beautiful. And Beckwourth was downright proud of himself, to have again secured an honor sought by many braves, the honor of taking a chief's daughter to wife.

During the night Beckwourth felt a stranger crawling onto his blankets. It was his first wife, sobbing piteously and apologizing abjectly for her disobedience. She really did seem to have a heart as broken as her head, so he took her back. After three weeks, Beckwourth went back to his brigade with a load of plews. He took his two wives. "When you are among Romans," he says blithely, "do as the Romans do."

Bridger had left somewhat earlier, and in somewhat of a hurry. His story was more modest than Beckwourth's. Catching him alone in camp, some braves had insulted him unbearably. Provoked, he brawled with them and gave them a good licking. The braves crept back with friends, captured the Blanket Chief, tied him, and left him in a lodge. Then they held tribal counsel about whether to torture and kill him, or set him free to maintain their relations with the whites. Bloodthirst won out. But when they went back to the lodge, they found the Blanket Chief gone. He made his way back to his friends alone.

Old Pierre came back healthy too. The next spring, though, some Blackfeet caught him, killed him, and chopped his body into little pieces.

That winter and spring were bad for Sublette's men all over. In fact, the SJ&S records for 1828 are a litany of lives taken by the Blackfeet, one man ambushed here and another there. Lives that would have to be avenged.

Jed Smith set out for Spanish country on July 13. He had eighteen men, supplies, and two Indian squaws as lodge-mates of two trappers. Silas Gobel went with him. Robert Evans, though, who had too painful a memory of his struggle across the desert, went back to the settlements. Three of Jed's men were new to the mountains—Toussaint Marechal, Francois Deromme, and a "Spaniard" named Gregory Ortago. The rest were veterans: Gobel, Boatswain Brown, William Campbell, David Cunningham, Thomas Daws, Isaac Galbraith (a free trapper), Polette Labross (a mulatto), Joseph Lapoint, Joseph Palmer, John B. Ratelle, John Relle (a "Canadian"), Robiseau (a "Canadian half-breed"), Charles Swift, John Turner, and Thomas Virgin. Like the West itself, a curious melange of races, nationalities, and languages.

Jed had two choices of routes: He could follow his original southwestward path, or he could go the shorter way back across the Salt Plain. Since he, his companions, and his animals had just come off the Salt Plain as skeletons, he picked the more roundabout route. It was difficult enough.

From Bear Lake he moved across to Salt Lake and

back up to the Eutaw lodges at Eutaw Lake. The Eutaws willingly traded him a couple of horses and other necessities, and told him that several starving men had passed through last spring on their way to Taos. Along Ashley's River, he found their tracks. He pushed along his old route. The Indians who fled like mountain sheep the year before now came to him in droves, all telling about the story of the white men who had come through. He made his way over to the Lost River, across to the Virgin and down it. At Corn Creek, he discovered that the Indians who had fed him were gone, and their crude lodges burned. He made only a small detour to avoid the deep gorge of the Virgin River, came to the Colorado at the mouth of the Virgin, and found the old Pautch farmer still there. He turned down the Colorado, and moved by almost the same route as before to the Mojave villages.

After a first fright—they had had no reports of the approaching whites—the Ammuchabas proved as hospitable as before. Jed camped near some good grass, settled in to rest his horses, traded with the Indians for some corn and beans. His interpreter of the year before, Francisco, was still around. He told Jed that a band of Americans and Spanyards had been to the villages since Jed's appearance. They had come from the east, along the Gila River. Here they had quarreled and split up—one group following the Colorado and the other setting off elsewhere. That, thought Jed, would account for the tracks he had seen and the tales of the Eutaw Indians about starving whites. Other trappers, it seemed, were penetrating toward California.

After just three days' rest, about August 18, Jed and his men started crossing the Colorado. They made some rafts out of cane grass, loaded part of their provisions onto them, and half the men eased out into the broad river. When they came up onto the sand on the other side, the Ammuchabas struck suddenly on the east bank. They screamed hideous war cries, and attacked the ten men and two squaws. Silas Gobel was killed. So were Brown, Campbell, Cunningham, Deromme, Labross, Ortago, Ratelle, Relle, and Robiseau. The women were taken as prisoners.

Jed and the eight with him watched helplessly, nauseated at the slaughter. Quickly, he considered the desperate situation. The Ammuchabas would be swarming on them in a minute or two. He pointed at the landed provisions. "Throw what'll sink into the river," he ordered. As they were pitching, he told them what kind of country they would have to face on foot. "Get whatever you want and can carry," he told them. "Scatter the rest of it on the ground." The Indians would waste time, he thought, quarreling about who got what booty.

They moved fast into the desert. Jed didn't think they had much chance. No horses. No guides. No likelihood of game in the desert. No provisions other than fifteen pounds of dried meat. And the Ammuchabas closing in. He decided to go back to the river. There, at least, he could make them attack head-on, and he might find some cover. If nothing else, the whites could make the Indians pay for white blood. When they had got to the river, Jed thought they were lucky to make it.

They got into a stand of cottonwoods. The trees were slender and close together. Jed set the men to chopping some of them down to form a little breastwork. They tied their knives onto the ends of small poles to make paltry lances. Then they waited. Some stood still. Others moved about with odd jerks. "You think we can make it, Jed?" one of them asked. Jed looked straight at him. "I think we can," he said flatly. He was lying.

The Ammuchabas were creeping up. Jed thought it was hopeless. He had eight men besides himself—with five guns between them. Some of the men were still sick from seeing their friends murdered. Four or five hundred Indians were working their way closer. Well, he could do no more than make it expensive for them. "No more than three men shoot at once," he instructed. If all the guns fired, they could be rushed before they could send another ball home. "And don't shoot unless you're dead sure of your mark."

Jed saw a few Indians ease out from behind their cover. He picked his best marksmen and told them to fire. Two Indians killed and one wounded.

Suddenly all the rest of the Ammuchaba braves fled. Jed shook his head in wonderment. For the moment, at least, they were all right.

They waited and watched until dusk. No sign of the Indians. Jed figured they would try to sneak in by dark. When the sun was down, the brigade pulled out and started into the desert. They walked all night to the first spring. Still no sign of the Ammuchabas. They were safe, more or less. They had lost ten men. They didn't have enough food to cross the desert. Worse, they had no way to carry water. They would have to find the springs and the pools dead on. Otherwise they'd die of thirst.

Jed and the men lay all day by the spring. The Mojave Desert, in late August, was much too furnacelike to chance walking during the day. Jed mulled over the surprise attack by the Ammuchabas. They had given no sign of hostility. He didn't understand it.

What Francisco, the interpreter, hadn't told him was that the band of trappers who had come through had fought a battle with the Ammuchabas and killed a number of them. The Indians had nursed their wounds and waited for the next white men.

Jed led the men across the desert all night. Unable to

see, he got lost. When the sun came up, they had found no water, and he didn't know where the trail lay. They couldn't spend the day on the blazing sand without water. Jed was more nervous than he wanted to let the men know. So he left seven of them, and told them which way to walk in case he didn't come back in a reasonable time. With one other man who was a good walker, he set out to hunt for water.

By luck and his mountain man's sense, he found a spring. Most men would have called it a miracle. Jed breathed in deeply. His body ached back at him, and twitched. He decided to send his companion back to fetch the others and got some sleep. When the party came up, he let them rest and climbed one of the high, rubble-like hills to get a look at the country. About five miles off to the left, he saw the route he had taken a year before. And there, he remembered, he had found water.

At sundown they started walking again. Jed bore toward the old trail and struck it beyond the first spring. He urged them on until about ten the next morning and found the next spring along the trail. They stayed there all day and all night.

At dawn the following morning, Jed left the old trail and struck out the short way to the huge Salt Plain where the desert swallowed the Inconstant River. His guides had mentioned the short route last year but had said that it was too rocky for horses.

The sun and wind parched their faces. Their lips split. Their minds spun fantasies of water. They wondered whether they would ever wet their tongues again. From time to time they hacked open cabbage pears. Though they grew on utterly barren ground, the cabbage pears were juicy. The men sucked the slivers, desperate for even a bitter liquid. Jed encouraged them constantly and urged them on.

An hour before sunset a man collapsed on the scorched earth. Immediately another pitched down beside him. They were dizzy, they said. They were sick at their stomachs. Their bodies hurt fiercely. Even getting back to their feet seemed far beyond their strength. Taking another step was more than they could even imagine doing.

Jed knelt down and tried to persuade them to try. They were close to the sink now, he said, and he knew a spring at its edge. If they could just walk a little farther. They swore they couldn't. Jed had no water to leave them, he explained, and it made no sense to leave food. He couldn't say they would have much chance if they stayed behind. They said that there was nothing to be done about that. All right, he decided. When we find the spring, I'll send water back. Sun's down in an hour or so. Follow our trail then, if you can. He pointed out the direction where he thought the sink was.

So Jed and the other six walked away. They were miserable about moving on, but each was agonizing in his private hell. Each had to try, desperately, to save himself. Jed had his doubts about sending water back. It might be dark before he got to the dry lake. He wasn't sure he could find the spring without light. Even those who kept moving wouldn't last long without water.

He made the sink of the Inconstant just at dusk. The old trail was drifted over with sand. He saw nothing to show where the spring might be. Then, walking up to the edge of the salt flat, he stumbled straight onto it. Mountain man's luck, he thought. Or Providence. The men charged the water like beasts, slurping it up, dunking their heads, stripping off their buckskins and splashing it all over their bodies. They couldn't even talk with their tortured lips and tongues. After a few minutes two of them filled a kettle and started back in the dark. They found the other two still lying where they had fallen, giving up. They drank and staggered on to the spring.

After a rest, Jed got them going again in the dark, across the Salt Plain. The moon was up in front of them. The salt gleamed, irridescent and eerie. Where each man stepped in the thin crust, he left a black moccasin print in the glaze of white. Only Jed had been on this salt flat before; the others lost all sense of direction. Jed walked right to the holes he had dug for water the year before, and they settled down for the rest of the night.

At dawn, he struck west across the salt flat toward the mouth of the Inconstant. Now last night's beautiful white crust looked like a snowfield, blazing instead of freezing, and the glare tortured their eyes closed. When he found the river, it was even drier than it had been the year before; the standing pools were lower and saltier. He forced the party on, thinking that they would find more water as they went upriver.

Abruptly, eight miles from the mouth, he saw two horses. Mountain luck again, by God. He had to have them. He went on alone and found two lodges of Indians. Quietly, he moved close. He didn't mean to give them a chance to run away. He surprised them. They were Pa-Utches. He gave them some knives, cloth, beads, and other foofuraw. They traded him the horses, candy they had made from cane grass, and crocks for carrying water. Now, relatively speaking, he was well fixed.

They wound up the Inconstant in comfort, able to dig holes and to take the water with them. When they got to the mountains, where the river came down from ten-thousand-foot peaks, bare of snow this time of year, he left the river and circled to the right toward a pass. They walked through a broken, other-worldly landscape of strange rock formations and desert plants. When they had topped the pass, they came down into grassland and saw the herds of the San Bernardino Mission. Jed had three cattle shot and the meat dried for the journey north. They were in shinin' times again.

They had crossed the desert in nine and a half days, compared to fifteen days on horses the year before. Jed was pleased enough that they had crossed it at all.

Jed sent word to the mission of his presence and of the cows he had killed. He didn't plan to go in. It was too far, and he suspected there might be more political trouble. An overseer from a nearby farmhouse came into his camp, though, and invited him to spend the night. He was handsomely treated, and he traded, with what was left of the supplies they had shouldered across the desert, for enough horses to get his men mounted.

His party was reduced, though. Virgin had been injured in the Mojave villages ruckus, so Jed left him behind with instructions to catch up in San Francisco. Galbraith, a free trapper, chose to stay in this paradise. Resting five days, Jed wrote the kindly Father Sanchez about what he was doing, presuming that Sanchez would inform Governor Echeandia. Then, with six men, he rode north through the San Joaquin Valley to the Appelaminy and his stranded brigade. They arrived on September 18. A remarkable journey in just over two months. And ten men dead on the banks of the Colorado.

Rogers and his companions had gotten anxious. Jed had promised to be back by September 20, and he barely made it. And after four months of waiting, they didn't get a speck of supplies. Instead of bringing traps, horses, powder and lead, and trading goods, he came empty-handed—except for the bitter news of the massacre.

But the brigade had had a fine summer. No Indian trouble. Deer, elk, and antelope as thick as huckleberries in June. A pleasant climate. The place lived up to its name. The Indians were scarcely Indians: Not only did they not steal, their chief actually returned a stolen horse and some lost traps. He would bring them meal and berries, and the trappers would give him fresh meat, which was something of a rarity for these red men. Some Spanyards had ridden out and asked some questions, but they went away without making trouble after Rogers told them that the party was stuck.

Now Jed had to have provisions. He could trade the plews stashed all summer on the Appelaminy. So he took three men and rode to the mission at San Jose, a three-day journey, and presented himself. Father Duran, the president of the mission system, merely took Jed's horses, let him do without food for two days, and made him wait until word could go to and come back from Governor Echeandia. The father was suspicious of Americans who fished about the country; he thought they might sway the Indians from the true faith. After two weeks of waiting impatiently, Jed and his crew were taken under guard to Monterey, the residence of the governor. They were clapped in the guardhouse for a day, and then Jed confronted Echeandia. Why did you come back? Echeandia demanded. Why did you return by a route which you told me was all but impassable? Why didn't you come straight across to the Appelaminy, instead of the long way around? Why didn't you inform me upon your arrival at San Bernardino?

Jed explained his supply mission, his choice of the

lesser evil in routes, and his notification of Father Sanchez, which he thought would be forwarded to the governor. Echeandia turned up his nose at all this and judged that it was a very mysterious situation. This time Jed would have to go to Mexico. Jed said that he was prepared to leave immediately on an English ship. The governor replied that that was fine: He would have to pay his own expenses. Jed objected strenuously to paying his own way to prison. In that case, answered Echeandia, you can wait for a Spanish ship—two or three months from now. Jed was exasperated. He refused to go.

Within a couple of days, some helpful American residents offered a sort of solution. Under British law, if there were four captains of ships in port, they were allowed to represent their country until their government could be contacted. Maybe the same could be done under American law. It was a dubious proposition, but Echeandia saw it as a way out of responsibility. Four captains, eager to help an enterprising countryman, vouched for Jed and took responsibility for his actions until he could get out of California. Meanwhile, Jed was forced to write to Rogers and order him to San Francisco so that all the Americans could be watched. Jed took a ship to San Francisco, went about the business of buying horses and mules, and wrote to Thomas Virgin telling him to rejoin the party. He sold his plews to a shipmaster—over fifteen hundred pounds of them—for two and a half dollars a pound. That would give him the money to get a new outfit. Then Virgin showed up. He had been imprisoned, starved, abused, and forbidden to speak to anyone. Jed was fed up with California hospitality now. But the Californians had one more obstacle for him. His bond provided that he had to cross out of Spanish territory at San Francisco at the mouth of the Buenaventura. (He now knew that this Buenaventura flowed from Mount Joseph, not the Salt Lake.) But the river was much too big to ford at that point, and the commandant at San Francisco's Presidio refused to let him have any kind of boat for the crossing. Neither would he allow Jed to go up the river to a passable point on the river. He would just have to wait for further instructions from the governor.

Jed had had more than he was willing to take. He promised to wait, went back to his camp, and wrote three letters—to the commandant, the governor, and the American Embassy in Mexico, expressing his indignation. He had plenty of that. He had lost two of the three hunting seasons since he left the rendezvous of 1826, one to dry country and the other to political folderol. In a year and a half of effort, he had produced next to nothing for SJ&S. And he had been manhandled for three months by the Mexican authorities. Now he was going to take matters into his own hands by moving his men into wilderness, up the Buenaventura. He would cross it at some reasonable place above, and get out of California for good.

He moved the brigade out on December 30, 1827. It was raining and miserable. But Jed sat in his tent that night and wrote in his journal: "Having been so long from the business of trapping and so much perplexed and harassed by the folly of men in power I returned again to the woods, the river, the prairae, the Camp & the Game with a feeling somewhat like that of a prisoner escaped from his dungeon and his chains."[1]

As he wrote, he could hear a faint neighing over the soft tapping of the rain. The horses. He wondered again how many of them he'd be able to get to the mountains. The horses and mules were now the key to his two California expeditions. He had gotten the idea months ago: California was overrun with horses, so many that the Spanyards drove the wild horses into pens and let them starve to keep them away from mission pasture. Horses and mules sold for ten dollars a head in California. They were worth fifty dollars a head or more in the mountains. Jed had been able to make one use of the delay at San Jose: He had bought over three hundred animals. He was driving fifteen or twenty thousand dollars in horseflesh toward the mountains. A windfall for SJ&S—if he could get them there. He had no idea what the country ahead was like.

The next morning he found out that it was bad. The drizzle kept up steadily. The country was inundated. Every low spot was a marsh or a lake and the animals could barely move. Jed crossed a river without losing a single one, but he knew his luck wouldn't hold. He took to staying where he was for several days at a time, moving only to find new grass. He was losing more time.

The water was so high that it made trapping difficult. All right, Jed would have bullboats made. He sent the men elk hunting to get hides. He had only forty-seven traps left—there were none to buy in a country that hadn't even heard of beaver trapping—but he would do what he could. The men took sixty-one plews in less than a week. Then four trappers came back in their skin boats with thirty-three more. Spirits perked up some. Reed, who had been a troublemaker the year before, and Pombert came in with twenty-two. If Jed couldn't move, he would wrestle with the horses and the weather while the men got plews. He sent the two back out with instructions to meet him on another river in eight days.

Jed kept trying to move the horses on. At a crossing they waded out and got mired down in mud. Men splashed in to help the horses back to ground that was only squishy. Man and animal ended up soaked and covered with mud. The country, during this rainy season, amounted to a huge slough, mire after canebrake mire. As they moved upriver, the horses and mules sank to the knee on every step. The whole landscape was turning into a quagmire.

Finally he found a spot where he thought the river could be forded. He chopped down trees and carried the provisions over. He had to force the animals across by building a pen and driving them into the water. On the other side they labored into such a mire that he lopped down more trees for them to walk on. It was ugly, messy work.

The Indians were friendly and quite naked. They brought several nice salmon into camp, and Jed gave them tobacco. A couple agreed to move north with him. For other provision, Jed sent his trappers out for the plentiful deer.

When they were ready to go on, Reed and Pombert were not to be found. After waiting and searching, Jed realized that they had deserted. What hurt was that they took eleven of his few traps with them. He wasn't going to get a lot of trapping done now. The horses and mules were his main resource. And in this country, they were a great nuisance. He had to hope for drier weather and firmer land.

He didn't get it. He spent whole days scouting for a dry route, and found nothing. Horses constantly got lost or mired down, and days were lost searching for animals, with fitful success, and pulling them out of the mud. The country was a morass of water and slime. Fortunately, the Indians stayed amiable. They helped him build boats and rafts to float his provisions. Sometimes, the brigade spent an entire day crossing a pair of sloughs divided by a few dozen yards of higher ground. The flooding water continued to make trapping difficult. Occasionally, the Indians stole a trap or two. By the last week of February, eight weeks out from San Jose, the party was floundering along at an average of less than five miles a day.

On February 26, came a bad incident with the Indians. Turner and Marechal, seeing some Indians around their traps, called out to them. Instead of coming, the Indians fled. The trappers fired, killed one, and wounded another. Jed reprimanded them severely and, since he couldn't watch them all the time, forbade them to set traps. On March 1, the brigade rode up to a lodge. The Indians were so frightened that they scattered in all directions. Trappers caught up with a squaw and made her some presents, but when Jed checked a ten- or eleven-year-old girl who had fallen down, he found she was dead. He was amazed that men who called themselves Christians could look so fearful as to scare Indian children literally to death. Leaving various presents to indicate his sorrow, he moved on.

The land seemed to be turning into water—pond after slough after lake. Trying to force a way, they drowned two horses, and recovered only six of the ten traps on their backs. The men would spend some time taking elk and bear, and then push forward a miserable few miles. On March 9, Rogers and Hanna went hunting for a wounded bear, and the bear attacked Rogers. He was wounded terribly, in ten or twelve different places. Jed treated the gashes with soap and sugar, and waited ten days for Rogers to be ready to travel. By March 28, after three months on the trail, they came into the vicinity of what would become Sacramento. Moving up the valley, Jed could see mountains to the east and west, and Mount Shasta, snow-topped, to the north.

Now the Indians were changing. They were still naked, but less miserable and destitute. A little further north Jed found an arrow in the neck of one of his horses. He told the men to grab their guns, and they found a band of Indians showering the herd with arrows. They fired and wounded three. Jed saw the Indians on hilltops during the day, yelling. When they camped, he took several men and went to within gunshot of the hill. He tried to tell the Indians by signs that he was friendly, but they strung their bows for a fight and screamed their hostility. Jed meant to act like a Christian, but he had also been through two massacres. He ordered the men to fire, and two Indians fell. The others ran off. He kept having trouble with them for some days. He and Arthur Black shot at one band creeping up on the horses, but missed. The guerrilla warfare continued. Once they chased a band and killed two men. Another time they wounded several.

They were struggling through the low mountains of what is now northern California, scrambling through the brush on steep hillsides, and moving along deep ravines. Because of the horses, it was treacherous going; they were coming up lame. In a bad pass, the horses jostled each other, struggling to keep from being crowded off. In the near panic two were pushed off a cliff and drowned. Five more traps lost. The going got so rough and rocky that at one point, they spent four hours traveling one mile. The month of April passed in fits and starts, bad passages through steep and stony mountains, and a search for a good route that seemed not to exist.

May passed in a chorus of miseries: The country was impossibly rough. The horses cut their hooves and legs on the rocks, got scratched in the brambles, were weak with hunger and fatigue, and often could not travel. They got lost continually, and Jed spent days searching for them. They spilled off precipices and drowned in the crossings. Jed tried to follow the Klamath River, but the steep sides regularly forced him onto ridges. Sometimes he had to retrace his steps. His scouts reported that they were close to the ocean and he turned that way, only to find the going horrible. He was pleased by one observation—the redwoods, which he called the noblest trees he had ever seen. And he was interested by the Indians, who used axes and lived in rectangular huts of split pine. While Rogers and Virgin were scouting one day, these Indians shot arrows at Virgin, and he wounded one. Rogers was so distressed at their general predicament that he prayed in his journal: "Oh! God, may it please the(e) . . . to still guide, and protect us, through this wilderness of doubt and fear. . . . Oh! do not forsake us Lord, but be with us, and direct us through."[2] This northward scramble had already taken five months, longer than the first crossing of the Great Salt Plain to California.

Just before June arrived, Jed decided that he had to make for the ocean, but the few miles took him two weeks: Fog reduced visibility to almost nothing; rain made the sides of the hills slippery. Two men were trying to make a route by lopping down trees. The brigade could find almost no game, and seemed to be missing what little they shot at. They were beginning to starve again. Jed traded for some mussels, eels, fish, and berries from the Indians, but that food seemed only to tease the stomach. They killed a young horse one night and feasted. Before they got to the ocean, Jed fell into luck and shot three elks. The men gorged themselves on the meat, raw.

When they struck the beach, Jed hoped the going would be better. It wasn't. Sometimes the beach was too stony; sometimes it was flooded by high tide. He marched along the ocean, or along a low ridge, or through the marsh and mire of the flatlands. The tidal rivers regularly turned out to be too deep to cross. The Indians occasionally killed his horses. He lost twelve or fifteen head crossing the Rogue River—drowned, he guessed, by the sheer numbers of animals in the water at once. He had lost twenty-three animals, he noted, in three days by various accidents. He

saw some beaver sign, but the tides ruined the trapping.
He remembered that he was due at rendezvous about now.
No use thinking about that.

They moved north along the coast, still foundering.
Coming to sizable rivers, he had to travel inland a way to
find a ford. He met a new tribe of Indians through here
who called themselves Kelawatsets, and who knew the
white man: They had British trading goods. Jed and
Rogers were relieved, because they could expect Indians
used to dealing with whites to be more pacified. These,
though, showed an unsettling inclination to kill the horses.
Greatly outnumbered, Jed decided not to press the issue
beyond a peaceable discussion. He was glad to find out
from the Kelawatsets that he was not far from the Willamette Valley and from the Tillamook Indians, who were
on intimate terms with the British. The Kelawatsets described what they called a passable route to the valley of
the Willamette, or Multnomah.

One disturbing incident: While the Indians were helping the brigade cross a river, an axe disappeared. Jed and
another man grabbed the Indian who had stolen it and tied
him up. While Jed held a rope around his neck and demanded to know where the axe was, his men trained their
Hawkens on the other fifty Indians. Finally the bound Indian showed them the axe, buried in the sand.

He was a chief, though, and had been mortally insulted. At his lodges, he cried for vengeance on the whites.
Another chief overruled him.

Two days later, on July 14, Jed left the brigade and the
horses where the Umpqua River met its north branch. As
was his habit now, he was going ahead to scout the best
route. He paddled up the north fork in a canoe with an
Indian guide, the Englishman Leland, and Turner. Before
he left, Jed told Rogers not to let the Kelawatsets into

camp. Jed had violated this rule of his often lately, but he didn't trust these Indians and wanted to take no chances. There were too many of them.

When Jed left, Rogers let the Kelawatsets into camp anyway After all, they had good relations with other whites. One of the chiefs—the one who had ruled for peace a day or two before—mounted one of the horses to ride around the camp in style. Black saw him and decided the Indian couldn't be trusted. He made the rascal get down.

Now this peace-making chief felt humiliated and outraged. The two hundred braves waited until the whites were drying their guns from the thunder shower of the day before. Then they attacked. Two wrestled with Black for his gun and cut his hands with their knives. He saw an axe swinging toward his head, jumped aside, and felt it whack into his back. He sprinted for the woods. His last sight of camp was of men falling under axes everywhere.

A little later, paddling back downriver, Jed began to look for sign of his men. Strange that he didn't see them. He knew camp was close. His Indian guide spoke a few words to another Kelawatset on the bank. Abruptly the guide turned around, grabbed Jed's rifle, and dived into the river. Kelawatsets jumped from their hiding places along the bank and shot at the canoe. Jed, Leland, and Turner paddled desperately for the opposite bank, and made it. They got to the cover of the woods and then climbed a hill to get a look at the camp. Not one of his men could be seen. And not one had come running at the sound of gunfire. Either they had been cut off by an attack, Jed gathered, or they had been massacred.

Arthur Black stumbled around the woods in a daze. He could not let himself see clearly what he had seen on the Umpqua, and he could not deny it. His mind went into a stupor. He reeled and fell. He couldn't sleep for terror. He couldn't move, either. He staggered around, helpless.

After four days he got to the ocean within several miles of the scene of the massacre. His mind was clearing. He had to walk north and try to find Fort Vancouver. He had no horse and no rifle and it was maybe a hundred miles away. He would have to try.

He stumbled along the coast until some Indians found him. When they stripped off his clothing and took his knife, he could hardly care. He kept walking north. Finally, he chanced on some Tillamooks, and they offered to guide him.

When Black was brought to Fort Vancouver on August 8, three weeks and four days after he ran into the woods by the Umpqua, he couldn't speak. He was still horror-struck. He sat down to try to collect himself. McLoughlin, the Hudson Bay Company head, was waiting for him to tell what had happened. After a while, he managed to get out, still incoherently, that he was the only survivor of a massacre of Jed Smith's party. Smith and the rest, he stammered, had been murdered by Indians on the Umpqua.

The next morning McLoughlin sent Indian runners to the Willamette Indians to ask them to bring in any whites who might still be alive. The following day he equipped a party of forty trappers to go looking for survivors. As they were setting out, Tillamooks arrived with Smith, Leland, and Turner. They had followed the same route as Black.

Smith got the story from Black now. Fourteen men and an Indian boy had been murdered. Of the men who had been with him since 1826, only Black was still alive. Of those in the 1827 reinforcements, only Turner. All his plews were lost, and all his horses. He thought of each one of the men vividly: The pious Rogers, who had been so offended by a woman's boldness that he refused a señorita;

the negro Ranne, who had been sick recently with swelling in his legs; Virgin, the old man he'd been so glad to see after he got out of the Spanyards' prison. Marechal, Swift, Palmer, Reubascan, Lapoint, McCoy, Gaiter, Hanna, and Laplant, who had been his translator; Lazarus, Daws, and even Marion, the Tillamook boy he had recently rescued from slavery. Jed had hunted and trapped with all these men. He had tramped across a barren desert with them, and waded through floods with them. He had gone hungry and thirsty with them. He had yarned with them around a big fire. He had spread his blankets next to theirs. Now all dead.

He was sick at heart. And mad as hell.

SIXTH INTERLUDE

Mountain Craft

WHEN THE EMIGRANT, THE SOLDIER, AND THE gold-seeker came to the Rocky Mountains in the 1840s and 1850s, they floundered in danger and discomfort where the mountain man had lived, for several decades, in relative safety and ease. The difference was in the trapper's mountain craft.

To say that the newcomers were short on know-how and experience is facile and not appreciative of the facts. The mountain man certainly had developed a large repertory of skills: He was his own wrangler, naval architect, meteorologist, hunter, blacksmith, tailor, butcher, merchant, guide, diplomat, and practical psychologist, among the other trades he practiced. And he had adapted all these skills shrewdly to the circumstances of mountain, plain, and desert. But mountain craft was more than a set of skills.

Men acquire skills by controlled and critical repetition. The mountain man learned to trap beaver by a huge number of specific actions, applying what was grasped in each one to the next, and modifying his techniques to fit different circumstances; finally, a broad range of techniques and an acute observation of terrain brought him a knack for trapping that might have seemed magical to the uninitiated. He taught himself how to travel long distances in rough country safely, quickly, and comfortably by the same method. He discovered that ridges were the safest approaches and exits from unknown territory. He learned what terrain gave least resistance in what weather. He memorized the patterns of ridges, canyons, passes, and creeks in areas of millions of square miles. In any given situation he could consider the immediate weather, the likely weather for the time of year, the whereabouts and moods of the Indians, the movements of game, and the availability of wood and water, and add them into a sum that was a precise route covering hundreds of miles, with options for changing conditions. These skills were the product of repetition refined by judgment.

The catalogue of skills was awesome: He could look at a trail and tell which tribe made it, how many of them there were, what mission they were on, whether they were going to it or returning from it, how many horses they had and whether the horses were burdened, how many women and children were with them, how long ago they were here, and where they were now. Such feats of sign reading stupefied newcomers, but they were commonplace among the trappers. Kit Carson won a national reputation, thanks to Frémont, for such acuity, but he had many equals among the mountain men.

That kind of sign reading, in fact, was a comparatively gross skill. A trapper could look at three ducks swimming down a creek and know without thinking whether they were just looking for food normally or had been scared by men upstream. He could see by the way a herd of buffalo was running whether it was moving naturally, or whether it was fleeing a band of men up the left-hand canyon, or whether Indians were, in fact, chasing the buffalo for cover to get close to him. When he saw a branch floating in a stream, he knew whether it had fallen through natural processes or had been broken or kicked by a man. The chattering of birds could alert him to enemies. So could a broken bush or a deer standing strangely. He knew how to find water among sand dunes, and how to get game with no weapon but his bare hands. The mountain man had learned these special skills partly from the Indian. But unlike the Indian, he was not bound by ritual and tradition. He was more open to questions, to rethinking, to experimentation and adaptation. So he eventually surpassed his mentor in every way, from sign reading to horsemanship.

Yet these skills, meticulously acquired and kept on file for application in any context, were only the rudiments of mountain craft. The rest of it—the imposing bulk of it— was integration of these skills into a complex physiological and psychological mechanism that added up to a unified system of behavior.

A mangeur de lard *(a pork eater, a man not adjusted to mountain ways)* might have acquired any one or any ten of the skills that the mountains demanded. What he lacked was their interrelation, their programming. A

mountain man had developed a pattern of habitual screen-
ing, of automatic analysis of input, that gave him what
information he needed at any given moment. In a crisis,
that total of information would propel him into a course
of action, drawn from his catalogue, faster than an IBM
computer could have calculated it. And the mountain
man would have acted instantly, without conscious thinking-
out. If Joe Meek, for instance, riding along through
Blackfoot country, saw a minute but definite sign of immediate danger, it would trigger a progression of automatic protective actions, and Joe would probably be safe
in no more time than he would need to explain what he
had done and why.

What would have saved him? A set of habits, each
learned perfectly in itself, each become fully automatic
by the training of muscles and nervous system, and then
organized into a hierarchy—and set in motion, without
conscious direction, by what he saw and what he knew of
the circumstances.

An integrated set of skills: Like those a man develops
to ride a bicycle, where balance is a matter of motor concentration, and thinking about it is ruinous. Or like
those a man develops to read music at the piano, where
instructions are translated into action much faster than
the mind can acknowledge them consciously. Or like those
of skillful driving, where the driver assimilates large
amounts of information and acts deftly on it without
conscious analysis.

Mountain craft involved integration of particular
skills into a set of automatic responses to be triggered by
observation. That integration was what distinguished
the mountain man from the greenhorn who learned any
number of single mountain skills.

It also created a barrier between mountain man and

greenhorn. The emigrants of the 1840s, when they had former trappers as guides, found them offensively taciturn. They had no way of grasping that when a trapper rode ahead of a wagon train, his concentration was all-absorbing. Every foot of ground within his sight, every sound within his hearing, was an encyclopedia of what had happened there, and an omen of what was about to happen. All his senses, all his mind, every nerve-ending in his body were reaching out to gather every possible bit of information. A movement on a ridge three miles away, which might last for a fraction of a second, could tell him about fresh meat or approaching enemies. At any moment he might simply be sure, without necessarily being able to say why he was sure, that now was the time to bring the wagons close and check the rifles.

The greenhorns more or less knew that every yard of the Oregon Trail was dangerous, and the knowledge made them so afraid that they kept their eyes on their saddle-horns. The mountain man knew the dangers and the survival techniques—knew them much more intimately in specific, moment-to-moment consciousness. What he knew made him tingle with awareness. It kept his programming at the ready. In a crisis that paralyzed the greenhorn with fear, the mountain man's programming launched him into a burst of nearly automatic action.

Any man who survived for several years as a trapper, taking responsibility for his own survival alone in the wilds, had been schooled thoroughly by the Rocky Mountains. He had acquired the most complex wilderness skills ever known on this continent. He had been graduated from Rocky Mountain college, a pragmatic university that gave no degrees, but flunked men into their graves.[1]

VII

A Choice of Allegiance

JEDEDIAH WAS READY TO MAKE WAR ON THE KELA-
watsets. By chance, John McLoughlin, the governor, was
about to send a Hudson Bay Company brigade south, led
by Alexander McLeod, when Jed arrived. He and his
three men joined the party. Several days out, they got bad
news in a letter from McLoughlin. His runner reported
that Jed's property was scattered all over the territory. Their
chances of getting it back were poor. McLoughlin was
sympathetic to Jed's desire for revenge. He wrote that he
knew well that "such barbarians . . . have no horror or
compunction of Conscience at depriving their fellow
Man of Life." He also knew well that if the massacre went
unpunished, the barbarians would feel free to maraud as
they pleased. But, he added, it would do no good to attempt more than they could do against such large forces.
McLeod, he said, knew the Indians, and McLeod would
have to decide what to do. In his letter to McLeod, he observed that if some reprisal was not made, "our personal
security [will] be endangered."[1]

The brigade, twenty-two Hudson Bay engagés, fourteen
Indians, and the four SJ&S men, rode through drenching
rain. They heard reports that the happy Kelawatsets were
waiting to massacre them in the mountains.

As it turned out, the first Indians they met ran away.
After some persuasion from the Indians accompanying
the white brigade, though, they came into camp and
eventually brought their old chief for a talk. The old man
asked if the whites had come to wage war. McLeod as-

sured him that they only wanted to establish peace and to recover Mr. Smith's property. The old chief gave them thirty-four of Jed's horses and mules.

On October 21, in sluicing rain, the party rode into the Kelawatsets' village and demanded the stolen goods. They got over six hundred pelts, along with guns and various other odds and ends. A week later, scouting around for other thieves, they came on the site of the massacre. Jed saw the skeletons of eleven of the fifteen missing men bleaching in the sun. If he had held out any hope, he gave in now. The other four bodies were probably in the woods nearby. He just looked, without speaking. He had survived three massacres, but forty men had died.

The brigade collected furs, horses, and other articles all over the countryside. About the first of December, they started back for Fort Vancouver through the flooded landscape—the rainy season had arrived again. Jed had spent nearly a year floundering in the Northwestern rain forests. He had almost nothing to show for it. Except for huge losses and fifteen dead men.

The British were generous enough to Jedediah at the Fort. Although they had lost the fall hunt in helping him, they proposed no charge for either their setback in furs or their actual expenses. They offered him a fair price for his damaged plews and his horses; they even offered free transportation through Canada in the spring which would allow him to reach St. Louis in midsummer. They were being magnanimous to a defeated enemy. But Jed, as always, was impatient to be on with it. On March 12, he set out up the Columbia by boat for Flathead Post. He had heard reports of American trappers in that area, led by his partner Davey Jackson. Two of his men had quit. The one who went back to the mountains with him was the tenacious Arthur Black.

They debarked at Fort Colville and made their way uneventfully to Flathead Post. From there they worked north along Flathead River until they found Jackson. The reunion was glad but restrained. Jedediah made fast friends, but he didn't make a show of it. The first night they started into their serious business. Jed had almost two years of company business to catch up on.

The years '27 to '29 had been good ones for the company, excepting that Sublette and Jackson had lost a lot of men, as had Jed. Bill Sublette had taken the furs down to St. Louis himself last fall and had stayed the winter planning to meet them at rendezvous. Jim Beckwourth, the mulatto, had left the company and gone to live permanently with the Crows. (Apparently, a trapper had told them a wild story about the great foe of the Blackfeet: He had been born a Crow and kidnapped; the whites had later taken him in. The Crows, always friends to killers of Blackfeet, welcomed him as a long-lost son.) Jackson, in his usual quiet way, had just finished another good hunt. Robert Campbell, the Irish aristocrat who was Jedediah's close friend, was leading the other brigade east of the continental divide, in Crow country.

They marched south along the west side of the divide toward rendezvous. This year it would be at Pierre's Hole, a sumptuous spot just west of the Tetons, as Jackson Hole lay just east of them. Sublette arrived in late summer, full of news.

He had met Campbell on the Popo Agie, just east of South Pass. Bob had over $20,000 worth of plews, and he had gone to St. Louis with them himself. Since his brother was not managing the family estate back in Ireland very well, Bob was going home to straighten things out. The men had been sent back into the area of the Powder and Tongue Rivers for the fall hunt under Milton Sublette.

The three men considered: The company had survived a bad period, the time of 'Diah's western explorations. It was out of debt and had about $28,000 in the bank, in fact. Not much for three years' work, and the estates of the men who had been killed would still have to be paid; but pretty fair, considering. They had made a major effort to find new beaver country to the west, and had failed. Now it was time to look to taking advantage of the beaver country they knew.

Jed listened to the conversation with half an ear. He heard them enthuse about the coming season, and heard as well what Sublette and Jackson didn't say in so many words: That SJ&S needed one bumper year, a year of hard trapping in proven territory, to make the difference between struggle and easy street.

Other things were pushing at Jed: The sight of the skeletons back on the Umpqua. The thought of too many friends gone under. The frustration of coming back from three years of trekking, empty-handed. The memory of parents who were now aging. The memory of a man killed on the Judith, another killed on the Platte, another on the Bear—a man dead, in fact, for almost every place he might trap in the entire West. Wherever he rode now, ghosts would ride with him. The words droned on, and he knew what he had to do: He owed his partners at least one highly productive year of taking plews.

While the partners were working things out, the rank and file had their blow-out. Joe Meek, a newcomer to the mountains that year, was seeing his first mountain carousal, and what a spectacle it was. A hundred-seventy-five trappers were there, a good many of them free trappers. And neither Joe Meek nor any other *mangeur de lard* had ever seen anything quite like these men.

They were a new American breed. That decision of General Ashley's back in 1823, from necessity rather than foresight, had created them by sublime accident. When Ashley sent his men to the mountains by land rather than by river, the pattern of the fur trade changed; the river man gave way fully to the mountain man. Under Jed Smith, the mountain men dropped the pretense of trading for beaver, which was all their licenses permitted, and relied almost completely on trapping. Then Smith led them to new country—first across Southern Pass into the valley of the Siskadee, then to Bear Lake, Cache Valley, and Great Salt Lake; then north and northwest to Flathead territory and Snake territory; then to California, and back by the Columbia.

Back on God's side of the Missouri, people still thought that the Rocky Mountains were an impenetrable barrier, and that the Great American Desert was uninhabitable. These men crossed the mountains casually, both ways, and they knew that a lot of that desert was their Promised Land. Hell, back on the civilized side of the Missouri, the government was still pretending that plews came from Indian trade. What did those greenhorns know?

And the men. They had started out as Falstaff's battalion, according to Jim Clyman, who picked up the ragamuffin bunch in grog shops and other sinks of degradation. They were social outcasts—some of them army deserters, some of them men with a legal charge over their heads, some of them bound boys or slaves who had run away—but men were pretty much the same out here. A black man who could shoot center and eat boudins with you and warn you about a Blackfoot creeping up wasn't a man you looked down on. Out here a man wasn't judged by whether he could read or write, or what his color was, or what kind of family he came from, or how much money he had back there, but by his skill. Social rank here, in rising order, was pork-eater, camp-tender, company trapper, clerk, booshway, and top rank—free trapper. The measure of a man was the extent of his skill—his mountain craft.

The mountains had tested Falstaff's battalion. They demanded the consummate in skill of survival. And they paid off fast: A man who exercised mountain craft got shinin' times; a man who didn't, left his bones in the sun. The mountains didn't care either way. Joe Meek was astounded at the craft: He heard about Hugh Glass, who had managed to find food for weeks without a knife or rifle while he crawled and hobbled three hundred miles to a fort. He saw Bill Sublette study an Indian trail and then tell how many Indians there were, of what tribe, what their mission had been, whether they were warlike, how long ago they'd been here, and where they were now. He heard how Jed Smith had found water in the Mojave Desert, like out of nowhere, because he just knew where it would be in miles on miles of sand. He saw Jim Bridger exercise the fine art of getting a beaver to come to medicine. Joe reckoned he had a lot to learn.

At this rendezvous Joe was seeing men who had graduated from the Rocky Mountain college with high honors. They might look like riff-raff. They might be a touch quick with their fists, and with their Hawkens. They might be liars. They might fornicate prodigiously. They might have their odd ways and their superstitions. They might look strange in their grease-blackened buckskins, and sound

strange with their mountain lingo. They might seem
too bullheaded to discipline. But they knew the West as
well as an Ohio farmer knew his back forty. They knew
how to survive. And from the look of the fun around Joe,
they knew how to live. Joe wanted to be one of them.

The rendezvous went through its usual excesses of
whisky, sex, fighting, gambling, yarning, and hell-raising.
While the men were having their fun, the partners made
an important decision. Where would they go now for beaver? Jed had seen enough of the areas west and southwest
of Salt Lake to rule those out. California was too far. South
was no good—too many trappers streaming out of Santa
Fe. Northwest, the Snake country was trapped pretty thin
by the combination of the Hudson Bay Company and
SJ&S. To the east, Milton Sublette was trapping Absaroka. What was left? Blackfoot territory. It was rich with
beaver. It was mostly untouched, since the Blackfeet,
Bug's Boys (the devil's children), were so hostile. But it
was the best country available. Smith and Sublette would
move north and try the Blackfeet. They would take the
sensible precaution of traveling in large numbers. And
Jed Smith would be the partisan.

Smith, Sublette, Bridger, and Joe Meek rode north,
over the divide, and into the area of the Three Forks of
the Missouri, prime Blackfoot country. Bug's Boys picked
at them all the way. In this kind of danger, Jed had to in-
sist on military discipline every minute. A large brigade
like this one moved in a long file. Hunters and scouts,
like Jim Bridger, roamed ahead on the flanks, looking for
Indian sign and for game. The booshway, Smith, rode at
the head of the column, leading the mule that bore the
company records. A gang of pack animals followed him,
watched by camp tenders. Behind the animals rode the
trappers, each leading another horse or two that carried

his possibles. A melee of squaws, children, and friendly braves followed the trappers, dragging their belongings along by travois, makeshift trailers of poles and skin. Last came the clerk, here Sublette, watching the rear.

A party of trappers this size was enough to intimidate even Blackfeet. The horses were vulnerable only when let out of the nightly circle to feed. The trappers were most vulnerable when they were out working the creeks. Instead of having them split up into small camps with either camptenders or squaws to keep the lodge fires burning, Jed kept the whole party in a single camp while they were in Blackfoot territory. The men worked nearby streams and stayed out for only a couple of days at a time.

After a first-rate hunt around the Three Forks, Jed turned east toward the Yellowstone. By this time, the Blackfeet had gotten too frustrated. They mounted a full-scale attack on the entire party. Not a man was killed, but the trappers were scattered. Looking for them in what was new country to him, Jed sent Black Harris to a hilltop to survey the area. When he got back, Harris reported soberly that he had seen the city of St. Louis and one man taking a drink.

Joe Meek had been cut off in the attack. Left with just his mule, blanket, and gun, he decided that his only chance was to head for the agreed on wintering grounds around the Wind River and wait for everyone else to show up. He left the mule and turned southeast, taking an occasional mountain sheep to stay alive. Unexpectedly, he wandered into the hot-springs area of Yellowstone. The whole country was sending up smoke from bilin' springs, he said later, he could smell burning gases, and the little craters were whistling. He decided that the place reminded him, by God, of Pittsburgh. Two trappers Jed had sent to hunt for Meek showed up and guided him back to the brigade. Joe admitted that he'd had some thoughts about that place being the back door to hell. But he observed that "if it war hell, it war a more agreeable climate than (I) had been in for some time."[2]

Still working their way east, the trappers got to the Big Horn and ran into Milton Sublette's band there. Together they trapped their way up the Big Horn to the mouth of the Popo Agie, where the Big Horn, for no good reason, changed its name to the Wind River. They found some wintering grounds and settled in. They built lodges; they shot buffalo, and dried the meat. And Jed began to do some serious thinking.

First, he and his partners had to consider their business prospects. That was simple: The fall hunt had been un-usually prosperous because the new Blackfoot country was so rich. They had just enough in the bank to bring up a new outfit from St. Louis. Then the take of 1829–30 would be profit, their first real cash-in. So Sublette would make another midwinter express with his old companion Black Harris.

But Jed was bothered by personal matters. He had been in the mountains for eight years. His mind and feelings were turning homeward. On the day before Christmas he thought of his parents, his brothers, and the man who had been his mentor, Dr. S. A. Simons, at their Ohio and Illinois homes, enjoying the good cheer of the season, the warmth of their mutual closeness, and the fellowship of the Christian Church. Jed missed them. He sat down to write to his parents:

He first reminded them that he had written several times and heard nothing in return since he left home. He had often been ready, he went on, to end his business and come home, but it would have been bad policy. It would be "the height of impolicy," he said, for him to make a definite time commitment now. But he promised to try to come as soon as possible. "The greatest pleasure I could enjoy, would be to . . . be in company, with my friends, but whether I Shall ever be allowed the privilege, God only knows, I feel the need of the wa[t]ch and care of a Christian Church—you may well Suppose that our Society is of the Roug[h]est kind, Men of good morals seldom enter into business of this kind—I hope you will remember me before a Throne of grace. . . ."[3]

Jed had been aware, from the beginning, that he was unlike most of the men in the mountains. He was learned, for one thing. He was serious—serious about his religion, serious about turning a profit, serious about writing a book and making maps. He didn't go for debauchery: He stayed away from Indian women and didn't join in the rendezvous carousing. He tried to practice his religion in a profane environment.

Jed was acutely conscious of his duty to his family, friends, church, and country. He knew what was expected of him. And he was beginning to feel delinquent.

He picked up his pen again to write his brother Ralph. After a matter-of-fact account of his adventures in the West, he wrote, "As it respects my Spiritual welfare, I hardly durst Speak. I find myself one of the most ungrateful; unthankful, Creatures imaginable. Oh when Shall I be under the care of a Christian Church? I have need of your Prayers, I wish our Society to bear me up before a Throne of Grace. . . ." He went on to send a couple of thousand dollars home for Ralph to distribute among his parents, the doctor (Ralph's father-in-law), and Ralph or others who might be in need.

He was bothered, though, by his own failure to be

upright. He wanted to say something to explain what he
had done, to show that he was not merely a vagabonding
reprobate. That he had made a profit would do, partly,
and that he had remembered his family with some of it.
But he wanted to say something moral: "It is, that I may
be able to help those who stand in need, that I face every
danger—it is for this, that I traverse the Mountains covered with eternal Snow—it is for this that I pass over the
Sandy Plains, in heat of Summer, thirsting for water, and
am well pleased if I can find a shade, instead of water,
where I may cool my overheated Body—it is for this that
I go for days without eating, and am pretty well satisfied
if I can gather a few roots, a few Snails, or, much better
Satisfied if we can affo[r]d ourselves a piece of Horse
Flesh, or a fine Roasted Dog, and, most of all, it is for
this, that I deprive myself of the privilege of Society and
the satisfaction of the Converse of My Friends! but I shall
count all this pleasure, if I am at last allowed by the
Alwise Ruler the privilege of Joining my Friends. . . ."
That was as close as he could come to speaking his pride,
or justifying his wayward course. It didn't seem good
enough. He went on: "Oh My Brother let us render to him
to whom all things belongs, a proper proportion of what
is his due. I must tell you, for my part, that I am much
behind hand, oh! the perverseness of my wicked heart!
I entangle myself altogether too much in the things of
time. . . ."[4]

The perverseness of his wicked heart weighed on Jed.
He sat in his tent that day considering. He knew that the
desire for profit would scarcely account for his eight years
in the mountains. He knew that he could have made money
and helped those who stand in need as a storekeeper or a
teacher. He knew that he had stayed in the mountains
partly from a love of wilderness, of grand country, of unfet-

tered movement, and of freedom from Society. He knew that his feelings weren't entirely what they should be.

Well, if they weren't, he could correct himself, do right, and hope for salvation.

Tired, Jed got up and left the tent. He found Sublette with Black Harris. They were packing up for the trip to St. Louis, laying in dried meat, making sure of the hide thongs on their snowshoes. He handed Sublette the letters, and Bill reminded him that two men were wanting Jed to write home for them. Jed nodded. Harris joked scoffingly that the letters would be packs of lies. Not a man of them would tell his folks the truth about the mountains, he said. The big man grinned at Jed. He himself fancied cheating the plains of his bones again, he reckoned, but he didn't care for staying in St. Louis longer than he had to. Jed knew that he would start by tying on a big one, then bed some riverfront whores, and then tell some newspapermen a few whoppers in the taverns. And he'd love it.

Jim Bridger was jawing with Tom Fitzpatrick and Joe Meek. Jed squatted and started asking questions about the territory for the spring hunt. Jim answered soberly, sketching river, canyon, and ridge patterns on a buffalo hide with the burnt end of a stick. Fitzpatrick eyed them casually—Bridger sitting cross-legged as he drew, his mind easily calling up details of thousands of square miles, relaxed and casual; Jed crouching on the balls of his feet, squirming a little as he watched and listened.

Meek looked from one to the other without saying a word. He felt like a child sitting with grown-ups. Jim and Jed were some. Joe had heard tell over and over, from every coon but Jed himself, about the trips to Californy, and he had learned the mountains at Jim's feet. But they were so different. Jim was a wild and natural cuss that made you feel like you were all right. You could booze with him, and take women in tandem with him. Jed was sort of distant and stern. You were afraid to have fun around him, and he never had any fun himself. It was like he allus had something heavy on his mind that kept him from being free and easy. Both men had the ha'r of the b'ar in 'em. But Joe didn't cotton to Jed, he surely didn't. Couldn't even talk to him without wanting to call him "Captain" Smith.

Jed stood up abruptly and walked away. Jim half grinned at Tom, but Fitzpatrick turned his head and followed Jed. Something riding him, maybe.

Meek, Bridger, and Fitzpatrick were not reflective men and were not in the habit of giving tongue to all that they felt. Had they done so they might have said that Jedediah Smith was not one of them. Bridger, Fitzpatrick, and Meek were well rid of civilization. They'd be damned sorry if it ever caught up with them, which it sure as hell wouldn't. No place in this country for families and schools and churches and stores. Never would be. Here, they were in a naturally shinin' place free of the things that cramped a man in, and what made sense but to enjoy it? They were like Adam in the Garden of Eden before the Fall, going about without any rules, learning all the new creatures and places, and living off nature's bounty like natural men.

But Jed Smith knew, and could have said, what he brought to the mountains they had left behind: The consciousness of sin.

Jed checked with the men who wanted to send words back home and went back to his tent. But he couldn't write. He stared at the paper. He dipped into the pot and picked small bits of meat out of the water. He found himself wondering what he had been doing for the last five minutes. At last he forced himself to begin scratching out the letters. When he had finished, he paused a moment and realized that he had made a decision. He would leave the mountains.

Wind River usually turned out to be first-rate country for wintering, with plenty of buffalo, wood, water handy, and tolerable shelter from the cold and the winds. The winter of 1829–30, though, was severely cold and drove the game to lower elevations. Jed followed the game several hundred miles east to the Powder River and stayed there until about the first of April. Then he started the brigade back for Blackfoot territory, with Jim Bridger as guide. As they moved west, they got caught in a heavy snowfall along the Big Horn. The traveling changed into a heavy slog. Crossing Bovey's Fork of the Big Horn, Jed lost thirty horses and three hundred traps, swept away by the high water. Moving on through Pryor's Gap, they came into Absaroka around Clark's Fork of the Yellowstone, then turned north to the Yellowstone proper and into Blackfoot land.

From here on, as they trapped north along the Musselshell and Judith Rivers, the Blackfeet hounded them. Jed doubled the night watch. Horses and traps disappeared constantly. He was gaining in plews, but losing his gain in animals and equipment. On the Judith, he gave the order to turn back. Meek remembers that the men were glad to get out of there, with a bountiful load of furs. They rode the long way, south to the Big Horn and back to Wind River. When they got to rendezvous, Davey Jackson was there with plenty of beaver. He and Jed had only to wait for Sublette with the new outfit and send down their best take yet.

Sublette had run into some trouble, though. John Jacob

Astor had gradually bought up the several companies trading with the Indians for plews along the Missouri. His St. Louis representative, Pierre Chouteau, pestered Sublette with questions about the mountain trapping while Bill was in town setting up his new supply train. Sublette was nothing if not a shrewd businessman. He could see that Astor's gigantic American Fur had in mind to come to the mountains to compete with SJ&S. Some tentative forays, in fact, had already been made. When he left St. Louis, he was carrying news to his partners of formidable new opposition from Astor, who had the advantages of huge amounts of capital and of exceptional ruthlessness.

He was also bringing a dozen wagons, a dozen cattle for meat until he reached buffalo country, and a milch cow. No one had even taken wagons to the Rocky Mountains before. Bill intended to show that a natural wagon road was there, and that less hardy folk could get West. Since rendezvous was on Wind River, Sublette did not take the wagons on across South Pass, but he would point out later to the government of the United States that he could easily have gotten ten wagons right across the Rocky Mountains.

His first news to Jed was sad: A letter from home said Jed's mother had died late the winter before. So he was already too late to see one of his parents again. The second news was major trouble: Astor. He would end what had amounted to a monopoly on mountain trapping. He would end their monopoly on supplying the precious manufactured goods. And Astor was coming at a time when the country had been substantially stripped of its beaver.

If Jed had had second thoughts about going back to civilization, these two pieces of news put them away. The partners decided to sell out. Jackson and Sublette, though, wanted to keep their hands in the business. They promptly formed a new firm to bring supplies to rendez-vous; they were making the exact move General Ashley had made when he sold out to SJ&S, four years earlier.

Smith, Jackson, and Sublette found buyers quickly. Tom Fitzpatrick, Milton Sublette, Jim Bridger, Henry Fraeb, and Jean Baptiste Gervais were eager to take over the business. They made the deal Ashley had made with SJ&S—they signed a note for the goods left at the end of rendezvous, payable in beaver at three dollars a pound. If notified by March 1, Bill Sublette and Dave Jackson would bring up next year's supplies and take the beaver down. The new partners called themselves the Rocky Mountain Fur Company.

The heads of the Rocky Mountain Fur were mountain men rather than businessmen. Ashley had been an ambitious politician who turned to the mountains to make money. His successors were a mixture: Smith, a mountain man par excellence, but educated and business wise as well; Sublette, a practical hand and superlative businessman; and Jackson, a first-rate brigade leader. Now the trappers would be led by their own: Bridger, who was illiterate, would be the field leader. Fraeb (pronounced Frapp) and Gervais were experienced partisans. Milton Sublette did not have the business head of his older brother Bill, but knew the mountains. Fitzpatrick, the intelligent, deter-mined Irishman, would be the brains of the new com-pany.

RMF was starting out some $16,000 in debt. But hadn't SJ&S done the same? And hadn't they made out fine? Didn't they set themselves up rich in four years? Fitzpat-rick, Milton Sublette, Bridger, Fraeb, and Gervais were old hands and good hands. They knew how to take beaver. Now, they thought, it was their turn to make out.

Unfortunately, they had planned without taking into consideration Astor, the multimillionaire who was prepared to capture the mountain fur business regardless of cost.

Bridger had now emerged as a premiere mountain man. He spoke various Indian languages easily. He understood Indians as very few trappers did. He was courageous, even daredevil, in battle. He knew the country so well that he could sketch it all out in the dust, and tell a booshway a new route just by remembering the lay of the land and figuring it out. He shot so center that he was said to have dropped twenty buffler in twenty straight shots. A companion described him a few years later:

The physical conformation of this man was in admirable keeping with his character. Tall—six feet at least—muscular, without an ounce of superfluous flesh . . . he might have served as a model for a sculptor or painter, by which to express the perfection of graceful strength and easy activity. One remarkable feature of this man . . . was his neck, which rivalled his head in size and thickness. . . . His cheek bones were high, his nose hooked or aquiline, the expression of his eye mild and thoughtful, and that of his face grave almost to solemnity. To complete the picture, he was perfectly ignorant of all knowledge contained in books, not knowing even the letters of the alphabet; put perfect faith in dreams and omens, and was unutterably scandalized if even the most childish of the superstitions of the Indians were treated with anything like contempt or disrespect; for in all these he was a firm and devout believer.[5]

The men had started calling him Old Gabe now. Some said that Jed Smith gave him that nickname, after the arch-angel Gabriel, because Jim always looked so solemn.

Jed, Bill Sublette, and Jackson set out for the settlements in early August. They were going home in clover: Their plews would bring enough that, after expenses, the three partners would divide about $54,000 in profit. Now they could set themselves up as wealthy businessmen.

Jed found civilization stretching westward. Independence, Missouri, was now a thriving town on the very edge of Indian country. It had grown because of the traffic to the mountains and to Santa Fe. When he got to St. Louis in October, the *Beacon* heralded the enterprise of SJ&S as a manifestation of westward expansion. "Messrs. Smith, Sublette & Jackson are the first that ever took wagons to the Rocky Mountains. The ease with which they did it, and could have gone on to the mouth of the Columbia, shows the folly and nonsense of those 'scientific' characters who talk of the Rocky Mountains as the barrier which is to stop the westward march of the American people."[6]

Westward march of the American people? That phrase would have stuck in the craw of some of the men Messrs. Smith, Sublette & Jackson had just left behind. They didn't want their country rutted by wagon wheels, frilled with skirts, and swept with brooms.

Smith, Jackson, and Sublette were mountain men, true enough, and they understood the desire to keep the church and the general store out of that country. But they were also responsible businessmen and citizens. So they promptly sent a letter to the Secretary of War. They spoke of the ease with which they had taken wagons to the mountains; they further pointed out that the route on the other side of South Pass was easier than on the eastern side, so that wagons could go all the way to the Great Falls of the Columbia with no difficulty. Jed described the British Fort Vancouver in all its particulars, and pointed out the threat of a foreign military establishment there. They also noted the baleful influence of the British on the Indians and the British attempt to trap out the jointly occupied territory; they concluded that the joint-occupancy treaty was unfair to Americans.

Newspapers immediately reprinted the letter all over the country. And, in late 1830, the enticing possibilities of major westward expansion into huge reaches of unsettled territory were put before the masses of Americans for the first time.

Jed still had business to attend to. He wanted to write his book and make his map of the West. First, though, he had to arrange some kind of settling down. He sent his brother money to buy Jed a farm in Wayne County, Ohio. He might become a farmer. Meanwhile, he needed a place in St. Louis. One of his brothers had already arrived— Peter—come to find out whether Jedediah was still alive. Austin came as well: when Ira showed up, Jed enrolled him in a seminary in Illinois and wrote home that St. Louis was no place to send youngsters, since it provided entirely too many temptations. To give himself, Peter, and Austin a place to live, he bought a lot and a house on Federal Avenue. He added two black slaves, a man and a woman, to make it into a home. He was setting himself up to live the life suitable to a distinguished man of affairs.

Jed, a Christian in the Puritan tradition, regarded making money as one of a man's positive duties, and thought of unused capital as an evil. He now had to decide on some use for his capital. Well, he might go to Ohio and that farm eventually, but he wanted some business venture in the meantime. The role of gentleman farmer may have pulled at his fancy, but not strongly enough. He hired Samuel Parkman, a young man who had gone to the mountains in 1829 and come back with Jedediah, to copy out his journals and help him make his maps. That was one important enterprise.

He also thought that he might go into a partnership with Robert Campbell. He discovered, though, that his Irish friend had gone home to Ireland; Robert's brother Hugh, who lived in Richmond, Virginia, informed Jed that Robert's health was failing again. He wrote to Hugh with good wishes for Robert's well-being and a fervent wish that the two friends might be together again. In the spring, he added, he would still have capital to start a business with Robert.

Peter Smith had wanted to follow 'Diah to the mountains. Another young man, J. J. Warner, came to Jed for advice on how to become a mountain man; Jed talked him out of such a pagan life. Austin was also casting about for something to do. So Jed began to think of the West again—not Absaroka and Cache Valley, this time, but Santa Fe. Maybe he could explore the possibilities of trade with the Mexican provinces.

He missed the mountains. Writing to Hugh Campbell on November 24, just a month back from the mountains, he admitted that "I am much more in my element, when conversing with the uncivilized Man, or Seting My Beaver Traps, than in writing Epistles."[7]

He decided to put off going home. He did miss his father, his teacher Dr. Simons, and his brother Ralph. But that could wait. Business, he told them, was too pressing. He didn't add that the lure of wild country was too strong.

He made up his mind for Santa Fe. That was less risky

than beaver trapping, even though the route lay through Indian country. He knew the business of supplying, and plenty of trappers were operating out of Santa Fe and Taos. He could get Peter, Austin, and J. J. Warner started in the world, give them a taste cf the trail and the mountains, and still not be shot at by Blackfeet. At first he thought that he himself might not go along—he'd just handle the business end. But by the end of January, Jed had determined to hit the trail again. He wrote General Ashley for help in getting a passport.

He could explain it all to himself. He was making a good investment; he was going into a business he knew; he was giving a hand to young men of enterprise. Besides that, he could go beyond Santa Fe and see the Southwest. That was the only part of the entire West he did not know first-hand; a trip there would let him complete his map. He didn't have to believe that he was giving in to the perverseness of his wicked heart, or to an uncivilized love of wild places.

Sublette and Jackson, meanwhile, had been waiting for Fitzpatrick to arrive with confirmation of their deal to take supplies to rendezvous in the summer of 1831. But Fitzpatrick had not shown up. They had already arranged to buy the provisions and equipment. Stuck, they elected to go with Jed. Legally, the two parties would be separate and Sublette-Jackson would get an independent passport and hire their men and sell their goods independently. But the outfits would travel together as far as Santa Fe. So, by late March of 1831, Jedediah Smith, who had tried to commit himself to the settlements by buying a farm, a fine house, and two servants, was back in the mountain trade with his old partners.

They set out from St. Louis, on April 10, with twenty-two wagons, including one bearing a six-pound cannon, and seventy-four men. Before they reached the frontier, two more independent wagons and nine more men joined them. Near Lexington, Missouri, they camped for final preparations. Jed took the precaution of making a new will, since he was heading back into Indian territory. But they still had several hundred miles of beautiful rolling plains before any possible danger.

Then they had a surprise in camp: Tom Fitzpatrick rode in. He was headed for St. Louis, two months late, to contract with Sublette and Jackson for supplies for the 1831 rendezvous.

The Irishman explained: Fraeb and Gervais had gone to Snake country; Bridger, Milton Sublette, and he had moved back to the Three Forks area, again in strength, to cash in on Blackfoot country. They had made a good hunt; but during the winter they had heard nothing from their other two partners. Finally they decided to take a chance on buying a new outfit anyway. But Fitz hadn't gotten away until March to make the express to the settlements. What could be done about the outfit?

Jackson and Sublette were not carrying exactly what they would have taken to the mountains. They were supplying two towns as well as possibly some trappers. They decided that if Fitzpatrick would go along to Santa Fe, they would supply him there. Sublette and Jackson would let him have two-thirds of the outfit, and Smith the other third. The credit of the Rocky Mountain Fur Company was good with these old friends. But Fitzpatrick would have to get the goods to rendezvous on his own. And since it was already into the first week of May, he would be plenty late.

So they set out for Council Grove. They had no troubles that they weren't used to—drizzle for days at a time, miry ground, and willful mules. At Council Grove they stocked up on wood for axles—the country was barren from here on—and got organized into disciplined units for traveling safely through Indian territory. Before long a war party made a charge on the wagons, but the cannon scared them off. A little later the clerk for Sublette and Jackson dropped behind the party to hunt and was killed by Pawnees. The Santa Fe Trail was not looking as trouble-free as it was supposed to be. This expedition, though, had an unsurpassed congregation of masters of the craft of the plains and the mountains. Jed Smith, Bill Sublette, David Jackson, and Tom Fitzpatrick were four of the half-dozen most skilled mountain men living.

They followed the Arkansas River southwest for over a hundred miles to come to the place where the route forked. The round-about way was easier and safer—along the river to the mountains and then due south, through Raton Pass, to Santa Fe. The short way was quick but treacherous. It was a straight line across the Cimarron Desert. It was a scorched country without water, without any landmark, crisscrossed by buffalo trails that disguised the wagon road and could lead a party the wrong way and into a torturous death by thirst. They took the Cimarron Cutoff. If anybody knew how to cross a desert and find water when he had to, it was Jed Smith.

In the confusing maze of buffalo trails, even these old hands lost their way. Soon they had spent three days without water. The animals were about to die. The men were delirious with thirst. Discipline was breaking down and small groups were wandering through the desert in a desperate search for water.

So Jed did what needed doing. Taking Fitzpatrick with him, he pushed ahead of the wagon train to try to find a water hole or a spring. He knew that the Cimarron meandered out there somewhere. Even if it was as sporadically wet as the Inconstant River, he would find a hole and dig for water.

The two men came to a hollow that should have had water. It was dry. Jed told Fitzpatrick to stay there, dig for water, and tell the main party in which direction he had gone. He was going to look further ahead. It was a dangerous choice in Indian country, because a lone man was an irresistible temptation. But Jed had to take the chance.

He found the dry bed of the Cimarron fifteen miles further on. It was dried to sand in most places, but here and there were holes filled with liquid. Jed's mind said caution: Buffalo holes would make good hunting spots for Indians and were likely to be watched. But his body cried out for wet. He rode down, let his horse walk in, and waded in himself.

After his pain eased, he got back on his horse. He would be able to save the wagon train now. But when he turned, Jed saw a band of fifteen or twenty Comanches blocking his way. He realized they had crept up while he was splashing in the water. He knew his chances were slim: The Comanches had a reputation for savagery.

His one hope was to make a strong front of it. He rode straight up to them and made signs of peace. They paid no attention. Since he had his gun cocked, the Indians fanned out to either side, away from the line of his rifle. Jed watched to make sure they didn't get behind him, and again tried to talk to their leader.

His horse was fidgeting backward. Suddenly the Indians began shouting at the horse and waving their blankets to frighten it. The horse wheeled and turned so that Jed's back was to the flank of braves. Instantly, one of them fired and hit him in the shoulder. Jed gasped, his breath knocked away. He turned the horse around to front, leveled his Hawken, and killed the chief.

He grabbed for his pistols. A lance knocked his arm away from a handle. Two more blows, like sledgehammers, crushed his chest. He felt a falling, back and sideways, like falling in a dream, falling without stopping. He forced his eyes to register: Blue, a vivid blue. He couldn't think what the blue might be. It darkened. And the sense of falling slipped away.

Jed Smith's brothers and friends waited and waited for him. Finally, for the safety of the caravan, they moved on. They hoped that he would miraculously survive whatever had happened, as he had always survived, and catch up with them on the trail. When they got to Santa Fe, on July 4, they heard the story of his death. Mexican traders had gotten it from the Comanches. Peter and Austin bought Jed's rifle and pistols from the traders. Jed's body was never found.

Jed Smith had made his traditional Christianity a deep principle within himself. But the love of wild places had rooted into him and become a deeper religion. His place of meditation was not the oak pew but the lone wilderness, as his eulogist said. His altar was the mountaintop, in a sense truer that his eulogist meant. His sacraments were mountain skills. At the age of thirty-two, he had lost his life in the service of his true church.

Yet was he modest, never obtrusive, charitable, "without guile," . . . a man whom none could approach without respect, or know without esteem. And though he fell under the spears of the savages, and his body glutted the prairie wolf, and none can tell where his bones are bleaching, he must not be forgotten.[8]

Jed Smith had made a great pilgrimage to discover and know intimately the West he loved. For that mission he had risked, in his own eyes, even his salvation.

Though he died young, his quest had been successful. He had found the way across the Rocky Mountains at South Pass. He had led his men the length and width of the Great Basin. He had pioneered the overland route to California. He had become the first man to cross the Sierra Nevada. And he had been first to travel by land from California to Oregon. If the trappers were light years ahead of the American government and American people in their knowledge of the West, it was because Jed Smith had shown them the way. As an explorer of the West, he had come to rank with Meriwether Lewis and William Clark. Such were the accomplishments of the public man.

The private man had met his own standards in enterprise, courage, integrity, and fairness. He had challenged the dangerous and the unknown with a fierce energy, and had thrived in them. He had spent his days living and feeling in the particulars—the creeks and meadows, the ridges and peaks—of the country he loved most, the Rocky Mountains.

A decade or two later, newspapers publicized the trapper garishly. Dime novelists idealized mountain men into heroes for wide-eyed boys and dreaming fathers. Kit Carson and Jim Bridger became epic figures, American versions of Odysseus. But then, when he should most have been remembered, Jedediah Strong Smith was forgotten.

~~~~

SEVENTH INTERLUDE

Mountain Mating

WHEN ALIEN PEOPLES MEET, THE SAYING GOES, FIRST they fight and then they fornicate. The trappers and Indians did both, as mood and circumstance might dictate. The opportunity for some great sex was probably one of the primary lures of the mountains for the whites, and the squaws seem to have relished it with the trapper, in or out of marriage, avidly enough to fulfill his wildest fantasies.

Compared to white attitudes toward sex, Indians were utterly uninhibited. They suffered from no embarrassment, shame, or secretiveness about it. With rare exceptions, they had no concept of chastity, in the sense of abstinence before marriage. Teenage girls and boys alike were expected to take their pleasure where they could find it. (Adultery was a somewhat different matter.) Adults coupled freely in front of children or anyone else. One prominent chief was often seen walking about his village naked, displaying an erection. Public ceremonies in which men and women copulated with someone other than their own husbands or wives were common among the plains tribes. And the American Indian was completely innocent of the notion that something he enjoyed sexually might be "wrong." "Wrong" would have been an incomprehensible concept to them in that context.

They were just as uninhibited in other matters where white culture invokes strong taboos. Homosexuals, called berdashes, populated every tribe and drew no censure; they were thought to be following visions given them in childhood; many were even warriors. Sex with an animal was perfectly permissible, too. So was sex with a recently killed enemy, usually as a final humiliation.

On the other hand, Indian marriage had conventions alien to the white newcomers. Polygamy was common. Wives were a sign of wealth, so a brave accumulated as many as he could afford. Romantic love was a notion the Indians simply did not have (again like most "primitive" peoples). Marriage was a necessary living arrangement, predicated on economic considerations; accommodation, duty, and obedience rather than love ruled it. Divorce was easy for both sexes: A brave simply told his woman to get out; a squaw simply left to live with another man. (For a woman to be single was out of the question.) For men, adultery was natural; for women in some other tribes, it was a punishable offense—an offense not against love or the marriage bed, but against property. A brave could dispose of his female property as he liked—lend her, trade her, or sell her. A squaw was not to give away what belonged to her man. Some tribes were amiably tolerant of adultery; but the Blackfeet killed straying squaws, or cut off their noses. (Prince Maximilian of Wied observed that in the Blackfoot tribe he saw, half the women had no noses.)

The trappers, brought up in a society where women covered even their ankles, sat sidesaddle on horses to disguise the fact they had legs, and never, ever referred to the biological difference between male and female human beings, naturally looked forward to any meeting with friendly Indians as a sexual field day. They pursued the squaws with an enthusiasm quite incomprehensible to the Indians, who had no way of knowing that the whites were plucking forbidden fruit.

And the willingness of Indian women was proverbial.

Records of it extend all the way back to Vespucci's visit to the New World in 1497. The squaws of the plains and mountains were as sensual and fun-loving as any. They also were inclined to regard white men as creatures with extraordinary medicine. Crow women were especially fond of white men, which doubtless accounts for part of the trapper's long-time affection for the Crows.

Aside from general sexual appetite, a squaw had plenty of reason to bed with a white man. It was hospitable, a way to show the friendship of herself, her father or husband, and her tribe to any trapper. Or she might want the baubles she sometimes got—trivia to the trappers, but great wealth and magic to her. Or her man might want the firewater, the tobacco, or the knife he could get for her. To expect compensation for the loan of a woman was as reasonable as to expect it for the loan of a horse. The guilt-ridden notion of prostitution never entered in.

And the white man was lustily eager. The trappers had come from a sexually repressive society, and desires must have been expressed explosively.

Think of their elation at discovering that, in many ways, squaws were preferable to white women. They were often strikingly attractive; they had high standards of cleanliness for the circumstances in which they lived; they were clever at using scents and other small allurements. But, mostly, they liked to do almost anything sexually. They liked to do things that only whores would do back in the settlements—and that many states still have laws against in 1973. There were blasts of wish-fulfillment.

Once the first flush of enthusiasm passed, many trappers settled into permanent or semi-permanent relationships with squaws. Becoming a squaw man, though, was a luxury usually reserved for the free trapper. It was ex-

pensive. He had to come up with a dowry in horses, buffalo robes, furs, or other goods. At every rendezvous, he had to buy his squaw enough foofuraw to make her outshine all the other squaws; keeping ahead of the Joneses applied in the mountains, too. And, worst of all, he had to be generous to all her relatives, who turned out to be an entire village, if not an entire tribe. To reaffirm his friendship to each one, he had to come up with an interminable number of presents.

He may still have gotten a bargain. He got a companion and a lover; and his woman had been well trained in obedience and domestic skills by her people. She dressed his furs. She made his clothes from skins with a skill that was beyond him. She made his lodge into an orderly home. She provided mountain cuisine, took care of his animals, skinned his kill, carried his water and wood. And as a bonus, she warmed his home with the mythic tales of her people and with superbly scatalogical jokes.

For the squaw, the arrangement was even better. When she acquired a trapper for a husband, she acquired high social status and unimaginable wealth. And she assured herself of better treatment than she would have gotten among her own people. A trapper might lodgepole her occasionally to teach her submission, but that would be mild compared to what her mother and sisters endured.

If he chose to divorce her, no one would be offended or censorious. He would simply tell her to go home. Perhaps he would even send a few presents along with her to prevent hurt feelings. And then her father could collect a second dowry by selling her to another man.

The mountain men learned to adopt the attitudes of their mentors, the Indians, in these matters. Listen, for instance, to Ruxton's fictional Killbuck recalling his "marriages" for a trapper tempted by a Taos girl. (And notice that, Indian-fashion, he begins his dissertation on marriage by counting his coup):

"From Red River, away up north among the Britishers, to the Heely (Gila) in the Spanish country—from the old Missoura to the Sea of Californy, I've trapped and hunted. I knows the Injuns and thar 'sign,' and they knows me, I'm thinkin. Thirty winters has snowed on me in these hyar mountains, and a niggur or a Spaniard would larn 'some' in that time. This old tool!" (tapping his rifle) "shoots 'center,' she does; and if thar's game afoot, this child knows 'bull' from 'cow' and ought to could. That deer is deer, and goats is goats, is plain as paint to any but a greenhorn. Beaver's a cunning crittur, but I've trapped a 'heap'; and at killing meat when meat's a-running, I'll 'shine' in the biggest kind of crowd. For twenty years I packed a squaw along. Not one, but a many. First I had a Blackfoot—the darndest slut as ever cried for fofarrow. I lodge-poled her on Colter's Creek, and made her quit. My buffler hos, and as good as four packs of beaver, I gave for old Bull-tail's daughter. He was head chief of the Ricaree, and 'came' nicely 'round' me. Thar wasn't enough scarlet cloth, nor beads, nor vermilion in Sublette's packs for her. Traps wouldn't buy her all the fofarrow she wanted; and in two years I'd sold her to Cross-Eagle for one of Jake Hawkin's guns—this very one I hold in my hands. Then I tried the Sioux, the Shian, and a Digger from the other side, who made the best moccasin *I* ever wore. She was the best of all, and was rubbed out by the Yutas in the Bayou Salade. Bad was the best; and after she was gone under, I tried no more. . . .

"Red Blood won't 'shine' any ways you fix it; and though I'm h— for 'sign,' a woman's breast is the hardest kind of rock to me, and leaves no trail that I can see of."[1]

VIII

War in the Mountains

AUGUST 1831: RENDEZVOUS IN CACHE VALLEY. THE partners were worried. Bridger and Sublette had made two good hunts in Blackfoot country, and when they found the brigade led by Gervais and Old Frapp (Fraeb), the second force turned out to have plenty of plews, too. But the competition was buzzing around like gnats.

In the fall, an American Fur Company outfit had come to the Three Forks region under William Henry Vanderburgh. They were out of Fort Union, which Kenneth McKenzie had built for the Company in 1829. Vanderburgh's men were promptly routed and sent home by the Blackfeet— which gave the RMF hands a chortle or two. Then Vanderburgh had managed to follow Old Gabe's outfit through part of its spring hunt, which was a damned nuisance. When Frapp and Gervais showed up, another American Fur bunch was following them; it had trailed them all over Snake country. Now, while the RMF men and the free trappers were waiting for their annual supplies, the American Fur trappers were contentedly camped nearby.

Old Gabe was some riled. The partners could see what the masterminds of the Company operation, McKenzie and Chouteau, had in mind. They already had the river trade in hand. Now, with their huge resources, they intended to grab the mountain trade on top of that. Bridger and his partners had one big advantage: They knew the mountains and they had the skills to trap them. So the Company developed a simple strategy: Trail the RMF men everywhere they go. Learn the territory. Train the river men to be mountain men. They might lose a lot of money and some lives in going to Rocky Mountain college under the involuntary tutelage of the mountain veterans. But Astor could afford it. After their free lessons, they would pour in men and money and take over the mountains.

The tactics would likely work. Bridger had proved enough of an Indian to lose Vanderburgh for part of the spring; but he doubted that he could do that indefinitely.

The biggest worry of the partners, though, was their business leader, Tom Fitzpatrick. He was over a month late to rendezvous already. The men were getting restless. Where was their whisky? Where was their 'baccy? Where were their trade goods? Where was the foofuraw they could dangle in front of the squaws and the young girls? They hadn't had any fun in a year, and they were getting tired of waiting. Some of the Indians had already left in disgust.

Luckily for the partners, the American Fur partisans didn't have any supplies either. Because RMF had some whisky left, the partners had tempted some trappers away from the Company. Now, an uneasy truce held forth over the two camps. Lucius Fontenelle and Andrew Drips, the Company leaders who had trailed Frapp and Gervais, had gone down to St. Louis in early summer to get an outfit, leaving Vanderburgh in charge. Bridger wasn't worried about Fontenelle and Drips: They'd be lucky to get to their men before winter.

But where in tarnation was Fitzpatrick? Had the little red-headed Irishman gone under? Even powder and lead were low now, and the trappers were grumbling. Old Gabe and Frapp decided to do something about the situation: They went to a Crow shaman and paid him two horses to divine Fitzpatrick's fate. The medicine man began his ceremonial divination. He called for dancing, drumming, and singing. He consulted the powerful objects in his medicine bag. He listened to the birds that came to him in visions. He went into a trance. After several days of mystical consultation, he came up with his answer: Fitzpatrick was alive, but he was traveling the wrong road.

Bridger and Frapp were mightily relieved. Frapp immediately took the year's furs and started east to find Fitz. Bridger divided up the trappers into three brigades under Milton Sublette, Gervais, and himself. While Frapp hunted for Fitzpatrick, they got started on their fall hunts, desperately low on essentials.

Frapp moved across the Siskadee, through South Pass, down the Sweetwater River, and to the North Platte. In September, near the mouth of Laramie Creek, he ran onto Fitzpatrick with the pack-train—traveling, sure enough, the wrong road. Fitz, of course, had detoured all the way to Santa Fe with the Smith-Bill Sublette-Jackson trading expedition, had got moving out of Santa Fe in July, and was just now getting on the usual route to the mountains. He was bringing a small outfit and forty new men. (One of them was a young hand who had had some experience working out of Taos, Christopher Carson.)

Frapp and the reinforced party turned around and rode west with the supplies. Fitzpatrick went along for a while, then reversed toward St. Louis. With competition getting serious, RMF had to be sure of an outfit for 1832.

Meanwhile, during that autumn, RMF was taking its

usual good harvest of furs west of the mountains. They made winter camp on the Salmon River, and glory be if Frapp didn't show up with a load of supplies. Gabe pointed out wryly to skeptics that the old medicine man had surely earned his pay. Now on fat times while the Company men were on poor times, they could have a field day. They bribed away furs and trappers with their fixens all winter. Poor Drips showed up with supplies too late to be of much help to the Company.

But two more ominous pieces of news came by mountain grapevine to the RMF leaders. Fontenelle had gone to Fort Union and intended to bring a caravan to rendezvous from there; he would have several hundred miles of head start on the RMF outfit. And McKenzie had done what not a beaver of them had been able to do: He opened trade with the Blackfeet. He had built a fort at the mouth of the Marias River, in the heart of the territory of Bug's Boys, and was trading them rifles, powder, lead, and whisky for plews.

It was a rough year for the Company brigades in the field. RMF was luring their men away. And the Blackfeet were putting a lot of pressure on everyone: Armed by McKenzie, they had decided to wipe out their old enemies, the Flatheads, and their new enemies, the whites. So Company guns were sending balls into Company men.

That made no difference to McKenzie. He had his orders from the men who lived handsomely, far from the danger, in St. Louis and New York: Wipe out all opposition. He had instructions to buy all the plews in the mountains, at whatever price; to hire all the trappers, even at outrageous wages; to befriend all the Indians, by whatever means; and to harass RMF.

If American Fur lost money for several years, that made no difference. John Jacob Astor, having made a small fortune in fur as a young man, had turned his financial wizardry to other areas, principally to New York real estate. He continued to finance his fur business, though, and made one major effort to get established in the West: In 1811 he sent two parties to the mouth of the Columbia River, one overland and one by sea, to found Astoria. For various reasons, the enterprise failed, and the post fell into the hands of the Northwest Company, which later merged with the Hudson Bay Company. For some years then, Astor was content to let his associate, Ramsay Crooks, run the lucrative fur business east of the Mississippi.

In the mid-1820s, American Fur decided to add to its empire the fur trade on the Missouri River and in the Rocky Mountains. With Astor providing the funds and Crooks masterminding the operation, they bought out the minor firms of the Western trade and made executives of the former owners, Pierre Chouteau and Kenneth McKenzie. Chouteau and McKenzie were ordered to seize the Western trade at any cost, to enlarge the virtual monopoly American Fur held in the East. If they had to pay nine dollars for plews that would sell for half that price in the East, Astor had the capital. Until RMF was destroyed or bought out, price was no object.

That was why the gigantic arm of American Fur had been stretching up the river—first to Fort Union, then to Fort McKenzie in Blackfoot country. McKenzie was even making plans to build a fort at the mouth of the Big Horn, in the center of Absaroka, in the summer of 1832. He intended to secure the friendship and trade of the Crows, the long-time friends of the opposition trappers, for American Fur.

McKenzie was a character, and he was already beginning to be nicknamed the King of the Missouri. He lived in high style at Fort Union. He dressed his Indian mistresses in the latest fashions that St. Louis had heard tell of from New York. He smoked fine cigars. He drank fine wines and brandies. He had the shrewdness to be an agent of John Jacob Astor, and the ruthlessness: When he was told about an Indian raid on one of his brigades, in which all the men had been saved, but all the horses lost, he raged that it ought to have been the other way around.

Bridger and Sublette trapped southeast from their Salmon camp that spring and headed back toward Cache Valley. To their disgust, Vanderburgh caught up with them at Gray's Hole. His men trailed the RMF men up every little creek, setting their own traps. And Bridger ran into more trouble: Milton Sublette was stabbed in a fight with a half-breed.

Old Gabe wanted to be showing Vanderburgh his heels, and he could see that Milton was going to go under. So he left Joe Meek to bury their friend—just as Gabe himself had been left with Hugh Glass more than eight years earlier. That gave him twinges of painful memories; but Gabe had lived down that story by now.

He took off and used his various tricks to cover his trail. But Vanderburgh was getting wily too, and he refused to be shaken off. He stuck with Bridger all the way to rendezvous at Pierre's Hole. And to make it worse, he had recently gotten Drips's supplies; he turned the tables on Bridger by bribing away RMF plews and men.

Back on the Bear River, Milton Sublette was coming around. Meek tended him for forty days while he recuperated. Then they broke camp and took off after Bridger. But they rode right into a band of Snakes. They figured that Milton wasn't well enough for a cross-country chase, so they took the best alternative. They rode straight into the camp, ducked into the chief's tent, and gave themselves up to his hospitality. Full Indian council got underway. In long speeches, full of recollections of the valor of the speaker, the braves declared themselves for or against the killing of the trappers. The palaver went on for hours. They decided for ritual execution.

While the braves were outside getting ready for the ceremony, and relishing the idea of a great blood celebration, one of the dissenting chiefs sprang Meek and Sublette from the lodge. He led them across a creek and into a thicket. There a young Indian girl was holding their horses. That was the first time either Joe or Milton saw Umentucken Tukutsey Undewatsey, Mountain Lamb. She seemed to each of them the most beautiful girl in the mountains. But they had no time to linger over her now. They galloped off. A year later Milton would marry her. When Milton left the mountains, Joe would marry her. And she would become known by all the trappers as the loveliest woman in the mountains.

JUNE 1832: RENDEZVOUS AT PIERRE'S HOLE: Milton and Joe rode into rendezvous late. They found Bridger, Frapp, and Gervais camped in Pierre's Hole with the hundred or so men who worked for RMF. Settled happily beside them were Vanderburgh and Drips with nearly as many men. RMF, which was coming to be called the Opposition, had reaped a bumper crop—some $60,000 in plews. The Company, on the other hand, had not got much; their partisans were still catching on.

Still, the difference between fat cow and poor bull for the Opposition lay in one place: The trade of the free trappers. The partners needed those plews; they also needed the profits on their trade goods. All the trappers were ready for a blow-out, but they couldn't get started until one of the two supply trains arrived. So the difference between profit and loss for the Opposition lay in a simple question: Who would get to Pierre's Hole first—Tom Fitzpatrick, Bill Sublette, and Robert Campbell for the Opposition, or Lucien Fontenelle for the Company? The race was on.

The partners sent out two men to find Sublette, Campbell, and Fitzpatrick and put the whip to them. Vanderburgh and Drips sent men after Fontenelle. The RMF men came back on foot, having been robbed by Crows; they'd seen no sign of Sublette. The Company men came back without finding Fontenelle; but they had spotted the RMF outfit, apparently in the lead.

In midmorning of July 8, the camp was roused by a hundred rifles volleying from the south. The trappers answered back with their Hawkens. It was Sublette riding in—hooves clopping, packs and saddles creaking, dust coming up like from a herd of buffler, and, over it all, the trappers bellowing, "Hurrah for Bill Sublette!" The four partners grinned at each other and jumped on their horses to meet the coming train.

They had a grim surprise. "Whar's Tom?" Bridget asked Bill. "Ain't he hyar?" returned Sublette. Jim and Milton looked at each other. Campbell told them Tom had ridden ahead from the Sweetwater. He had in mind to tell his partners that the RMF outfit was on its way. If the Company had beaten the Fitzpatrick-Sublette train, Tom figured, maybe they could stall their trappers and some of the free trappers until it arrived. But he had not shown up. The trappers got straight in to whooping it up, but their celebration was dampened a little, and the partners were glum. Tom was one of the great men of the mountains. He was also the brains of RMF. If he had gone under, they were in trouble.

The Opposition sent out the routine search parties, but without much hope. Any young Crow hot for coup would have taken the scalp of Broken Hand, whether or not the Crows were supposed to be friendly. And Bill had run into a large, migrating band of Blackfeet as he came in. They were actually Gros Ventres, but they lived with the Blackfeet and behaved like Blackfeet, so all their enemies considered them the same as Bug's Boys. They had been south visiting their cousins, the Arapahoes, and had left blood all along their trail back north.

Fitzpatrick had taken the kind of calculated risk that mountain men took routinely and with a daredevil spirit. The Indians were always hostile and any kind of mistake could let the country itself be just as murderous. Any bit of bad luck would let the danger of Indian or territory slip from behind its facade and put a man under. Tom was as expert as any of them. But he had had over four hundred miles to go—up the Sweetwater, through South Pass, over to the Green, across the mountains at its head, across the Snake. That was a lot of risky country. Especially for a man alone. Well, the mountain men shrugged off the bad luck of their friends. A coon could turn up a bad card any time.

Tom Fitzpatrick is tired. The sun has been up for a couple of hours, but he's still riding. Since he left Sublette, he has ridden mostly at night. He can't afford to chance being seen by Indians in the daylight. He rides all night on one horse and leading the other, then switching. During the day he sleeps. Not long after dawn, he labors up some little draw to its head, finds a thicket, hobbles his horses where they can graze, and flops down. In midafternoon he wakes up and waits for sunset again to get started. Since these are the longest days of the year, it has sometimes been a long wait.

He has pushed hard, and now he must be well ahead of Sublette—maybe a week, he judges. Being wary, he has seen not a speck of trouble. He has kept off to the side of the main trail up the Sweetwater, crossed South Pass on its northern flank, angled northwest to the Siskadee, staying always in the timber near the edge of the hills. Yesterday, he came into the maze of canyons and ridges west of the headwaters of the Seedskeeder. Now that he is well off any recognized trails, he is risking a little more travel in the daylight. It is full light now, and he has not stopped. It's about time to sleep.

He hears the yelps before he sees them. Indians. Damn, he's been careless, riding up so close without seeing them. He'll have to run for it. No matter who they are, they'll be boiling for this easy a trophy. He lets go the trailing horse and kicks his cayuse up a draw. This valley is small. He has no choice but to ride up one draw, over the ridge into another, rip through the brush, and hope that the draws will eventually come together in such a way that he can lose the redskins, at least momentarily. He can tell from their shouts now that they are Blackfeet. Cuss his luck. And his carelessness.

They stick on him. He has to kick his horse up steeper and steeper draws. Doesn't look like a way out of this. Soon he is pushing the beast nearly straight up a mountainside. The horse will have to go. He jumps from the saddle and starts running up the slope, straight toward the rising rocks.

Then he hears the yells below. The Blackfeet have found the horse, and they could smell blood now. He slips into a chimney and desperately covers the crevice with rocks and brush. Nothing for it but to hide and hope.

They swarm up the hill. Some of the braves stop to paint themselves. War is religious, after all. Gros Ventres, he can see. They set up their howling. This yelping is their way of calling on their gods for protection. The songs have been revealed to each brave as the medicine that will make him invulnerable in battle. They put on their strong medicine— feathers, small bones, claws, small pieces of dung, whatever they've seen in their dreams as their great power. They begin to recite ceremonially their great deeds of the past. Well, it slows them up anyway. Tom feels calm and clear. He'll be able to take some with him if they find him.

They keep it up all day. They scramble over the rocks above him, trot across the grass below him, always whooping. A couple of times they get close enough to scratch. A couple of times they go back down, and call up some more medicine, and swarm up again. Tom figures he has one advantage: To him, all Blackfeet are stupid.

When dark begins to fall, he takes a line by the stars that will keep him away from their camp. Then, in full night, he steals out and starts crawling around them. He crawls straight into their lodges. Disgusted, and judging that it isn't his night, he creeps back to his hole. The next day is an exact repeat, the Blackfeet scampering all over the place, sniffing, yelping, like a pack of dogs that doesn't have the scent. They won't quit, though. An easy white scalp is temptation enough to keep them from whatever they were doing for days.

The second night he sneaks out again. This time he calculates better and gets around the camp. During the day he hides in a thicket, and sees them again. The third night he gives them the slip, he reckons, for good.

He sets out for rendezvous on foot, moving by day now. He can take game, so he'll make it.

When he gets to the Snake River, he makes a raft to get his possibles across and keep his powder dry. The upper Snake is a mean river, though; it takes his raft apart. By the time he pulls himself out on the west bank he has nothing left but his Green River. He'll have to eat roots. Tom can't get much lost in this country, though. Pierre's Hole is a touch west and then straight north.

But he's getting weaker. Roots don't keep a man's strength up. On his fifth day out from the Snake, he stumbles across a hulk of buffler left by the wolves. He eats the meat raw. Soon his moccasins are shredded from walking on rock. He cuts his hat into strips and ties them around his feet. Still, they bleed.

He is half delirious, emaciated, weak as a new calf, staggering, when he sees the trappers. He realizes that they have seen him already. He can stop trying now. They will take him to food, rest, and even a drink. He grins to himself. He is only a couple of hours from rendezvous. He has made it on his own.

They put him on a horse and lead him to Sublette and Old Gabe. Sublette, he finds out, rode in just this morning. Beat the Company outfit, too. So there's whisky to make a toast with.

Now the debauch really got going. The trappers would drink until they threw up, and then drink some more. The clerk for Sublette and Campbell cut the whisky a little thinner every round, but the whites and Indians didn't know and didn't care. (The stuff was a mixture of one gallon raw alcohol to three gallons crick water; tea or tobacco, ginger, red peppers, and molasses were likely to be tossed in for flavor.) Eye-gouging brawls broke out sporadically. Guns popped like firecrackers on Independence Day. One trapper grabbed a kettle of alcohol, started reciting a version of the baptismal ceremony, and dumped the liquid over a lanky, red-headed trapper's head. A third man lifted a stick out of the fire and put the redhead ablaze. The gang pitched in to beat out the fire, but the poor fellow nearly died.

The men promptly began to chase the fantasies they had entertained all winter long. Two hundred lodges of Indians were at rendezvous, with seven or eight Indians per lodge, so the braves came to drink and barter away their women for the night. Beads, bells, cloth, some tobacco—almost any fragment of trading goods represented great wealth to the braves. Some men would roll up for the night with the squaw, some would take her on the spot and move on. Some dealt baubles to free-lancing teenage girls instead of their fathers.

Besides his own men, Sublette had brought some real greenhorns along—Nathaniel Wyeth, a Massachusetts ice merchant, and his crew of nineteen. Being reputable fellows, they were more astonished than most *mangeurs de lard* at these goings-on. They listened to the yarns with big ears. They saw gambling aplenty, and heard what a serious business it was for Indians.

A Crow and a Sioux had once sat down for a serious session of the hand game. The Sioux had bad luck; he lost almost every bet until his weapons, his clothes, even his medicine, were gone. Calmly, he wagered his scalp on the next guess. He lost. His foe stood up, cut a ring around the head just above the ears and across the forehead, put his shoulder on the Sioux's shoulder, and yanked the scalp off with a sucking pop. The Sioux made not a sound. Bleeding, he stood and asked that the two meet again in the same place for another session. It was agreed.

At the return match, the luck ran the other way. The Sioux, his skull gleaming in the sun and his forehead welted red, seemed to win every bet. He took all the Crow's belongings. At last he took the brave's scalp. Now they were even. But the Crow refused to quit. He wagered his life. He lost. He made no protest as the Sioux raised his knife and made no sound but a whoosh of breath when it whacked into his chest. For years the Sioux wore both scalps, his enemy's and his own, dangling from his ears.

The Wyeth recruits also listened agape to Bridger's fabulous stories—about the box canyon he could leap across on his horse because the law of gravity was putrefied; about the mountain that was such clear glass that birds dashed their brains out on it; about the wonders around Yellowstone Lake, the back door to hell. These greenhorns had plenty to marvel at.

Wyeth was trying to find out from these master trappers where the beaver were. This ingenious and energetic Yankee, sitting in civilized Boston, had calculated a way to make a fortune in furs. These woodsmen were doing it uneconomically; he was sure he knew how to turn big profits out here. He had raised capital, recruited men, and made his way to St. Louis. Bill Sublette had offered to escort him to the mountains: Such an obvious greenhorn would provide no competition for the men who understood the mountains. Back in Boston, where men were reasonable and Ralph Waldo Emerson was making sense of the world, Wyeth's neat little plans looked like a sure bet. Sublette laughed quietly, knowing that the reality of the Rockies was something Boston didn't dream of. Wyeth quickly found out Sublette was right. But now that he was here, he was going to learn the business.

Gabe amused him with yarns, but RMF wasn't about to tell any newcomers their trade secrets. They had enough on their hands with the Company. Innocents were not welcome—neither Wyeth nor the band that Sublette had passed back on the trail, a brigade led by an army officer named Captain Benjamin Bonneville. What right did these greenhorns have in the mountains anyway?

The partners were concerned about American Fur. This year RMF had done nicely: Because Sublette had gotten to Pierre's Hole first, they had been able to get all the trade of the free trappers. But it was a momentary victory. Next year the Company might be first. They couldn't afford to keep taking that kind of risk. Fitzpatrick, Bridger, both Sublettes, Campbell, and Gervais talked it over seriously. Then they walked over to see Vanderburgh and Drips.

It was a simple and friendly proposition they said. RMF would divide the mountains with the Company. That would keep the two from tripping over each other's feet; it would eliminate the raids on each other for men and furs; it would let them spend their time trapping instead of running from or chasing each other.

Vanderburgh scarcely pondered before he declined. He and Drips didn't know the mountains well enough, he offered, to be certain that RMF was giving them a fair shake. It was a lame excuse; any free trapper could have said for sure whether the split was square. But Vanderburgh and Drips had their orders from McKenzie: *Écraser toute opposition*. After two more hunts they might know the mountains well enough that, instead of making a deal with the Opposition, they could wipe it out.

The partners went back to their tents in a temper. Jim was ready to fight, by God. He outlined the coming year's hunt: Milton Sublette and Gervais would make a huge sweep west, a circle including the Salt Lake, the Humboldt River far to the west, the lower Snake, and the Salmon River area. Bridger and Fitzpatrick would work the Yellowstone and the Three Forks. Frapp would stay on the Siskadee. In short, RMF was going to trap every worthwhile stream in the mountains in 1832–33. They'd see Sublette at rendezvous on the Siskadee next summer.

Sublette had decided to add some fighting of his own: He intended to build posts on the upper Missouri to compete with American Fur—one next to every Company outpost.

That was the plan. As they got ready to spread out for the year, hoping to lose the Company outfits that hounded them, Vanderburgh and Drips cussed Fontenelle and waited for him to show up. Finally, long after rendezvous, they went looking for him and found him still on the Siskadee. He had big news: The Company had managed to get a steamboat all the way to Fort Union at the mouth of the Yellowstone. That would put a different color on things—a new form of transportation for men, goods, and furs.

Benjamin Bonneville straggled up to the Siskadee even later. He decided to build a fort there in the heart of beaver country—another nuisance to Bridger and company. "Hell," Jim fumed, "where was they when we come to this country, larned it, larned the Indians, larned the ways, larned what shines and what don't? Safe in their Missouri River forts," he scoffed. "Safe on the other side of the Mississippi, some of 'em. In Boston."

Before Gabe could get his brigades gone, there were still some shinin' times to be had. The hand game went on for drunken hours, and the dallying with squaws took up some time. The trappers were game to show the *mangeurs de lard* what they could do on horseback, with their

Hawkens, with their fists, and in any other form of competition they could concoct. They took time to show off
their new clothes, fresh from St. Louis. (The clothes would
be worn out pretty quick anyway.) They had to trade with
the squaws for what they needed—those same buckskins,
cut from hide that had been used for lodges the year before;
if it had been smoked in that way, it wouldn't shrink painfully when it got wet, or bag so badly when it got stretched
after the wetting.

Many of the trappers were squaw men by this time and
for them, rendezvous was an expensive proposition. A
"married" trapper had to turn his woman out like a human
Christmas tree, cover her from tip to toe with the frip-
pery that the squaws adored. What it meant to a squaw to
be "married" to a trapper, after all, was to be rich. And
she would parade her riches like a child in front of her
envious relatives.

This squaw was likely to be a lovely spectacle. She might
be a Shoshone girl—the mountain men thought the Shoshone women the most beautiful in the mountains—with
small, delicate hands and feet and finely formed limbs.
During their teenage years, Indian girls were often re-
markably lovely. This girl would have brushed her black
hair glossy with a porcupine-tail brush and scented it with
an ointment she made. She would have colored the part
line with the vermilion her rich husband had just bought
and her forehead, nose, and cheeks would show finger-tip
circles of color as beauty spots. She had blended herbs,
grass, pine needles, and flowers to perfume her body and
garments. Her costume was splendiferous: She wore a
dress of doeskin, beaten thin and whitened. The skirt was
fringed with tiny bells. The bodice was decorated with
colored quills and ribbons in the shape of a flower. A wide
leather belt, geometrically beaded, cinched her waist. Some

designs in paint and colored cloth topped off the ornamentation. She would have put these finishing touches on her clothing as soon as her man got the materials from Sublette and Campbell, and would preen in them like a show horse all during rendezvous. She probably frustrated a good many hot-blooded trappers: Though her sisters, and even her mother, might be available for any sort of fun, she was not. She was a valued piece of property, not to be passed around, and she knew it.

During these last days of rendezvous, 1832, the locale itself was among the joys to be savored. Pierre's Hole was a romantically beautiful spot, one of the most beautiful in all of the Rockies. It sat below the Grand Tetons on the west as Jackson Hole sat on the east, spectacular ornaments for a spectacular range. Opposite the three spiky Tetons stood a western wall of mountain, the Big Holes. Pierre's Hole was greener and more timbered than Jackson Hole. The light in the mornings now had no direct source, but filtered through a limitless clear sky. It was a pale, misty, soft light that favored the cottonwoods, the aspen, the dwarf oak. The Teton kept a hazy mysteriousness until midmorning, when the sun came over the peaks and gave a brilliant sheen to the light. It was a good time to be alive.

Bridger and Fitzpatrick moved out first. On July 17, Milton Sublette, Wyeth, and Frapp rode south out of the Hole. And smack into one of those migrating villages of Gros Ventres.

The hundred whites and their Indian companions marched on to within a mile of these Blackfeet and stopped to wait and watch. They were sure enough of a fight to send an express back to rendezvous immediately for reinforcements. (Along with free trappers and Bill Sublette's outfit, Vanderburgh and Drips were still there, fidgeting until Fontenelle showed up.) One of these villages had shot up Bill Sublette's camp on the way here, another had chased Tom Fitzpatrick. Their hearts would not be good. When the Gros Ventres sent a war chief toward the trappers holding a medicine pipe, the trappers didn't take the ruse. These Blackfeet were stalling until they could invoke their various gods and powers to make them invulnerable. A half-breed and a Flathead met the chief, shot him point-blank, and took his scalp.

Just then Bill Sublette came up with reinforcements. The Gros Ventres were boiling mad now, and screamed their taunts at the whites. They were forting up behind a makeshift cover of fallen trees.

Sublette took over. He got sixty volunteers to attack with him. He and Bob Campbell made wills to each other verbally. Sublette split the volunteers into two units and instructed them to get straight up to the breastwork and attack from two sides.

When they did, they got the hell shot out of them. The Blackfeet, well covered, poured balls into them. Two free trappers were killed in the first couple of exchanges, and Sublette was shot in the arm. The trappers, better shots with better rifles, picked off their share. But they also shot some of their Flathead allies approaching from the opposite side.

They backed off a little and kept up occasional fire. Words were also weapons. Each side told the other they were cowards, that their fathers were quaking rabbits, and so on. Ten whites and Flatheads went under during the afternoon. At last Sublette decided that attack was foolhardy and useless. He gave the order to burn the Gros Ventres out. The Flatheads objected to the waste of perfectly good scalps and booty, but they were overruled.

The Blackfeet started their death songs—magic

incantations meant to ward off even the surest death—
and intensified their taunts. One of them cried that hundreds of lodges of their people were coming up behind
and would rub the whites and their allies out. (And a lot
of Gros Ventres were in the area.)

By the time his words got translated into English,
perhaps through a Flathead, they had undergone a sea
change. The news spread like fire in dry brush. While
the trappers were fighting it out here, hundreds of Gros
Ventres were attacking the main camp back at rendezvous. All but a handful of the trappers galloped off to
the rescue. When they came back, embarrassed, it was
too late to execute the burning that day.

The next morning they found that the Gros Ventres had
slipped away in the dark. The Flatheads scalped the dead
left behind, including women and children, and exulted in
the litter of plews, robes and other wealth that was abandoned along the trail of retreat. Five whites and seven
Flatheads had been killed, and at least twenty-six Blackfeet.

Sublette and Campbell waited back at rendezvous while
Bill convalesced. They also kept their eyes open for more
Gros Ventres, but none showed up. The unlucky Gros Ventres, though, did manage to blunder into a large band of
Crows, who massacred them. When the migrants straggled home to their Blackfoot friends, they had an unhappy
story to tell; it just added to the Blackfoot vengefulness
for the coming year.

Blackfeet were only one of many annoyances for RMF in
the season of 1832–33. The presence of intruders was
another, and Tom Fitzpatrick wrote to Ashley, now a congressman, advising him and hoping he would use his

influence against the newcomers. Bonneville and Wyeth were in bad straits, though. Wyeth's men had mutinied; half were going back to the settlements with Sublette and Campbell. Wyeth was taking the rest to Fort Vancouver to continue his education in the trapping business. Bonneville was inept; in the next couple of years, he would lose men, horses, equipment, plews, and money until he drove himself far into bankruptcy.

The major annoyance was still the Company. After Vanderburgh and Drips finally found Fontenelle with their supplies, they took off after Bridger and Fitzpatrick. To the veteran's digust, they caught up with the RMF brigade quickly (in late September) and stuck with them. Well then, Gabe and Fitz would provide a fancy chase. Through the mountains north of Yellowstone the RMF partisans would slip over a ridge, down a draw, and into a decent spot for plews—only to have the Company show up a couple of days later, dogged as ever. All right, we'll make it cost 'em. Gabe and Tom headed east down the Missouri, into an area where no beaver were to be found. Still the Company stuck. At least the Company men were on lean times. The outfit ahead got most of the game.

When RMF headed back to Three Forks, Vanderburgh and Drips decided that they'd better do some trapping. So they split up; in a neat division, RMF and two Company brigades divided the three forks of the Missouri between them. But Gabe and Fitz knew more about Blackfeet, and how to deal with the niggurs, than their competitors. They knew not to halve their strength, as the Company was doing. Vanderburgh's bunch got ambushed in a gulley; Vanderburgh himself was killed, along with another trapper, and others were injured. Drips's outfit also got shot up and lost some horses as well. The Blackfeet were having a lot of fun this autumn. And Gabe and Fitz were shaking their heads knowingly, figuring that the Company had it coming.

Milton Sublette, meanwhile, had fallen on starving times out near the Humboldt River. Joe Meek, who was with him, learned to eat crickets, and even to stick his hands in an ant-hill, wait till they were covered with ants, and greedily lick the critturs off. By the time Milton, Meek, Frapp and company got to the wintering place on the Salmon, where they met Bridger-Fitzpatrick, Drips, and Bonneville's stragglers, they had made a poor hunt.

The winter was uneventful except for one episode that Meek got himself into: Joe was out hunting with three other trappers, Hawkins, Clement, and Doughty, when they spotted huge grizzly tracks in the snow in front of a cave. Doughty proposed to get onto the rocks above the cave and shoot the varmint if any of the other three had the stuff to roust him out. All three volunteered for the fun of bear-baiting. The rest of the story, as Meek told it to his biographer:

On entering the cave, which was sixteen or twenty feet square, and high enough to stand erect in, instead of one, three bears were discovered. They were stand-ing, the largest one in the middle, with their eyes star-ing at the entrance, but quite quiet, greeting the hunters only with a low growl. Finding that there was a bear apiece to be disposed of, the hunters kept close to the wall, and out of the stream of light from the entrance while they advanced a little way, cautiously, towards their game, which, however, seemed to take no notice of them. After maneuvering a few minutes to get nearer, Meek finally struck the large bear on the head with his wiping-stick, when it immediately moved off and ran out of the cave. As it came out, Doughty shot, but only wounded it, and it came rushing back, snorting and running around in a circle, till the well directed shots from all three killed it on the spot. Two more bears now remained to be disposed of.

The successful shot put Hawkins in high spirits. He began to hallo and laugh, dancing around, and with the others striking the next largest bear to make him run out, which he soon did, and was shot by Doughty. By this time their guns were reloaded, the men growing more and more elated, and Hawkins declaring that they were "all Daniels in the lions' den, and no mistake." This, and similar expressions, he constantly vociferated, while they drove out the third and smallest bear. As it reached the cave's mouth, three simultaneous shots put an end to the last one, when Hawkins' excitement know no bounds. "Daniel was a humbug," said he. "Daniel in the lions' den! Of course it was winter, and the lions were sucking their paws! Tell me no more of Daniel's exploits. We are as good Daniels as he ever dared to be. Hurrah for these Daniels!" With these expressions, and playing many antics by way of rejoicing, the delighted Hawkins finally danced himself out of his "lions' den," and set to work with the others for a return to camp.[1]

The mountain man's sense of drollery.

In the spring Milton worked Salmon and Snake country; Gabe and Fitzpatrick went back to Absaroka. Drips stayed around the continental divide in the Bitterroot Mountains, and paid ruinously high prices to the Indians for plews. When they all got to rendezvous, RMF had about $33,000 in beaver, and the Company about $19,000. If the Company was losing a fortune, it was still hurting RMF by every plew it took. Again, the trade of the free trappers would swing the balance one way or the other. And so, the race between Sublette-Campbell and Fontenelle was on once more.

JULY 1833: RENDEZVOUS ON NEW FORK: Sublette won for RMF again, by three days. Another blow-out: Captain William Drummond Stewart, late of the British Army and now traveling with Campbell, had not heard such ruckus-making in all his adventuresome life. Since he had spent it in the army, that was saying a good deal. Nor could he have heard so many different accents in one place—Spanish, English, French, Irish, Snake, Crow, Bannock, Nez Percé, and Flathead. The diversions were those he had long known, and on a scale at least as grand. Like sailors on liberty, the trappers drank, fought, gambled, and bedded women.

The mountain men had more reason than usual for their carousing. The rendezvous of 1833 was a buyer's market. In the first decade of mountain trapping, the companies had managed to keep a monopoly on selling goods and hiring men. This year, two major outfits were competing, and even Bonneville did his bit. Graduate mountain men could draw as high as $1500 for the next year's work, and plews were selling for as much as nine dollars a pound. They were not worth half that, back in the settlements. These prices would ruin any company. The American Fur trust was confident that they would ruin the small, indebted RMF first.

News was aplenty in the mountains this year. Bill Sublette and Bob Campbell were building forts on the Missouri, right next to the Company forts. In fact, Campbell had brought supplies while Bill set up on the river. Wyeth was back from Fort Vancouver, alone, but with ambitious

plans to return to the mountains and fight for a fortune. A
German prince was said to have come up to Fort Union
by steamboat to study the Indians. And here, right amongst
them, was a Scotch nobleman come to see the mountain
doin's. The tale had it that he was paying Bill Sublette
just to bring him up here and let him shoot some game.
He had brought fancy wines and gourmet foods with him,
to mix with elk roast and beaver tail. Wagh!

The partners and some of the trappers wondered, though,
what was becoming of the mountains, what with greenhorns
getting thick as pine needles underfoot.

The drunk was as boisterous as usual. When Joe Meek
was lying stuporous in his blankets, a rabid wolf came
into camp. He bit several men (some of whom later died),
but missed Joe. Joe would have been an easy mark, Captain Stewart pointed out to him. Joe agreed, but judged
that his alcohol content was so high that the bite would
have either killed or cured the wolf.

Financially, the picture looked bad for everyone. RMF
could do nothing but sign more notes payable to Bill Sublette; his goodwill, and long credit, now were all RMF could
depend on. Bridger was incensed: Those damn marks
on paper, which he didn't understand, were robbing him
of the money he had earned in freezing creeks and under
the noses of the Blackfeet. Since he was king of the trappers, why shouldn't he make the most money?

Truth to tell, Sublette and Campbell had a firm grip on
RMF. They also had a sort of hold on the Company. Though
they didn't say so, they were not necessarily building those
forts on the Missouri as serious competition for the Company. They guessed that the Company might be willing to
pay a good price to buy Sublette & Campbell out.

When rendezvous broke up, the partners were fretting.
They couldn't go on like this. But Nat Wyeth, always

enterprising, proposed a scheme to Milton that might save RMF—through only a little subterfuge.

The various brigades fanned out toward the most remote reaches of the mountains. RMF intended to concentrate on the country east of the mountains this year—partly to offset the effect of the Company's Fort Cass at the mouth of Big Horn. Milton Sublette, Fitzpatrick, and Bridger led their men east to South Pass with Campbell's train. Campbell was not taking the furs to St. Louis by the usual land route; he was going to the new fort Bill Sublette had put up next to Fort Union; from there the catch could move downriver by keelboat. Fitzpatrick would ride with Campbell as far as the Big Horn and then veer northeast to trap prime Crow country. Milton planned to go downriver with the furs on his brother's boat. Wyeth was with this large party; so was Captain Stewart.

It was an uneventful trip, but some comic relief cropped up in two encounters with irate grizzlies. Wyeth and Stewart, veterans though they were in their different ways, took turns in playing greenhorn and nearly went under. A hunter also managed to fall off his horse while chasing a buffalo. The monster charged the fleeing man—and missed; then charged again, and missed again. By this time the fellow got collected and killed the beast with a single shot. When they inspected the bull they found out what had saved the hunter's life: The bull was blind in one eye. And by mountain luck, the hunter had been on the crittur's bad side.

In camp on the Big Horn, while all hands were making bullboats to float down to the Yellowstone and the Missouri, Wyeth offered his little plan to Milton: Wyeth would supply the RMF at rendezvous for less than half of what Sublette & Campbell was charging.

He had a clever scheme. Wyeth had determined to outfit a ship for Fort Vancouver, take on dried salmon, and carry it back around the Horn for sale. That same ship could take, on its outward leg, plenty of supplies. The route from Fort Vancouver to any rendezvous west of the mountains would be shorter, easier, and safer than the Platte River route. Fewer men and fewer horses would be needed. Wyeth would take the RMF furs back to Oregon and deliver them to New York by ship.

Wyeth knew that the ship would not be in time for the rendezvous of 1834. So he would take the outfit to the mountains by land this first time—for about $6,500 instead of Sublette & Campbell's $15,000. Besides, that expedition would, in effect, give him free transportation back to the mountains with men and horses.

Milton listened well. He was impatient with the growing hold his brother had on RMF through IOUs, and he could see that Wyeth was a shrewd Yankee. So he and Fitzpatrick, acting for RMF (Bridger had already split off for his fall hunt,) signed a contract with Wyeth. Among other things, it provided for a small forfeit to be paid by either party in case of failure to follow through. They said not a word to Campbell.

Now Wyeth, Campbell, and Milton Sublette set out down the Big Horn in their bowl-shaped skin boats. At its mouth they were received rudely by Samuel Tulloch, head of Fort Cass for the Company. But at the mouth of the Yellowstone they got a nearly royal reception from the King of the Missouri, Kenneth McKenzie.

This was an ironic spectacle: Three representatives of McKenzie's competition for the mountain trade being hosted by a man who would have willingly helped them go under on a cold creek or in a dry wash. He was preparing to ruin the Sublette & Campbell fort only four miles away, at this very moment. But here the King was in his salon and in formal dress. He lived up to his reputation for grandiose style. The visitors got milk, bacon, butter, and cheese; fine wines and brandies were at hand; Assiniboin girls were also made available.

In showing off, in fact, McKenzie showed a little more than he should have. He had recently had a still brought up the river, and it was now producing a fine corn liquor. Wyeth was impressed—so impressed that he spoke to army authorities back in the settlements about it.

Liquor was a touchy issue with the U. S. government. It had always been illegal to trade liquor to Indians. Now it was illegal even to bring liquor into Indian country. But all traders with the Indians had always used liquor abundantly—each protesting that it was forced to keep up with the competition.

Until the summer of 1832, the government had permitted the importing of liquor for the use of the boatmen only. (Bill Sublette, for instance, in his race for Pierre's Hole in 1832, had taken along 450 gallons of alcohol for the use of the "boatmen" who managed his pack mules.) But now, in August of 1833, the government had a prohibition against taking liquor into Indian country for any reason at all. Naturally, the prohibition had only given a splendid opportunity to everyone's ingenuity at evading the laws.

The Company had the toughest time, though. The government could inspect boats coming up the Missouri at Fort Leavenworth; it was harder to keep track of whoever went by land. Thus McKenzie's still. It was his home remedy for a nuisance the government had put in his

way. But when Wyeth reported it, perhaps without mal-
ice, all hell broke loose. (Eventually the Company, as a
reprimand, was forced to dethrone the King of the Missouri.)

So Wyeth moved downstream, alone, after his pleasant
sojourn at Fort Union. Milton and Campbell joined Bill at
his new Fort Union and then got going down the Missouri
a little later. Though Milton said nothing about his deal
with Wyeth, the brothers were already squabbling about
business matters.

Fitzpatrick, after settling the deal with Wyeth on the Big
Horn, trapped his way east through the center of Crow
country—through the badlands and the low ridges of
mountains, across the Little Big Horn, the Rosebud, and
into the valley of the Tongue River. Here Captain Stewart, staying in the mountains this winter for sport, got his
first taste of the trapping routine: the small groups of men
setting their trap lines at dawn, taking the beaver at dusk;
the camp tenders and squaws cleaning and stretching furs,
and stamping them "RMF"; the relaxed companionship
of three or four men around an open fire in a wilderness;
the use of float stick and medicine.

Near the Tongue the brigade came onto a village of
Crows. Fitzpatrick had his duty to do: The Crows were
the oldest and most consistently loyal of the RMF's Indian friends, dating back beyond Smith-Jackson-Sublette
and Ashley-Smith to the early days of Ashley-Henry
and Jed Smith's winter on the Wind River. The mountain
trappers had always worked Crow country confident of
their safety, except for the matter of the horses that would
now and then pay tribute to the Crow notion of tribal

honor. Eager to maintain this friendship, Fitzpatrick went to make some presents to the village, a sort of toll for using Crow land this autumn.

He left Stewart in command of the brigade and rode some three miles to the village. The chief greeted his friend Broken Hand warmly, and Tom got started on negotiations to outbid the Company for Crow plews.

Meanwhile, though, a band of young Crow braves paid a courtesy visit to the rest of their old friends, who were under the supervision of a man who did not yet know Indian ways. The British Army veteran knew that Crows were allies, and had been told to treat them cordially. The Indians were positively effusive: They embraced the whites, told them dirty stories, clapped them on the back, laughed, clowned. Though Stewart told several men to stay alert and keep their guns at hand, the Crows bewailed this apparent lack of trust and demanded correction. They got it.

Suddenly every Indian weapon was out and pointed at a white man. Every Indian hand was on something valuable. Now the braves mocked and sneered at the whites, and nastily challenged them to do something about it. Stewart had been duped, but outmanned and outgunned at the moment, he had too much sense to try to stop them. It was a complete clean-out—all the horses, the trade goods, the plews, and traps—everything. They even got Stewart's watch.

Fitzpatrick, when he got back to camp, was outraged. The point was clear enough: Though the Crows were not yet ready to make war on RMF men, they were prepared for a sneak attack like this. He suspected that the Company had put them up to it. When he got back to the village, he was sure that it was Company skullduggery. For there sat his old acquaintance Jim Beckwourth.

Beckwourth had left Smith-Jackson-Sublette some five years before to become an adopted Crow. He had lived with them ever since, and was now a chief. He was also a Company factor, on the payroll to make sure that the people of Absaroka took their trade to Fort Cass and not to RMF. Though Fitzpatrick didn't know it, Crows had also harassed the Campbell outfit down on the Big Horn. The Company men in this area were provoking them to such tactics under McKenzie's instructions to wipe out the opposition by fair means or foul. Fitzpatrick, when he saw Beckwourth in the village, remembered him as a liar and scoundrel and promptly decided that his heart was as black as his skin.

Tom demanded that the chief give back the property. That gentleman explained casually that he sometimes had trouble controlling his hot-headed young men, but he would see what he could do. That turned out to be the return of some of the horses, rifles, and traps, but no furs and no trade goods.

Fitzpatrick was infuriated, but helpless. He took what was offered and hightailed it out of Crow country. He scouted out Jim Bridger to get equipped again and moved back to the Siskadee. There he wrote to the RMF protector in Washington, Congressman Ashley, to ask that the Company be stopped from open robbery and to hint that the mountains ought to be divided between the rival firms. All over the mountains, Jim Beckwourth was set down as a crook.

(Some years later Fitzpatrick found Beckwourth in a St. Louis bar and tried to kill him with a knife. Still later, in his autobiography, Jim concocted a wild story that showed himself as a helpful hero wronged by scandal.)

McKenzie gloated over the victory and the apparent destruction of Fitzpatrick's fall hunt. He did make the magnanimous gesture, though, of offering the RMF furs back to RMF—at a healthy price. Ashley did his bit in Washington, though, and used this story, combined with the reports of a still at Fort Union, to arouse the government and the public against Astor's fur trust.

As a matter of fact, the fur war was being settled this winter, not in the mountains, but on the eastern seaboard, in American Fur's posh offices in New York City.

Bill Sublette, when he reached St. Louis in his keelboat, moved on to New York. He had in mind to make a deal with the American Fur Company. He might have seemed to be in a bad bargaining position: American Fur was licking RMF in the mountains, and was in the process of giving Sublette & Campbell a brutal shellacking on the Missouri. But Bill had a certain leverage.

John Jacob Astor had a well-justified reputation for business acuity. In London, not long before, he had noticed that silk hats seemed to be coming into style—after a couple of centuries of beaver hats being the fashion. Astor built his fortune primarily in New York real estate; but furs had been the initial cornerstone of his empire. Though he was inclined to be sentimental about the fur business, he was also shrewd. Before Sublette arrived in New York, Astor had given notice that he was withdrawing from the fur business. So American Fur no longer had his limitless resources to call on for destructive competition.

The Company was also in political trouble from the scandals of the still at Fort Union and the robbery of Fitzpatrick. Sublette could call on the influence of General Ashley and therefore a great deal of credit from Eastern backers. He might be able to take advantage of the Company's doubly weakened position.

Sublette made his deal: The Company was to take over his establishments on the river and his merchandise there, in return for which the Company would withdraw from the mountain trade for one year. So RMF would temporarily have no competition in the mountains, and the Company would have none on the river. Sublette exulted over the deal. And it may have involved more than what he signed his name to.

By the time Sublette got back to St. Louis, he had found out about his brother's secret contract with Wyeth for an outfit. He was incensed. He made some small financial trouble for RMF during the spring, and he set out to destroy the agreement with Wyeth. Now he would exercise his financial power over RMF.[2]

Missouri had a bustling outfitting business that spring. Wyeth and Milton Sublette were getting ready to kick off, having rounded up their supplies in the East. Fontenelle, as usual, was preparing the Company packtrain. And now Bill Sublette was setting a Sublette-Campbell train for rendezvous, without a contract for the merchandise. This year it would be a three-way race for business.

Wyeth had with him three more symptoms of the greenhorn invasion of the mountains. Two scientists were making the trek to gather new knowledge: Thomas Nuttall, a Harvard botanist, and John Kirk Townsend, an ornithologist. Here also was Jason Lee, a preacher heading a Methodist mission to the Indians. Lee was pious, determined, and Calvinist. He was fully prepared to wage a hard war on heathenism.

When the various outfits got to Independence, the kick-off point, they saw yet another hint of greenhorn westwarding. A "sect of fanatics, called Mormons,"[3] recorded

Townsend, had practically tried to take over the town and been given the boot. Now they were causing a hubbub across the river in Liberty.

Wyeth suspected that he might somehow be undone by Bill Sublette, so he and Milton kicked off early, on April 28. Bill took his time, confident that he could outmarch Wyeth.

But Wyeth had learned the wilderness well. He drove his men at a furious pace. After a month he got a bad blow: Milton, who had had trouble with his leg for some time, got so sick that he had to turn back. Wyeth was deprived of his co-command and of his most trusted connection with RMF. Two weeks later, Wyeth got a second blow. He found the tracks of Bill Sublette: he had passed around him in the night. Wyeth might be skilled at plains travel, but Bill was a master. Wyeth immediately sent an express to Fitzpatrick at rendezvous; he promised to arrive by July 1, and added that he had sent a ship around the Horn to supply RMF during the winter or next summer at advantageous prices. He was scared.

At Laramie Fork, Wyeth got a surprise. Sublette, evidently cocksure of his lead and his influence with RMF, had taken the time to start building a fort here, to be called Fort William. He had left some men to finish it. Bill, having agreed to abandon his river enterprises, was trying to take his customers to the plains.

Wyeth drove on up the Sweetwater, through South Pass, and, on June 17, found Tom Fitzpatrick on the Siskadee. Wyeth had made amazing time across the prairies; he had beaten the usual arrival date by two weeks. But Bill Sublette had beaten him. And Fitzpatrick, here on Ham's Fork, shattered Wyeth's hopes. Paying a forfeit of $500, he canceled the contract for merchandise.

How had Bill Sublette come out the grinning winner?

Simple: He demanded that RMF pay off in fur the notes he held. So the partners bought their supplies from Sublette with a poor 1833–34 hunt. RMF had been helpless.

JUNE-JULY, 1834: RENDEZVOUS AT HAM'S FORK: Fontenelle made rendezvous last, as usual. The normal fun reigned, heightened by the presence of some greenhorns to show off in front of.

These *mangeurs de lard* were not delighted by the spectacle. If Stewart had had a sporting man's appreciation for hell-raising, the scientists brought the attitudes of self-consciously cultured Boston to the revelry of the mountains. Reluctant to speak their disapproval directly, and maybe fearful too, they recorded their chastisements in the privacy of their diaries:

Townsend, the observer and cataloguer of birds, was irked. The principal visitors to his camp with Wyeth, he wrote contemptuously, were Indians "who come with the furs and peltries which they have been collecting at the risk of their lives during the past winter and spring, to trade for ammunition, trinkets, and 'fire water.' There is, in addition to these, a great variety of personages among us; most of them calling themselves white men, French Canadians, half-breeds, etc., their color nearly as dark, and their manners wholly as wild, as the Indians with whom they constantly associate. These people, with their obstreperous mirth, their whooping and howling and quarreling . . . their dashing through our camp, yelling like fiends, the barking and baying of savage wolf-dogs, and the insistent crackling of rifles and carbines, render our camp a perfect bedlam." Ill himself, Townsend complained of having to listen all day to the "hiccoughing jargon of drunken traders, the *sacre* and *foutre* of Frenchmen run wild, and the swearing and screaming of our own men, who are scarcely less savage than the rest, being heated by the detestable liquor which circulates freely among them."[4]

Lee also thought the white men as savage as the Indians; instead of being irked, he was appalled. Here, after all, were the crimes against God that would send them to the hell of real fire and brimstone—fornication, adultery, all manner of lewdness, drunkenness, profanity, and even murder. "Another drunken crazy hooting quarrelling fighting frolic," he wrote. "My God is there nothing that will have any effect on them?"[5]

This devout was sickened to find white men participating in a war dance. He felt as a trapper captured by Blackfeet would have felt as the devils danced around him, whooping in glee. The idea of preaching them a sermon crossed his mind, but he abandoned it quickly. Wyeth had warned him that the trappers resented his presence, besides thinking it ridiculous, and would be glad of a chance to give him hell. So he discreetly kept his peace.

Yet another greenhorn thought the Indian girls lovely, but was shocked that ladies would sit a horse astride.

So the strangers to the Stony Mountains were not pleasured by what they saw. They must have gotten a chuckle, though, out of the stories they heard. Joe Meek alone could shower them out like sparks from an anvil. About him betterin' Daniel and that lions' den. About the time he yelled out "Blackfeet in camp"—for a joke, just to shake 'em up—and scairt some actual Blackfeet creepin' up on the horses right out of their cover. About the time a little coon name of Stanberry dared to argue with Joe about who was braver, and Joe settled it by banging a ba'r on the head with his wiping stick. About the time a grizzly come at him and Milton Sublette, and Milton run off to climb a tree and was found, when the b'ar was kilt, squeezing the trunk and sitting almost on the ground. Joe loved to laugh about Milton's method of climbing a tree.

The greenhorns might hear some blood-curdling yarns too. One of Bonneville's men liked to tell about when the Arikaras stole their brigade's horses. Two of the Injuns come straight into camp and set down to smoke while their pals snuck up on the cayuses. The trappers tied them fast, and offered to trade the hostages to the thieves for the horses. At first the niggurs offered one hoss for one prisoner. Refused. Then they decided horseflesh mattered more than their friends and took off with the horses, singing their mourning songs as they left. The trappers went right ahead and burned the Injuns alive.

One morning Kit Carson and some five other coons was riding on a plain where there was no cover, and no water for miles. Some Comanches come at 'em. Carson and the other mountain men cut the throats of their mules and dropped down behind 'em, in a circle. Fired half their rifles every time the Injuns got within range. The Comanches didn't like three dead braves on every charge. Their ponies didn't like the smell of blood from them mules, either, and kept shyin' off. Held 'em off all day that way, they did, and under a sun that damn near burnt 'em up. Come night, they snuck off on foot and started hoofin' for water. Seventy-five miles it was to a drink. And they all made it.

Lee and Townsend heard these stories with horror and fascination. (Nuttall had been West before, and cottoned more which way the stick floated.) Lee was not shocked—he was a tough man—but he detested men who could be proud of such actions. To have to do them was bad, but to repeat them with this boastful bravado. . . .

The men got their spirits dampened a little when they

got around to signing up for the next year. The war for trappers was over. The Company was out of the bidding now, since it had agreed to leave the mountains to its competitors for a year. What's more, 1833–34 had not produced many packs of plews. What's worse yet, the market price for beaver was down. RMF couldn't pay much for trappers in a bad market.

As a matter of fact, RMF couldn't afford much of anything. Bill Sublette's foreclosure on its debt had put it in a bad spot. It folded. Frapp got out of the firm for some merchandise which Sublette provided. So did Gervais. Bridger and Fitzpatrick formed a new partnership and signed Milton Sublette in by proxy. But they were fed up with Sublette & Campbell. They made a deal with Fontenelle to sell their furs next summer to the Company.

So the war was over. Bill Sublette's deal in New York, his beating Wyeth out of a firm bargain, and his foreclosure, had put the Rocky Mountain Fur Company under. Bridger, Fitzpatrick, and Milton Sublette made their paper outfit stand up for one year and then admitted what they really were—agents of the Company. The next summer, Bridger and Fitzpatrick signed on as Company partisans. They were master mountain men after all, superb craftsmen of their trade, and the Company was eager to have them. (Milton's leg problem turned out to be serious: He had the leg amputated in St. Louis; though he came back to the mountains, he died of the mysterious illness.)

Wyeth was effectively gotten out of the way. After he lost his contract for supplies, he learned that his ship bound for Fort Vancouver had been struck by lightning and missed the salmon season. Disaster. End of an enterprise.

Sublette & Campbell hung on for a while at Fort William. But the Company eventually bought the post, and it came to be called Fort Laramie.

So the Company, apparently withdrawing from competition in the mountains, had in fact gotten what it wanted there—a monopoly.

But if one war had just ended, another and more deadly war had just begun. Its advance scout was there on Ham's Fork, in the person of Jason Lee.

EIGHTH INTERLUDE

Exploration of the West

WHEN, IN 1803, THE UNITED STATES FIRST PUSHED *its borders west of the Mississippi River by concluding the Louisiana Purchase, no one knew what was out there. Spain, which had held the Louisiana Territory and still held the entire Southwest, settled the Pacific Coast and the Mississippi River Valley; and it had pushed into the interior at Santa Fe. What might lie between St. Louis and San Francisco was a matter of rumor, hearsay, and myth.*

The United States government went about the job of filling in the blank spaces on the map. William Clark and Meriwether Lewis were commissioned to cross to the Pacific via the water systems of the Missouri and Columbia rivers; their 1810 map accurately showed those rivers, the Yellowstone, and the Rocky Mountains at the point Lewis and Clark crossed them. Zebulon Pike pushed up the Arkansas River to the Front Range of the Rocky Mountains; his book, also published in 1810, introduced knowledge of a small, straight line in the huge reaches of the West. Major Stephen Long made a similar expedition across the plains to the Front Range, a little further north, and published his findings in 1823.

The next official information about the West, based on expeditions for the purposes of exploration, would come from John Charles Frémont some twenty years later. By that time, the entire West had already been mapped out—not in atlases, but in the minds of the men who traveled the plains, mountains, and deserts, the Rocky Mountain fur trappers. The discoveries were not made under official auspices or for national purposes; they were made by individuals who wanted to know, for business and for fun.

A glance at the maps will demonstrate the vast, complicated, and detailed knowledge that the mountain men achieved. Finley's A New General Atlas *was published in 1827, the year Jed Smith led the trappers across South Pass and into the interior West. It shows the Rockies mostly as a single chain, with some extra mountains about where the Front Range is; they represent guesswork, of course, because the Rockies are multiple chains; and Finley seems to know nothing of the Sierra Nevada. He has a large lake named Salado and another, named Timpanogos, somewhere near the vicinity of Salt Lake, both based on rumor. He lets a Buenaventura River flow from the Salado into San Francisco Bay, providing a neat but nonexistent water route to the Pacific. He makes plenty of other errors. He labels most of the Southwest "Unexplored Country." Such was the misinformation the mountain men were equipped with when they started over the mountains.*

Colton's Atlas of the World, *though published in 1856, has most of it right. The accurate information of Lewis and Clark has been supplemented massively; and the new knowledge has come almost entirely from the mountain men. They guided Frémont all over the West, and he anointed himself the Explorer by giving the information to a waiting government and public. Although he bestowed a kind of glory on one trapper, his principal guide, Kit Carson, he usurped most of the credit for himself.*

Frémont got that opportunity because of the untimely death of Jed Smith. Smith had made a manuscript map of the West, and intended to publish it, but the manuscript copies were lost. David Burr saw one, and part of Smith's knowledge got into his 1836 Atlas. The complimentary title Explorer should have gone to Smith. He had both qualities crucial to an explorer: The daring of a trailblazer who discovers places and routes, and the integrative understanding of a geographer.

Discovering a major geographical landmark, after all, involves more than merely stumbling upon it. It means being able to integrate that landmark into a larger scheme of topography, of the lay of land and watershed. Collectively, the Indians were acquainted with every mountain, river, and lake of the West. But they would have been helpless to render that acquaintance as a comprehensive map. They did not know how the piece that comprised their country fit into the whole puzzle. To do that required wider specific knowledge, and a grasp of abstractions which the Indians did not have.

After the pioneering venture of Lewis and Clark, which established the Missouri and Columbia water systems, the pattern of Western exploration looks like this: John Colter explored the Big Horn and Wind rivers, crossed the continental divide twice, and saw the Yellowstone area (all this alone). Jed Smith found South Pass and led his men into the valley of the Green River. (Probably he was not the first white man to cross South Pass; the British had preceded him on the Green; but he was working without knowledge of the prior visits, and he brought both to the attention of the American trappers and the public). From there, his trappers fanned out straight west, discovering the Bear River Valley and Salt Lake; Etienne Provost added a dimension by coming to Salt Lake from Taos. Smith followed the British north to Flathead House. Tom Fitzpatrick led General Ashley up the Platte to South Pass, establishing the first half of the Oregon Trail. Ashley went some distance down the Green. Smith rode west and north of Salt Lake, hunting fruitlessly for a waterway to California. His partners explored the Snake River from Jackson Hole, far to the west, and went into Yellowstone. Taos trappers traveled west to the Gila River in south-central Arizona.

In 1826, Smith led the way to California from Salt Lake, south to the Colorado River, and then west across the Mojave Desert and San Bernardino Mountains. Returning, he crossed the Sierra Nevada and the states of Nevada and Utah to Salt Lake. Later he drove from San Francisco Bay north to the mouth of the Columbia, and returned by known British routes to Flathead House.

At this point, the topography of the West was essentially filled in. The period of discovery is neatly bracketed: Smith crossed South Pass early in 1824; he got back from the mouth of the Columbia early in 1829. He had personally investigated most of the West. He had provided the leadership and the conceptual framework for the rest. During the next few years, the trappers would penetrate further into Idaho and work out what would become the last leg of the Oregon Trail. So the way would be prepared for the thousands of wagons to bounce and sway from St. Joseph to the Pacific. And the trappers would be able to turn the legacy of Jed Smith and his comrades over to Frémont and the government of the United States.

IX

Invasion

THE MONARCH OF A TINY HIMALAYAN PRINCIPALITY, in refusing to trade with the British, summed up succinctly the pattern of empire-building encroachment: First the traders, then the missionaries, then the armies, in inevitable succession.

Jason Lee was the first American missionary to venture to the mountains, and the harbinger of many to come. Traders, in the form of fur trappers, had indeed come first, but they had capitulated to the alleged enemy. Instead of converting the Indians to the white, American, Christian, work-ethic way of life, they had adopted Indian ways and abandoned the strict teachings they themselves were suckled on. They had, from the point of view of the missionaries, betrayed their function as wedges for the forces to come. Jason Lee marched forth to fight a war for what he believed to be the true light. He would have to defeat, he now saw, not only the ways of the Indians, but of the mountain men as well.

His westward pilgrimage had been fired by a strange incident in 1831. At about the same time that Jedediah Smith, Bill Sublette, and David Jackson wrote their letter about the unknown West to the Secretary of War, a delegation of Nez Percé and Flathead Indians arrived in St. Louis. They made their way to the Red-Headed Chief, William Clark, revered by plains and mountain Indians since the Lewis and Clark Expedition. By sign, since no one understood their language, they communicated to Clark that they had come to secure religious instruction for their tribes. They went home with nothing but the vaguest hope that, sometime, the white man would respond.

As Smith's letter was reprinted in newspapers all over the United States, so the Indian plea for Christ was picked up and trumpeted to the devout. The cry for help, uttered by longing and benighted heathen, spread like wildfire. One Methodist bishop proclaimed, "We will not cease until we have planted the standard of Christianity high on the summit of the Stony Mountains."[1] His words became a rallying cry.

The Methodists could not ignore an appeal from savages who had grasped their own want of grace. Their religious fervor did not preclude some appalling falsehoods. The original reporter of the plea, who never saw the Indians he described, drew a picture of a "Flathead" with a pointed head and claimed that the tribe bound the skulls of infants to produce this deformity. (The name of the tribe came from the sign-language gesture used to denote it, not from any unusual shape of their skulls.) Some impassioned writer even made up a touching piece of rhetoric and attributed it to one of the delegates: "My people sent me to get the White Man's Book of Heaven. . . . You make my feet heavy with gifts and my moccasins will grow old carrying them, yet the book is not among them. When I tell my poor blind people . . . that I did not bring the book, no word will be spoken by our old men or by our young braves. One by one they will rise up and go out in silence. My people will die in darkness and they will go a long path to other hunting grounds. No white man will go with them, and no White Man's Book to make the way plain. I have no more words."[2]

Thereupon, thousands of Methodists were determined to send the light of salvation to these supplicating Indians. Jason Lee was the first of their representatives. Unfortunately, what the Nez Percés and Flatheads wanted was not salvation; their desire would have been better served by an industrialist than a missionary.

It was a misunderstanding. A gross and dangerous misunderstanding. And a classic instance of the failure of an industrialized people to perceive the mental set of a "primitive" people.

All the Indians of the West had been impressed, more than anything else about the white man, by his trading goods. Rifles and pistols. Saddles. Bells and cloth and trinkets. Firewater. Mirrors. Powder and balls. Knives. These were mysteries. Every brave and squaw knew how to make a shirt from the skin of a deer, a robe from a buffalo hide, a soup or tea from a root. But where did the white man's marvel-making objects come from? From what plant, animal, or stone did they come forth? They could not imagine. It was mystery and magic. The white man must have superior medicine, superior gods—gods that accounted for the white man's power.

The Indians had their understanding of the world. Every being, animate or inanimate, had its own medicine, its own power. A man could use that power if he could divine its secret. He could protect himself against an enemy ball or arrowhead. He could bring rain. He could give himself long life, his tribe a bountiful hunt or crop. Through the medicine of things, a man could gain magical control of the world.

The Nez Percés and Flatheads had gathered, from the Hudson Bay traders, and from the half-christianized Indians HBC imported, that white power was centered in the white religion—just as Indian power was centered in the Indian religion. The whites had great medicine. It produced these tools, needles, beads, and a myriad of other wonders. From the moment they saw these miracles, they wanted to acquire this medicine for themselves. Then they would be able to conjure their own wealth. The answer was simple: We will go to St. Louis and ask to be taught.

So while the Methodists understood the Flatheads and Nez Percés to be yearning for the heritage of Moses, Christ, and St. Paul, they in fact wanted the heritage of Isaac Newton, Robert Fulton, and Eli Whitney.

When they got their missionaries, the Nez Percés and Flatheads would try with meek patience to comprehend the white wisdom. They would spend years reciting the words of the Gospel, praying, being baptized, making professions of faith, singing hymns—making whatever incantation was required of them. And wondering all the while when the magic would begin to bring forth baubles.

But let there be light among the heathen, intoned the Methodists. And let us pacify them while we're at it. White people may be wanting to go to Oregon.

Thus the Reverend Jason Lee to the rendezvous of 1834.

Lee was a hardy man, equipped for the outdoor life. He was never afflicted by any sense of his own sinful inadequacy for a task. He was afflicted instead with great zeal, with selfless and holy ambition, and with supreme confidence in his own rightness. He met there on the Siskadee with the representatives of the two tribes who had called for him, and who had come to rendezvous three straight years in the distant hope of getting a teacher of the white medicine. He spoke politely to them. But he would not promise to be their teacher. He was going on to Oregon; he could not say whether or not he might come back to his parishioners.

Lee was mute about his decision to abandon these suppliants and to change radically the task set for him by his mission board. A hint is given in a letter he wrote later to his nephew: "The truth is," he says cryptically, they are *Indians*,"[3] and draws a line under the term. Lee could see from the beginning that Indians were not going to become Methodists. Not, at least, so long as they remained Indians.

So there on Ham's Fork was planted the germ of Jason Lee's notion of his mission. To convert Indians into Christians, you first have to convert them into white men. You have to teach them to cultivate the soil, to wash with soap, to wear broadcloth instead of buckskin, to live in homes made of wood or brick, to eat at table with knives and forks; you have to induce them to learn carpentry, storekeeping, the alphabet; to get married; to live the same stable and productive lives that white men did.

That would never happen, Lee divined, here in the mountains. This harsh and awesome land—with its cracked and baked earth, with its spiny mountain ridges, with its abundance of buffalo and deer, with its inescapable wildness—would never be tamed, cultivated, scaled down to human dimension, turned into the farmland of New York or Ohio.

So Lee moved on to the gentle and fertile Willamette Valley. There he sent pleas back to the mission board—not for more clerics, but for lay people, for farmers, blacksmiths, carpenters, merchants, the practical men and women who could create and then populate a transplanted white civilization. Within a few years he would harness the water power, divide the land into farms and ranches, plant orchards, hayfields, and vegetable gardens, and start schools where children recited Scriptures. He would teach the Indians to mimic the doings of the whites. For he was right: The Indians would not become Christians until they became white men. The beginning, in short, was to destroy their culture.

Bridger rode out from rendezvous with a sixty-man brigade, headed north to defy the damned Blackfeet again, in the last prime beaver preserve left. With him were three skilled veterans, Joe Meek, Markhead, and Kit Carson. Carson, at twenty-five, was an old mountain man now. After some trapping west from Taos, he had come north with Fitzpatrick in 1831, trapped with Bridger awhile, and then worked the streams of the Front Range (which is in modern Colorado) as a free trapper. Though he never grew to even five and a half feet, he had the pound-for-pound fighting aggressiveness of a bobcat. If he was a little hotheaded, he was still a good man to have on your side in a skirmish, and a man no one messed with.

Markhead was a tough child, jovial, reckless, a lover of devilment. One of the familiar campfire stories let the trappers know he was dangerous. A no-good Iowa named Marshall, fired from one brigade and taken on by Captain Stewart as a retainer, had run off one night with Stewart's rifle and favorite buffler horse. Angry, Stewart exclaimed, "I'd give $500 for his scalp." Stewart sent several small parties after Marshall, and Markhead found him. He sauntered into camp that night with Stewart's horse and his rifle—with Marshall's wet scalp dangling from the barrel. Stewart was upset that Markhead had taken his rage so literally, but he paid the reward.

The mood of the brigade was low. Partly, they were disgruntled because plews were scarce. The competition between the Hudson Bay Company, Rocky Mountain Fur, and American Fur had forced the trappers to strip the country bare in order to stay in business—with the result they knew was inevitable. What was worse, it now seemed that there might not be a business to stay in. The price of beaver in St. Louis had hit bottom. A man had to take twice as many plews to earn as much as he used to. But there weren't half as many plews to take. They grumbled around the campfire, worried. Some of them asked Indian medicine men whether beaver would shine again. But they knew it would. Beaver just had to shine again. Wagh!

They got a miserable bunch of plews that fall, and lost eighteen horses to the Blackfeet besides. Carson, Meek, and Markhead chased the thieves fifty miles and came back empty-handed. Then Bridger himself took their trail and got nothing. During that year the Blackfeet killed five trappers of Bridger's outfit. The mountain men made more than a few Blackfeet come, in revenge, but it was poor revenge. To cap it off, they had a bad spring hunt too.

When they got to the rendezvous of 1835, at New Fork on the Siskadee, they sat down to wait for the supply train. And had a long, impatient wait. Drips was there with a brigade and, this time, the free trappers showed up in even larger numbers. It seemed, more and more, that a child would allow as how he could do better by himself, trapping creeks he didn't talk about to anyone else.

When the Company train did show up, a month late, it was not led by Lucien Fontenelle but Tom Fitzpatrick. The business of the mountains had been changing again. Sublette and Campbell had sold Fort Laramie to Fitzpatrick and Fontenelle, who had in turn sold it to the Company. Tom told Bridger that they might as well let their partnership go and sign on as Company partisans. Hell, Gabe didn't care. He didn't understand those business doin's anyway. That child just wanted to trap beaver, and maybe kill some Blackfeet. He knowed which way the stick floated there.

And so the Company had all the mountain trade. What there was of it. Beaver didn't shine now, with the price down and the men actually began to make money on coarse fur, like buffler. Why, they wouldn't have bothered about buffler hides even a couple of years ago. But they'd take what they could get.

Two more missionaries were with the late outfit, an old gent named Samuel Parker and a young one named Dr. Marcus Whitman. Whitman was a real doctor—had helped the outfit through a spell of cholera on the way up. Here he took an arrowhead out of Bridger's back that had been nestled there for three years: he had to cut it out of a network of cartilage that had grown around it. "Weren't you afraid of infection?" Dr. Whitman asked Bridger. "In the mountains, Doc." said Gabe. "meat don't never spoil."

Another sort of parson creaked his bones into rendezvous 1835: Old Bill Williams, also called Parson Bill, Old Solitaire, and a few cuss words as well. He had been a Baptist preacher at seventeen, and, later, a missionary to the Osage Indians. But Captain Stewart observed wryly that Williams had preached out all his religion before he came to the mountains, and got there without any. Stewart didn't have it quite right: Bill had some Indian religion, at least, a theory of transmigration of souls. He was so sure that his soul was going to come back in the form of an elk that he used to give the trappers signals to recognize him by, so they wouldn't shoot him.

Old Bill (and he actually was up in years—forty-eight in 1835) didn't have much truck with people. He did his trapping alone. He had done time with an expedition to the Heely, and with Joe Walker's California trek, but he preferred solitary trapping. He went over all of Colorado and Utah alone as casually as other men walked to the milking shed. He had developed a sharp eye for sign; when he saw that Indians were about, he would cache—simply disappear up a draw and be gone with no more trace than a mountain goat leaves on rock. His skill at stealing through the mountains and making Indians go under was so honed that he was becoming legendary even among the mountain men. Since he knew the country as sure as the best of them, he would come to rendezvous each year with an abundance of plews and trade them to the highest bidder. When they asked where he trapped, Bill said nary a word. He was tough, mean, and cantankerous: The word was that a smart child didn't walk in front of Old Bill in starvin' times. He was the perfect profile of the free trapper.

Bill and the rest of the boys got the usual drunk going, even if it wasn't quite as happy as some. A bully called Shunar, which was trapper for something like Chouinard, got to feeling his liquor and looking for someone to beat up. He had gotten tired of whipping Frenchmen, he growled. They were too easy. And the Americans were pantywaists. He wanted some bones to crunch. He stalked about camp, roaring for takers. The trappers held back. Shunar was a grizzly-sized piece of bully, and he had beaten up enough men to make them wary of him.

But Kit Carson, the smallest man in camp, stepped up. Carson had more than just Shunar's loudness to be mad about. He had been courting an Arapaho girl, and Shunar had tried to put the make on her roughly. Carson told Shunar that the camp was jam full of Americans who could whup hell out of him, and as the least of all the Americans, he could too. Carson would spill Shunar's guts on the ground for him.

This was getting serious. Drunk, but still swaggering,

Shunar went for his horse and rifle. Kit got on his own horse and grabbed a pistol. Shunar rode out shouting that he meant to kill. Carson rode straight to him until the horses were jostling each other. Then Kit asked Shunar if Kit was the one Shunar meant to kill. Shunar said no, but started raising his rifle. Kit waited for him to get it up. They both fired at the same instant. A hank of Carson's hair sprayed backward. Shunar clutched for his bloody gun arm, howling.

Later the yarns had it that Carson went back and killed Shunar, but the men were only fancifying a good story. Carson "married" the Arapaho girl.

Jim Bridger got married too. At the end of rendezvous, he didn't want to part with a Flathead girl he'd been romancing, so he took her with him to keep his lodge. She was the daughter of a chief, so he paid a good price; and he called her Cora.

Dr. Whitman decided to give the Flatheads and Nez Percés the teaching they had waited for. But he would need reinforcements. So he turned back to the settlements with Fitzpatrick. Samuel Parker judged that he could go on alone: Without God's providence, he would not be safe anyway; with God's watchful eye on him, he could travel as well alone as with Whitman. He would go north and west with the Indians who professed their love for him and scout the territory. As it turned out, Parker eventually went to Fort Vancouver and by ship back to New England. At fifty-six, he was too old for life in the wilderness. It was a notable loss for white-Indian relations, because Parker showed a sympathetic appreciation of the Indian perspective, and of the difficulty of christianizing Indians, that the other missionaries lacked.

He demonstrated remarkable courage and faith in setting out with a tribe of "savages" to ride from New Fork to the Pacific Ocean, alone and aged. Along the way he instructed them in such doctrines as marriage and immortality, and found them to be receptive, eager, and bewildered, like children. He perceived their plight truly: He saw some hope for "elevating" them if they were given time to make a gradual evolution to the white man's ways and not merely exterminated. They needed time, he wrote, and some guarantee of their basic rights and of the ownership of their land; they also needed some protection from the law and the courts, so that any riled mountain man could not kill one on whim. He had not much hope that all this would come about, but he saw it as the only hope.[4]

Parker started north with his Indians and, for a way, Bridger's brigade. When they got within sight of the Grand Tetons, in a place that made even mountain men worshipful in their way, the Reverend Parker got a chance to observe the sabbath properly. He held divine service there and tried gently, without damnation, to persuade the trappers that they were not fit to enter the house of the Lord. They listened respectfully, and Parker entertained a certain hope for their immortal souls. In the middle of his sermon, a herd of buffler topped a rise, and the men went for their rifles and horses. Here was fat cow for dinner, and shinin' sport besides. When they got back with their roasts, hump ribs, and boudins, Parker's mood had grown harsh, and he reprimanded them sternly for breaking the sabbath, fornicating, drinking, and gambling. They would have taken the message more to heart had the Reverend's mouth not been full of fresh meat while he talked.

When Bridger, Carson, and Meek rode into Jackson Hole, they were enjoying the relative luxury of married life—Jim with Cora, Joe with Mountain Lamb, and Kit with Grass-Singing-in-Wind. A squaw dressed plews, kept the meat simmering in the fire against the hour when her man would get back from the trap lines, packed, unpacked, and grazed the animals, and worked skins into new clothes. She made his lodge comfortable. The dirt was packed hard, the buffalo robe laid over a cushion of willow branches, every domestic item in its orderly place. She kept the coffee hot, with some kind of sweetening boiling in it. She made cakes of corn, puddings, teas, soups, and lots of other things a man wouldn't think of. If she had noisy relatives who visited constantly, she made up for it by telling jokes so dirty they could slay a tent preacher two canyons away, from sheer mortification. And she was ingenious at pleasuring a man under his buffler-robe blankets.

In winter lodge, she would also tell the ancient tales of her people, the peculiar blends of history and myth handed down from tribal poet to tribal poet until they became part of the tribal religion. For instance, the tale about where, in the beginning, the dance of the black bears came from:

A brave broke a medicine object on his leg, so the leg swelled up and crippled him. Though he had four wives, when the tribe left for a hunt, only the one he did not love stayed with him. If he died, she explained, she wished to die with him. She had to grub among the lodges for scraps of food. As she searched, she heard a voice singing sacred songs. On the magical fourth day, hunting for the singer, she found a rabbit snare. Perhaps it had been the singer. She had also seen something with long ears. Her husband thought it might be so, so he wove buffalo hair into more snares for birds and rabbits.

Trapping them against winter-long starvation, she saw something that was large and had long ears and a white tail.

Her brave told her how to trap a deer, and she did. Now they would survive the winter, and they were gladdened. The next two days she snared two more deer. On the third, besides getting another deer, she saw a man kill a buffalo across the river. She crossed on the ice and asked for meat, but he rudely said nothing. When the man left the front legs and the head, she dragged them back to her husband and told him what had happened.

The next day she saw a different man with a buffalo, and he gave her some meat. The third day she saw the first man again, and he treated her as he had before. On the fourth day she saw the generous man again, and again got meat from him. That night she told her husband that she wanted to follow the men. He gave her cornballs for food, and his medicine pipe. She said that if she did not come back in four days, he would know she was dead.

She followed their snowshoe tracks to a lodge of eagle-hunters. She was afraid to enter, for they might be enemies. Then she heard a voice speaking her own language. It was black bear language, as she would expect, because eagle hunters impersonate black bears. When she went in, she saw that they were not eagle hunters but black bears.

The bears were sitting in a circle. Those on the left combed their hair as the rude man did, those on the right as the generous man did. Though she sat with the ones on the right, the others began to quarrel about which of them would take her as his wife. The ones on the right gave her meat and then reprimanded the rude ones: We called her here, they said, not you. Our son is in trouble at the village and we want to help him. This woman is our granddaughter.

The woman then knew that the kind, older bears had called her. She gave them her cornballs and pipe. Ridiculing the younger bears from time to time, they smoked and ate ceremonially. Then they gave her meat to take home and snowshoes to help her along the way. First, though, they said, they would teach her a ceremony that she must teach her husband and that he must do in their name. She learned the songs and dances of the black bears and left. They promised to come to the village after four nights.

Her husband rejoiced to see her, for he had been weeping, calling, and thinking that she had been killed by enemies. When she gave him the piece of meat, it suddenly became as large as the piece it had been cut from. She told him her story. He was glad and ordered her to prepare a feast for the ceremony. Perhaps, she said, the black bears would cure his leg.

On the fourth night came the bears, carrying a buffalo skull and a pipe. The woman gave them a buffalo robe for the skull, another for the pipe, and another for each snare they had brought. The smallest of the bears, who was really a bent-stick snare, but had become a man and lived with the other eagle hunters, volunteered to doctor the swollen leg. He put bait and a snare over the ankle. A snake peered out of the ankle at the bait, but moved back into the ankle. Soon the snake put his head out again and began eating the bait. The bent-stick man snared it and tugged the snake out of the ankle. The man would be well now.

So came the black-bear dance to this people. "Only those who have the right to dance it and to keep the medicine bundle that goes with it can consecrate an eagle hunt. And only those have the right who are descended from the black bears."[5]

Jim led a mediocre fall hunt, but a better one in the spring. Beaver's goin' to shine again, the men told each other.

But when they got back to rendezvous at Horse Creek, on the Siskadee again, the sign was getting clearer. Men who could trail Blackfeet a hundred miles without swinging ten yards from their trail couldn't miss this sign.

When they saw the canopy of dust rolling up over the sage flats south of rendezvous, Joe Meek, three other trappers, and a dozen Nez Percés galloped out to meet the supply train. From a distance they began whooping their war cries. Closer, they fired a volley over the heads of the riders, and spurred their horses down the length of the train, which stretched the better part of a mile. When they came back front to clap Tom Fitzpatrick on the shoulder and greet Captain Stewart again, they laid their eyes on a sight more wondrous than Colter's Hell—two white women—the first ever seed on the mountain side of the Missouri river. For here came Narcissa Whitman, perched sidesaddle, and Eliza Spalding, jouncing uncomfortably on a wagon bench.

In camp, the ladies spurred quite a hubbub. The Indians, who had never seen a white woman, marveled at the dresses they wore, at the fancy stitching, and at Narcissa's blonde hair. (One Indian had earlier asked if the whites had no squaws, since the white trappers were always so keen after the Indian squaws.) The mountain men milled about, struck nearly shy by the presence of ladies. They had dreamed of white women for years, and here were two in the flesh. But they were put off as well: Petticoats and stays in the mountains? Manners and proper teas? Polite speaking? Wagh! The mountains were getting queersomer and queersomer.

Narcissa Whitman, who had married Marcus this past year and come west to assist with his mission, was enough woman to evoke a lot of buffler-blanket fantasies. About thirty, she was a handsome specimen, finely curved and filled out, and topped with spectacular red-gold hair. Far from being sternly disapproving of the mountain men, she openly delighted in them. On the trail she had gotten to hear the umpteenth version of the story of the putrefied forest, spun by no less a liar than Black Harris; Tom Fitzpatrick's yarn about the time he hid in the rocks from the Blackfeet for two days; the tale of John Colter's run from the same niggurs; and some more stories thrown in by Captain Stewart and Milton Sublette. Stewart had come again to the mountains for sport, and Milton was rebounding from the amputation of his leg with another trip west.

If Narcissa's charm was abundantly obvious, her invisible dedication was no less real. Beneath the vivacious smile smoldered a fierce determination to save souls; behind her full-blooded womanhood resided a passion for self-sacrifice in a holy cause. That passion, almost alone, had led her to marry Marcus Whitman: Single women were unacceptable as missionaries. At her wedding, she had worn black, as the bride of death, in a stark gesture of sanctified purpose.

Eliza Spalding was much less appealing—frail, emaciated, dyspeptic, self-righteous, intolerant, not resilient enough for wilderness hardship. Her husband Henry was a guilt-ridden missionary with the zeal that intense self-dislike can brew. To add to his bitterness he had the humiliation of traveling with Narcissa, to whom he had once proposed, while she was honeymooning with Marcus. Among the gifts the Spaldings bore to the mountains was an extraordinary capacity for condemning and quarreling with other whites, including missionaries. And they brought along a lay assistant, William Gray, who nurtured that capacity to an unusual peak of intensity.

What was called for, everyone agreed, was a wallop of a welcome. The Indians decided to put on a genuine rendition of a Wild West Show, donning their fanciest costumes for a grand ceremonial parade with horses doing their tricks and medicine paraphernalia in full display. The mountain men did their bit by fluttering around Narcissa for conversation and flirtation, even going so far as asking to be given Bibles for their leisure-time perusal. The good lady didn't think to inquire whether they could read. Bridger, of course, as the preeminent legend in the mountains, took care to pay his respects, to describe the country ahead for them, and to spin some yarns—like the one about eight-hour echo canyon, where a child could holler into the canyon when he went to sleep and be woke by the echo of his words eight hours later. Jim wondered how the ladies had survived the alkali dust, which turned eyes red, or the alkali water, which produced instant diarrhea, or the hot, dry wind which would crack their skin and lips and tan their faces to leather. The mountains was no place for a woman. But he'd be kindly to them, still.

Hudson Bay sent a brigade to this rendezvous of 1836. The Whitmans and Spaldings were to go under its escort to their appointed fields of spiritual cultivation. (Spalding actually stayed with the Nez Percés; Whitman set up his mission further west at Walla Walla.) The American trappers, who were in fact a mongrel mixture of nationalities and races, would have scrapped with the British again over territorial rights, except that there wasn't enough fur in Rocky Mountain creeks anymore to be worth fighting for. The St. Louis price of beaver was still down, and never going to rise again, some men said. Buffler robes paid more now. Rendezvous was a little subdued because of that, and perhaps

the presence of the ladies. The sign, unmistakably, was
that the mountains didn't shine like they used to.

Bridger rode out for Blackfoot country again, with a brigade
of sixty. Most of the American trappers went with him, except for those like Old Bill Williams who now chose to trap
alone or in twos and threes, moving like shadows through
the mountains. Right off, the Blackfoot skirmishes started,
and the men had to stay in camp more than they trapped. By
the time scouts reported a Blackfoot village camped on the
Yellowstone, the men were spoiling for a fight. They crept
up behind bushes that they pushed ahead, and made thirty
Blackfeet come before dark took away the fun.

Bridger was cheered by the birth of his first known
child, a daughter he named Mary Ann. But they passed a
depressing winter in their lodges. A couple of Jim's Dela-
wares decided to kill Blackfeet for sport, and did. The
Blackfeet got back by shooting up a meat-making party,
and the trappers avenged that by completely snuffing out
the next band of Blackfeet they met.

Jim was keeping a weather eye out for serious trouble
now. So when he saw a whole plain swarming with Blackfeet, only ten miles downriver, he ordered the brigade to
fort up. They make-shifted a six-foot breastwork around
three sides of the camp. Behind the camp stood a steep
bluff, in front of it the frozen Yellowstone. They waited
all afternoon, but no attack came. Bridger and Carson
set a strict watch during the night. That night did bring
something strange—a spectacular display of the aurora
borealis, farther south than usual. It lit the northern half
of the sky, in the direction the trappers were watching for
a Blackfoot assault, a lurid red.

Dawn, and still no attack. During the day, some Blackfeet stole close enough to throw sporadic and useless rifle fire toward camp, but nothing more. Gabe didn't understand it. He figured the Blackfeet had somewheres around 1000 to 1500 braves, and he only had sixty men. Uncommon for the Blackfeet not to hit them all-out with those odds. That afternoon he led a small scouting party out and found the Blackfeet camped about three miles down the river. They seemed to be holding council and arguing among themselves. Puzzled, he went back to camp and waited. Dark fell, and nothing happened.

The next morning, the Blackfeet started their damn fool sniping again from out of rifle range. Then, at midday, the lookouts on the bluff shouted out; they could see the whole Blackfoot army marching upriver on the ice.

The trappers tried to calm their squaws and their animals. They renewed the priming in their Hawkens. They stuck balls into their mouths for the ready. The Blackfeet stopped a quarter mile out and spread for a charge. Then, unexpectedly, a chief stepped out of the ranks, walked forward, and made the sign of friendship.

Mountain men weren't about to be taken by this ruse, not from Blackfeet. Hell, they had pulled it themselves. But why would the devils be stalling for time now? Everything was stacked on their side. Jim chawed on it a moment and then climbed over the breastwork and strode out to meet the chief, alone.

"Bad medicine," signaled the chief. He stretched his arms toward the northern skies that had reddened. Then he smacked his left fist with his right palm, sketched a medicine pipe in the air with both hands, and pointed his arm toward the distance. Sign for: Friendly. Smoke pipe. Leave. Soon the huge Blackfoot army was filing away to

the north. Gabe permitted himself a grin. He allowed it
was the queersomest thing he'd ever seen.

Bill Williams was moving slowly, his old, crop-eared
Nez Percé pony picking her way gingerly upwards. Eight
free trappers, including Markhead and Joe Meek, stretched
out behind him, leading their various animals. Bill cottoned best to trapping by himself. Since he was along this
time, the others let him take charge. He didn't work in
harness for anybody. Besides, they were riding up a fork
of the upper Yellowstone, and Old Solitaire knew the
country best.

As he rode, his face never seemed to turn to either side,
but his gray eyes flitted observantly over the whole landscape, taking in details. He turned away from the creek
once and made a wide circle before he came back. He
stopped to let the others come close, and said in a high,
cracking voice, "Do 'ee hyar now, boys? Thar's Injuns
knocking round, an' Blackfoot at that. But thar's plenty
of beaver too, and this child means trapping anyhow."
Strange for Old Bill: He was cautious, and usually cached
at the first Indian sign.

He nudged his old pony with huge spurs and eased on.
His body bent over the saddlehorn; his neck craned forward so that he looked humpbacked. His face was long
and thin, with a nose that made fair to tickle his chin. His
eyes peered out from underneath a black hat that shone with
grease. A buckskin shirt fell in large folds around his
gaunt body, and wet buckskin leggings clung to his sinewy
legs. Fixens were strung around his body: powder horn
and bullet pouch; an awl with a deer-horn handle and a
cherrywood case he carved himself; a squat bullet-

mould, its handles covered with buckskin so he wouldn't burn his fingers; an antelope horn, scraped transparent, filled with beaver medicine; a Green River stuck in his belt; and a Hawken resting loosely on the saddlehorn.

Old Bill was queer, but the eight followed him willingly. He knew fat cow from poor bull for sure. He shot with an odd wobble, but still plumb center. He lurched when he walked, like he'd been swigging too much Taos Lightnin', but he was cool and deadly in a skirmish.

Indians or no, the others were willing to try their luck if Bill was. They camped without a fire. The next morning eight of them spread out in pairs to trap, and Bill stayed back to guard the camp. Markhead went with Baptiste, Joe Meek with Marcellin, an old trapper with his young partner, and two Canadians together. Bill quietly set to work dressing a deer skin.

At midday, he was dressing another skin when he heard someone charging on horseback toward camp like a mad buffler bull. After a moment, he glanced up casually at Markhead, who had a face covered with blood and an arrow poking out of his back. "Do 'ee feel bad now, boy? Whar away you see them damned Blackfoot?"

"Well," Markhead managed, "pull this arrow out of my back, and maybe I'll feel like telling."

"Do 'ee hyar now? Hold on till I've grained this cussed skin, will 'ee? Did 'ee ever see sich a damned pelt, now? It won't take smoke anyhow I fix it."

So Markhead waited, some put out, until Old Bill coolly finished his chore. After Bill pulled the arrow, Markhead told Old Solitaire that Baptiste and himself had found three lodges with no one around and had helped themselves to what was in the pot. On the way back they got ambushed by maybe a dozen of the niggurs and had to run for it. Baptiste was dead. Bill observed that Baptiste, being only a *vide-poche,* was no account anyhow.

Pretty quick, two others rode up in a hurry with two scalps swinging from the barrels of their Hawkens. They had been ambushed out in a different direction, but had got the better of the coons. Seemed that the place was alive with Indians. Then the Canadians came in at full gallop with report of Indians. The trappers looked at each other and allowed as how they'd better get out of the area before they got shot in the lights. "This coon'll cache, he will," said Bill. Already packed, he threw his saddle onto his pony, grabbed the lead of his pack mule, spurred up a bluff, and disappeared.

When he topped the rise above the creek, Bill scanned the surrounding hills. He saw thin wisps of smoke suspended in the air at all points of the compass. Automatically, he headed his mare uphill, parallel to the creek, toward the distant ridge. This whole side of the mountain was infested with Blackfeet. Quickly he got back down under the edge of the bank. No sense in exposing himself on higher ground. Sometimes the bed narrowed, though, and rock walls formed a gorge. So he kicked her back up the slope. On this dangerous ground, the man and mare picked their way without seeming to pay attention. The mare moved as fast as the timbering and the steepness allowed. The man touched her along the route most concealed by trees. His eyes roamed the countryside for the tiny data of danger. His mind recorded them like a radar scanner, and transferred them by habit into light movements of his hands on the reins or his knees on her flanks. Occasionally, he brought the mare around some spot he seemed not to trust, without apparent reason.

He talked to the mare, urging her along faster by reminding her that she didn't want to be Blackfoot property. After a couple of hours it was dark, but he still pushed her on. They moved all night, slowing down as they climbed steeply toward the last long rise to the ridge. About dawn, Bill came into a narrow gorge where the banks were thick with bushes, cottonwoods, and ash. He guided the mare into the very thickest part, found a place where she could browse on cherry bushes with almost no chance of being seen, and sat his old bones down to rest. He didn't sleep, having in mind to keep his hair; that could wait for nightfall, and he'd put out again around midnight.

After a couple of hours, Bill heard someone coming toward him on foot. Two of the niggurs, from the sound of it. He pointed his Hawken toward the sound, checked the priming, and watched for the first glimpse of redskin. They were coming straight toward him, so they'd seen the pony. Branches sprang back and forth, and a head poked through no more than a foot from the muzzle of his rifle. A white man's head. One of the partners he'd slipped away from yesterday. Goddamn if they hadn't found his cache.

"Do 'ee hyar now," squeaked Bill, "I was nigh giving 'ee hell, I was now. If I didn't think 'ee was Blackfoot I'm dogged now." He grumbled about having been rooted out, but they explained that they had stumbled on him, by pure accident. while hunting. He followed them to their camp nearby, but muttered that more trouble was coming. He said nary a word about the way he slipped off on his own hook back down the mountain.

Bill, Markhead, the two American partners, and two Canadians set a guard and then slept soundly that night in the thicket along the creek bottom. (Their other companions had had to shift for themselves back at yesterday's camp.) They slept with their feet to a small fire made Indian fashion, just a few logs flat on the ground with their tips meeting at the center.

Bill sat up wide-awake at the first yell. His Hawken was still cradled in one arm where he had slept with it. The fire spewed ashes into the air when a ball thumped into it. In one quick move Bill sprawled behind a bush out of sight and peered up toward the top of the rock wall that the creek cut through. Balls were knocking branches off trees all around, and thocking into trunks. Out of the corner of his eye he could see the two partners flopped next to him, and he heard Markhead and the Canadians get cover facing the other wall of the gorge. From the yelling he judged there must be a hundred of the coons, hot for blood and sure of counting coup. He waited. In the half-light he couldn't see a single Indian up above on the rocks. Only the flashes from their gun barrels told their positions, and they were all well shielded behind rocks on the top, over a hundred yards off. Blackfeet got excited when they shot, and were stupid besides, so he didn't figure to go under from their rifle fire. But they was one behind every boulder on that sheer cliff just above him. One of the niggurs was shooting damn near straight down, and had already brought blood on the grizzled old trapper next to Bill.

Presently the crittur got so eager he overplayed his hand. He leaned too hard on his boulder while taking aim and toppled it over the edge. The younger partner took quick advantage and shot the divil center. His body came bouncing down the cliff and into the bottom near Markhead. It was the first shot the trappers had sent off. Markhead, a daredevil, jumped out from behind his bush, ran to the body, made a savage arc with his knife, and whooped as he held up the scalp. Half the Blackfeet must have fired at him as he yelled. And they exposed themselves to get their shots. All five of the trappers shot and hit. They'd show the niggurs how to make shots count.

After a moment the Blackfeet started running off like crazed sheep, yelling and showing their backs to the trappers. Again the Hawkens let go, and again some Blackfeet came. Mebbe they'd learned their lesson and quit.

After a couple of minutes, though, Bill saw smoke coming up from the thick bottom downstream. He calculated fast. Ordinarily he would just have set a backfire and put a stop to it. But if he did, he didn't think he'd be able to put it out. The wind was coming up mean through the gorge. The flames were moving like a thirsty horse to water, and the smoke was already clouding right around them. They packed in a hurry and moved out—because of the smoke, they rode straight up to the plateau above.

The Blackfeet were waiting on their ponies. They charged, and stampeded the pack animals right off. Bill was nigh jerked out of the saddle by the lead line when his mules bolted. More mounted Blackfeet were coming on from in front, and the ones along the gorge were running out from behind. "Do 'ee hyar, boys?" Bill piped. "Break, or you'll go under. This child's goin' to cache." Bending low over the saddle, he drove the mare right back into the smoke toward the creek bottom. The others scattered just as fast.

Bill rode around the fire, choking on the smoke, and cached quietly for two days, sitting still as a stone and scanning the area for Blackfoot sign. Then he slipped out, found the Indians' trail, and followed it. He wasn't about to let them have his mules on the peraira. Caching in deep gorges during the day and riding their trail at night, he caught up and struck his coup. He was vexed that he couldn't get back his plews as well, but no sense in stirring up the hornets' nest. He trapped alone the rest of the

season and showed up at rendezvous with mules over-
loaded with beaver.

The two partners had stuck together when they cached.
Finally they started west over the Bitterroot Mountains
toward Snake country. But the older one got lamer by the
day. The Blackfoot ball had lodged in his groin. It got infected, and he couldn't walk or ride at all. They were exhausted from trying to move through the heavy snow
against the relentless wind. They stopped and built a
shanty to rest until the leg got better. They knew they were
stuck for the winter, and that it would be starvin' times—
the game had moved to lower elevations for pasture.

After they had eaten their horses, they took to eating
parfleche, the soft skin of their bullet pouches and moccasins. The younger partner hunted, but saw no game; he
was getting exhausted and low as the older man. On the
fourth day of munching parfleche, the old man called
him over. "Boy," he whispered, "this old hos feels like
goin' under, and that afore long. You're stout yet, and if
thar was meat handy, you'd come around slick. Now, boy,
I'll be under, as I said, 'afore many hours, and if you don't
raise meat, you'll be in the same fix. I never eat dead
meat myself, and wouldn't ask no one to do it neither; but
meat fair killed is meat any way. So, boy, put your knife
in this old niggur's lights, and help yourself. It's poor
bull, I know, but maybe it'll do to keep life in. Along the
fleece there's meat yet, and maybe my old hump ribs has
picking on 'em."

"You're a good old hos," the young trapper answered
mildly, "but this child ain't turned niggur yet."

So the old man wheezed out a plea for the young one to
be on his way, to try to get down the mountain and find
game. The young man refused. He didn't add that he was
too weak to make it that far.

He staggered out to hunt again. He knew it was useless, and thought he might not get back to the lodge because he was nigh too weak to walk. Less than two hundred yards away from camp, he stumbled on a scene he could hardly believe. An old bull lay on the peraira, foaming and bleeding onto his shaggy beard, lolling his head, about to give up. Two wolves squatted next to him, their tongues dangling, waiting for him to go under. For a moment the trapper thought maybe he was seeing specters. Then he considered how to get close: He wouldn't be able to trail the bull if his first shot wasn't center. Dizzy and faint, he crawled toward it. Finally he stretched out on the snow, propped the barrel of his Hawken extra careful, and fired at the brisket. The bull raised its head, shook convulsively, and rolled over.

He barely had the strength to sink his knife into the flesh to cut the meat away. Driving off the wolves, he dragged himself and a little meat into camp. They ate the liver raw and dipped into the gallbladder for flavor, and then kept stuffing. It was poor bull for sure, but it did to keep life in.

They survived the winter and when the snow melted got moving toward South Pass and the road to rendezvous. They were starving again now, since they'd run out of powder and lead. They were roasting rattlesnake steaks when Captain Stewart found them near the crest of South Pass. If they had seen a bellyfull of sights in the mountains, none was stranger than this fancy-dressed Scotsman, come to do his shooting for fun. But he offered them meat aplenty, and gave them an outfit on the peraira. Wal, that was some. Wagh![6]

Jim Bridger's eyes narrowed underneath the visor and fixed on Joe Meek. Wal, he'd give it a go. He kicked his pony hard and galloped forward, holding the borrowed lance high. Meek charged toward him in the same fashion. Gabe lowered his lance as the horses thundered close, but made sure it missed Joe. Joe playfully clanked his lance against the ribs of Jim's breastplate. The trappers whooped, hollered, slapped their thighs, cheered, and jeered. The foes wheeled their horses for another round of jousting. Here came Joe Meek, free trapper, dressed in trapper buckskin, full tilt at Jim Bridger, Old Gabe, partisan, cased in a suit of armor with helmet and visor, tassels streaming from the peak. If this wasn't some!

On the sidelines, Captain William Drummond Stewart of the British Army guffawed with the rest. Nearby, a New Orleans artist, Alfred Jacob Miller, was sketching furiously. Stewart, soon to be a baronet, heir to ancient lands of Scotland including Birnam Wood itself, had come to rendezvous for the fifth straight summer. He had brought his usual delicacies—brandies, wines, cigars, canned gourmet items—and he had toted along a suit of armor, one of the symbols of Stewart's heritage, for his old friend Jim Bridger. It was a sight. The most respected man in the mountains, a man who would have made a soldier of fortune or a knight errant in other times and circumstances, Stewart thought, decked out in the gallant equipage of another age. And Jim, why he strutted like a proper representative of King Arthur, or like an Indian pleased as a child with a coat from a U. S. Army uniform.

But an artist? Stewart, suspecting that his brother, the baronet, had not long to live, and that his own sporting days in the Rocky Mountains might be near an end, had hired Miller to sketch the grand scenes of trapper and Indian life. Later, he would convert them into huge oils to decorate Murthly Castle and remind their owner of these days of splendor. (Stewart would take his favorite hunter,

Antoine Clement, to Scotland as well, along with some buffalo to give a new style to ancestral grounds.)

Old Gabe didn't know much about armor, but he did cotton to surprising subjects. Later he would even develop an interest in Shakespeare. Copies of Byron, Scott, the Bible, and Shakespeare had always made their way about the mountains in possible sacks, as a substitute for endless card games of euchre and seven-up in winter lodge. The old illiterate now had a young man who knew the letters to read Shakespeare to him, and the mind that could hold half a continent in firm and detailed grasp proved that it could also hold verse. After Jim listened to a passage, he would spill it right back word for word, lapsing only occasionally into trapper, and creating as incongruous a fabrication of language as the one Huck Finn heard on the Mississippi. But after he listened to *Richard III,* Jim would have no more of Shakespeare. His morality didn't hold with a man who would kill his own mother.

Jim liked Stewart's joke with the armor, though, and he didn't mind having Miller sketch him in it astride his horse. The Snakes also cooperated with Stewart and Miller; they staged a grand parade and show of trick riding, skilled shooting, and counting coup for the artist to sketch. They scoffed at the belief of some Indians that having your likeness drawn mysteriously robbed you of your medicine.

The superstition held true in a certain way, though. Miller was a kind of news-magazine photographer, carried West to catch a way of life before it disappeared. The sign was all bad again this year: Another poor hunt; the country all trapped out; the price down for what few plews there were; a lot of *mangeurs de lard* like Miller in the mountains. An old hand and sophisticated man like Tom Fitzpatrick shook his head sadly at the spectacle. The trapper was being recorded for posterity and was going under in the same breath.

Tom had brought the 1837 supply train out for the Company again—a smaller train than last year's, as last year's had been smaller than the one of 1835. Old friends were around: Etienne Provost, fat as a porpoise, had come out with the train; so had Black Harris; they had met Lucien Fontenelle, now a gentleman and a dandy, at Fort Laramie. The old stories were good for another round: Miller noted down the one about Hugh Glass and the grizzly. Markhead told about the time he bragged himself into following Old Ephraim into a thicket to kill it with nothing but a hatchet and as payment got part of his scalp torn off. The boys even told Miller about the mythical herb that gives immunity against snakebite, and the greenhorn swallowed it.

But tale-telling, after a while, begins to ring of living in the past. And Tom, who was keen, knew enough to know that after a decade and a half, his trade was putting out to pasture. New forts were springing up all along the Platte and even the Arkansas. The trade was swinging from the rendezvous system back to fixed posts, where it had started. And buffler robes outshone plews. Fitz was only thirty-eight years old.

After a while Stewart moved his outfit out from rendezvous, which was again on the Siskadee, between Horse Creek and New Fork, and up into the Wind Rivers Mountains to live out some scenes for his painter and his memory book. Another party put out from rendezvous early, taking a risk every mountain man warned them against. William Gray, the vindictive and self-righteous lay assistant of the mission to the Nez Percés, was going back to the States to round up more money and more hands so that he could get his own mission going. Arrogantly, he started through Indian country with only two other whites and five or six Indians.

Somehow they got as far as Fort Laramie without trouble. There, Fontenelle warned them to wait for Fitzpatrick and the security of the Company train. Sioux were everywhere, he said, and their hearts were bad. But the mule-headed Gray was invited to dinner at the Fort by a Sioux, so he decided that their hearts were good.

Near the forks of the Platte he got his comeuppance. Sioux chased them across the river and against a bluff where they tried to hole up. No use. The Sioux came on for hair. A french trader happened to be with the Sioux and asked Gray out for a parley. There he told the missionary that the Sioux braves were willing to spare the whites' lives but were determined to spill the blood of the Indians with Gray. As Gray and the other two whites stood with the trader, the Sioux charged the Indians of Gray's party and murdered them. Gray later claimed that he was taken by surprise by the maneuver. But every mountain man knew that Gray had sacrificed his red companions to save his own skin. So did the chief who had entrusted his son to Gray's care for the trip east.

Jim Bridger, for once, couldn't figure out which way the stick was floating. The fall 1837 hunt had been lousy. Crow country was burnt out now. The men likkered themselves into a winter-long stupor. In the spring of 1838, Jim had turned his brigade, sizable as ever, toward the Blackfoot country. And they had ridden all the way to the Three Forks without a single skirmish, without even seeing a Blackfoot. It made no sense.

Crossing from the Gallatin to the Madison Fork, Jim

suddenly cottoned why. They came on a lone tipi and found it filled with nine Blackfoot, dead, all scarred by smallpox. The trail of the village that had left these bodies wound up the Madison. But Jim moved his men away from the river and back into the mountains. They complained like hell: Every man of them remembered a dry-gulched friend he wanted to get square for. Jim had fought these Blackfeet half his life. The numbers weren't more than three to one against the brigade—good odds for mountain men. Was Jim losing his gumption? He turned them around to chase the village.

When they got to within about three miles, fifteen volunteers rode out and snuck up on the village. From the top of a ridge they sent volleys into the tipis while the Injuns ran around confused, and then skedaddled back to camp.

The Blackfeet finally got mounted, followed them, and set up about three hundred yards from camp—out of rifle range for either side. The Indians shot anyway, at random. They worked themselves to fever pitch with war cries and insults to the whites: The trappers should wear skirts because they were women who started a fight and then hid. The Blackfeet invoked their gods, called up their medicines, and assured themselves of long life and many coups. Finally, twenty trappers, led by an Iroquois who wasn't about to let anyone get away with calling him a woman, charged the hundred and fifty Blackfeet on horseback, routed them, and chased them all the way back to their village.

Trapper honor was satisfied, but the Blackfeet were not. After a quiet night, Gabe started moving his men toward the mountains again. The Blackfeet, though, had sent a horse patrol to cut the trappers off. So the Iroquois got thirty men, flanked the mounted Blackfeet, got to within thirty yards under thick cover, and led a surprise charge. Surprise always seemed to whip an Indian. The braves slapped their ponies and galloped headlong for the village. The trappers whooped and kept after them all the way. With a good scrap under their belts, they finally went back to trapping.

Moving south and west, they reached Henry Lake and another Blackfoot village—small enough to squash without half trying. As they were getting primed for the squashing, a half-dozen Blackfeet came out timidly, unarmed, and asked the whites to smoke and trade. Gabe could scarcely believe it. Blackfeet peaceable? But then he saw why. Smallpox had done worse for them than trappers ever had. Most were dead, and those living were skeletons. Jim smoked agreeably. Little Robe, the chief, said that the whites had given his people smallpox. Jim chastised him for his bad thoughts. But he was stuck for an explanation. So he yarned one: Jim Beckwourth, the divil, had deliberately sent the Blackfeet as a present a blanket infected with the disease. Gabe's little act of vengeance on Beckwourth, who had robbed Tom Fitzpatrick nigh five years ago, took hold in the Blackfoot memory.

In fact, the Blackfeet had picked up the disease at Fort Union. One of the steamboats had brought the infection. The Crows heard about it and stayed clear of the fort. The Blackfeet, hungry as always for rifles and ammunition, came in to trade. Quarantine had yet to be invented. So the Blackfeet spread it among all their villages. It devastated the most warlike tribe in the mountains with hellish thoroughness.

Bridger led his men on south to Horse Creek for rendezvous. But instead of a supply caravan, he found only a scrawled note tacked onto a log storehouse: COME ON TO POPO ASIA. PLENTY WHISKEY AND WHITE WOMEN.

Gabe's boys roared into camp and greeted their comrades with a fiendish ruckus. The ladies were properly horrified. Then, a dozen or two ran to feast their eyes on the white women, who looked a poor lot. A Snake girl with small, high breasts and fine thighs shined better any day. They took to waving their Blackfoot scalps and pounding their Indian drums in front of the ladies. Then they broke into a war dance round the scalp, whooping it up, one of the women wrote, "like emissaries of the devil worshipping their own master."[7] The next night they staged another war dance for the ladies, this time done up fine in war paint. Their faces blackened, or brightened with scarlet, orange, yellow, and brown, their buckskins greaseblack, drunk as lords or devils, they scared hell out of the women. They were celebrating the ravaging of the Blackfeet by smallpox.

The trappers had other reasons as well for making ferocious devilment. Drips had brought the caravan up, and had switched the place to the Popo Agie River, just east of South Pass and the continental divide, because it was closer to the States. No profit for the Company in rendezvous now, so any savings was to be taken. Plews were harder to come by than ever, and the price still down. The rumor spread that the Company didn't mean to send another supply train to rendezvous. All right, by God, they'd make this one the biggest, drunkest, meanest, happiest, struttingest rendezvous ever.

That notion suited Captain Stewart, come to the mountains for another big-game hunt, just fine. He was about to

have to return to Scotland to take over the responsibilities
of his high estate.

It didn't suit the missionaries at all. They were four
couples who had struggled out with Drips to bring God to
the heathen. On the way they had tried to bring Him to
each other as well, bickering incessantly, complaining,
getting sick, and growing so obnoxious that Drips asked
them to please travel alone. They declined, and kept up
their quarreling. They were dedicated and determined
people; they were also self-righteous, intolerant, and un-
adapted to plains life.

All of them were newlyweds honeymooning four to a
tent. Two couples had apparently married because they
wanted each other, but the other two had made marriages
of policy. Of these, Mary and Elkanah Walker had stood
in a predicament: Both had a calling to save souls, but
neither had a mate. The mission board, judiciously rec-
ommending marriage for missionaries, played the part of
matchmaker. They got engaged two days after they met,
but they managed to wait eleven months before they got
married. The other couple was William Gray with a new
helpmeet, Mary.

The presence of Gray, who had taken to affecting the
title "Doctor," aroused the rough and sinful mountain
men. They didn't recollect much about the Ten Commandments that Gray went by, but they sure as hell knew
their own. And Gray, in his little caper with the Sioux,
had broken the first of them: He had traded the lives of
his friends and followers for his own. The trappers paid
no allegiance to the writing in law books or to robed
judges, but they had a mountain notion of justice. They
went to the tent to work it on Gray. The two women were
terrified by the drunken brutes. One husband parleyed
with the trappers at the tent flap, claiming he didn't

know where Gray was, while Gray hid among the blankets in the darkness. His life was saved by luck: They didn't see him. The trappers went back to boozing. Didn't make sense to count coup on a pantywaist missionary anyhow.

In a temper equal parts bad and boisterous, the trappers lit into their rendezvous bust-out with a frenzy. Stewart helped make the merriment more real by flinging his dollars about smartly. The men fought, gambled, shot, and rode wildly. They declared an informal rutting season with the squaws, and fornicated grandly, not giving a damn about the prissy missionaries or their hatchet-faced wives. And finally they sobered up to a sobering reality. The least observant of them could see hard times acoming.

The Company—long since Pratte, Chouteau but always thought of as American Fur—did hire for one more hunt. Only half of last year's number signed on. Bridger led it, of course, but Drips tagged along to keep Jim from passing out so much Company whisky to the men. Jim worked the Snake country in the autumn and the Three Forks in the spring. It was the most miserable year yet for fur.

They limped into the Horse Creek grounds for rendezvous. On July 4, 1839, none other than Black Harris brought in the supplies. The train was a depressing sight—nine men and four mule carts with goods—a far cry from the high times of caravans that stretched nigh a mile across the plains. And Harris was bringing about as many greenhorns as hands. Here were a scientist and free-lance preacher venturing west, plus something new—emigrants bound for Oregon or Californy. The spectacle made the men dispirited. For the first time they could hardly raise themselves to drink or gamble. Beaver just didn't shine.

And the Company was not going to outfit another brigade. The trappers who had once been able to defy any war party would now have to trap in bands of a half-dozen or less, slip through the mountains hoping that no Indians saw them, and tote their skins to the forts once in a while to trade. Most of them had nothing but stiff joints from standing in icy creeks to show for their years of work. And a few scars, compliments of the Blackfeet. But, on the whole, they'd keep at their trade for what they could scrape out of it.

Wal, Jim Bridger wasn't ready to knuckle under. He didn't mean to skulk around the mountains where he had not long ago led a small army. The Company owed him $3,000 in back wages, he said. He'd use that, find some more money, and back his own outfit. And so, after seventeen years away from civilization, Jim left his wife and daughter with the Flatheads and turned his cayuse toward the settlements.

Those settlements had grown considerably westward since Jim had seen them, but were still a long way from the mountains. He didn't take any interest in the city of St. Louis. He wanted to get back where he belonged. He asked Tom Fitzpatrick to go in with him. No deal. Tom had stayed out of the mountains for two years, and saw no future in beaver. He talked to Bill Sublette and Bob Campbell. Bill liked to keep his mountain memories alive: On his plantation at Sulphur Springs Bill had deer, antelope, and buffalo, and even grizzlies in chains. But Bill and Bob had known when to become bankers and suppliers instead of trappers, and when to get out of the mountains. They were wealthy and influential men now. They said there was no future in fur. Finally, Jim wheedled a few thousand out of Chouteau for a two-year hunt. With Old Frapp as his partner, he kicked off for the mountains in the spring of 1840.

He made his fall hunt with a fair-sized brigade on the Siskadee, taking in a toluble number of plews in a trapped-out country. The next summer, he bent with the times to let Frapp take an outfit to hunt buffler instead of beaver. In July, he saw a sight to amaze his old eyes. Across the Siskadee came Tom Fitzpatrick with a big caravan. Not a caravan of supplies for trappers, but of missionaries and emigrators. There were about seventy of these emigrators, and they were headed for Oregon and Californy. Gabe had no patience with the greenhorns, and Tom confirmed that they had to be wet-nursed along. They did trade with Jim, though, for buckskins, meat, and mules. The biggest amazement was that Tom Fitzpatrick, Broken Hand, once an Ashley man and later the owner of a trapping company, had hired himself out as a nursemaid. But Tom told Jim that the future was in guiding emigrants, not trapping. Jim sniffed at that. What could the emigrators want with a country where only sagebrush would grow, and rattlesnakes slept coiled around the roots of most of the sagebrush? It just wasn't for them, and never would be.

More bad news came: Frapp had been rubbed out in an attack by Sioux and Shian. Jim took the trail after the niggurs, but they were long gone before he found their sign.

He hunted the Salt Lake and Bear River areas that fall, and the Snake country the following spring. Two of his parties were wiped out, one by Crows and another by Sioux. In June of 1842 he was ready to head for the States with thirty packs of beaver. Fitzpatrick, back from Oregon, traveled with him eastward. And at Fort Laramie, the two veteran trappers ran into more emigrants, over a hundred of them, with their white-topped wagons spread all over Laramie plain. Jim again traded with them;

the critturs didn't cotton anything, and came west with all the wrong fixens, or broke what they needed on the way. Fitzpatrick turned west again as their guide.

A few days later Gabe struck something else new—an expedition of topographical engineers of the U. S. Army under a lieutenant named John Charles Frémont. Jim camped with them to talk about the country ahead, and accidentally scared hell out of the men with his casual description. Frémont and his guide, Jim's old second-in-command Kit Carson, were out of camp at the time, but Jim left some words for Kit about how to avoid the riled-up Sioux.

Back in the States, he again got backing from Chouteau and turned straight back for high country. By spring 1843, he was on Black's Fork of the Green, named for a child Jim recollected well, Arthur Black, who had gone with Jed Smith to Californy. Jim had a fort built here in a pleasant valley with plenty of grass, plenty of water, and groves of cottonwoods and willows. In a corner of the fort he set up a forge and an anvil—the tools of the smithing trade he had quit twenty years before. The fort was sitting right on the route to Oregon. Jim knew the country better than any man above ground, and he was sure those wagons would be coming right past his gate. He figured to do some trading with the emigrators.

Herds of people did come that summer: An emigrant train bound for California and led by old trapper Joe Walker; a train headed for Oregon and led by Dr. Marcus Whitman, the missionary who had dug the arrowhead out of Jim's back—it had more than a thousand emigrants; and another Frémont expedition, guided by both Carson and Fitzpatrick.

Wal, Jim wasn't ready to say trapping was gone beaver

just yet. He'd heard about a lot of beaver sign way up north of the Missouri on the Milk River. He put together a brigade for a fall hunt there.

But the Milk River was as dry of beaver as the rest of the Rockies. The hunt was a complete bust. Gabe took his men in to winter at Fort Union, and there he admitted that the sign was unmistakable. He dictated a letter to Chouteau asking for a new kind of supplies.

I have established a small fort with a blacksmith's shop and a supply of iron on the road of the emigrants on Black's Fork of Green River, which promises fairly. They, in coming out, are generally well supplied with money, but by the time they get there are in want of all kinds of supplies. Horses, provisions, smith-work, etc., bring ready cash from them, and should I receive the goods hereby ordered will do a considerable business in that way with them.[8]

Fort Bridger was the first post ever constructed in the Rockies, not to trade with the Indians or the trappers, but as a way-station for emigrants.

Jim Bridger made his mark, and with that gesture he said that trapping had gone under. He signed the end to the life he had lived and relished and flourished in for twenty-one years. He committed himself to a changed order. When the free trappers, all over the mountains, heard, they gaped at each other across the campfire and muttered, "Ain't that some? Old Gabe gone to keepin' store. Wagh!" Jim was thirty-nine years old.

NINTH INTERLUDE

Trappers and Indians

ANY ENCOUNTER BETWEEN A "CIVILIZED" PEOPLE and a "primitive" people results in attitudes so bristling with prejudice and misunderstanding that the ethics of human relations becomes a Gordian knot. The very terms civilized and primitive express the prejudice of the case, because they have no meaning from the perspective of the "primitives." It is not surprising, in the long view of history, that such encounters are invariably bloody: The white European has attempted to impose his culture on the African, the Asian Indian, the American Indian, and so on. Sometimes his motives have been generous—he saw himself as a civilizer, raising the savage from material poverty and spiritual benightedness; sometimes they have been self-serving—he wanted goods and slave labor. In either case the white miscalculated grievously because he sought to plant, by force, a concept of the world in ground where it could not possibly grow. The white was as ignorant as the primitive in his total inability to understand a world-perspective foreign to his own. And the white with generous motives generally proved a more cataclysmic destroyer than the white with selfish motives. Still, where there was no possible basis for mutual understanding, bad feeling, rule by force, and bloodshed were the inevitable outcome.

A historian who attempts to say just what was right and wrong in such an encounter is guilty of blindness. The story of the relationship of the white man and the Indian in America can only be told from two incompatible

points of view. The service of Dee Brown's Bury My
Heart at Wounded Knee: An Indian History of the West
*is that Brown has committed himself to expressing the
Indian perspective, as his sub-title indicates. This book,
likewise, tells the story of the mountain men from their
own perspective and not from some independent, "objective" pedestal of judgment. To try to evaluate the way
the mountain men and Indians treated each other "ob-
jectively," could only mean to evaluate it from a perspective that participates in the cultural bias of neither. Such
a perspective may some day be formulated. But it seems
to me that we speak meaningfully only when we look at
the encounter from the well-meaning, deep biases of both
sides.*

*By 1806, when Colter, Dixon, and Hancock took up resi-
dence in the valley of the Big Horn River, white-Indian
relations in America had had a long and sorry history. A
glance at an old map of the United States will reveal
large areas of the Ohio Valley marked prominently: RE-
SERVED FOR INDIANS. We know what happened to that
land. The settling of the West followed the same pattern:
Huge land areas were granted by treaty to the Indians
for as long as the sun shone and the waters flowed. The
grants held good until gold was discovered on Indian
land, or until some ranchers felt the need for more pasture.
The white man may or may not have intended to keep the
promises of these treaties; but he consistently broke them.
Some of the tribes of the plains and mountains were
marginally aware of that pattern when the mountain
men arrived. And certainly the mountain men had been
born to the premise of expansion wherever they wanted
to go.*

Misunderstanding breeds contempt. If a man has no

*notion of why another man behaves as he does, any dif-
ferent behavior will seem foolish; and the other fellow's
failure to grasp the "obvious" undermines respect and
goodwill. The Indian held the trapper simultaneously in
contempt and in awe. Awe, because the trapper had magic
that made such wonders as mirrors; contempt, because
he would give away an object of such powerful magic in
return for something so commonplace as a five-minute sexual servicing. That list could be expanded indefinitely. The
trapper held the Indian in contempt because the Indian
prayed when he should have fought, because he thought
himself made invulnerable by a string of bear claws, and
so on. Neither had any way to comprehend the other's
mind-set.*

*It is surprising, in this context, and in the larger con-
text of white destruction of Indian culture, that the
mountain men and Indians treated one another as fairly
as they did. The mountain-man era was not just another
phase of domination and exploitation of the Indians
by whites. It was an exception to that overwhelming
pattern.*

*Consider the reasons: The trappers came to the moun-
tains in miniscule numbers; Colter's party was three
men; Lisa's was only a handful; Ashley's first expedition,
in 1822, was made of about a hundred. So few men could
not possibly force their way through the mountains. The
plains and mountain tribes numbered in the tens of thousands each. On the east side of the Mississippi, an indi-
vidual white had the power of the United States Army
behind him; the trappers had no such advantage. So they
were compelled, from the beginning, to try to get what
they wanted by friendship, persuasion, and trade. They
paid tribute for the use of Indian lands; they paid in*

goods for services and products. The Indians did not re-
sist the trappers, on the whole, but welcomed them; all
the tribes wanted the tobacco, firewater, armament, and
foofuraw the white man brought.

An important chief is supposed to have said that he
never feared the coming of the white man until he first
saw a plow in a Conestoga wagon. The remark must be
apocryphal: No Indian would have known what a plow
was used for. But it expresses a figurative truth.

The basis of friendship was not only trade. The trappers were friends to the Crows because they were willing
to be enemies to the Blackfeet. This was policy, at first,
rather than inclination, and the pattern held in relationships with various Indian tribes. Virtually all the tribes of
the plains and mountains had hated and fought each other
since time immemorial. Truces were rare, alliances tenu-
ous. Warfare was integral to Indian culture; it was deeply
involved with Indian machismo and therefore with the Indian concept of manly virtue. A tragic seed of the later
white conquest of the Indians was that the tribes hated
each other more than they hated the intruder. Throughout
the years of the Indian wars, Sioux would join whites to
fight Crows, only to find Crows helping the Long Knives
when the Long Knives wanted to fight Sioux.

The fact remains: Most Indian tribes were friendlier to
the trappers than they were to each other. And the trappers cultivated these friendships, trying to be the ally of
all and the foe of none.

The one major exception was the Blackfeet. With very
rare lulls, the Blackfeet and the trappers took to their rifles every time they saw each other. That enmity may
stem from the fact that Lewis and Clark killed a Blackfoot; more likely, it began when the Blackfeet saw John

Colter on the side of the Crows in a pitched battle. The major causes, though, were two: The Blackfeet battled implacably with anyone, white or Indian, who was not a Blackfoot. And they would not accept a white as their friend if he was also friend to their enemies—which meant every tribe they knew of. After a while, the trappers began to relish answering in kind, and Jim Bridger became famous for his love of killing Blackfeet.

Modern, race-conscious America may argue that regardless of how the trappers acted, they felt and projected racist scorn for the red man. To say so is to drop context radically. The talk of the trappers was full of "racist" references to everyone not like them: John Bull got it as fully as the "niggur" who got it as fully as the red man who got it as fully as the "greaser" who got it as fully as the "Frenchy." It was directed at anyone from as far away as the next county, or at anyone of slightly different social standing. But the mountain men also were developing frontier democracy, and they lived it probably more completely than any coherent group of men in the West. Despite their talk, they accepted the Irish Tom Fitzpatrick and the Irish Robert Campbell as their leaders, educated Jed Smith as a kind of great man, mulatto Jim Beckwourth as a comrade, and the Englisher William Stewart, Scottish titles and all, as a regular fellow. The mountains had a way of leveling all men to equal stature, and of persuading everyone to respect a man according to his skills, not his birth.

And the attitude of the mountain men toward the Indians evolved from calculated strategy into felt identification. Between 1822, when the Ashley men first went West, and 1843, when the first hordes of emigrants came, the trappers in a way became Indians themselves. They dressed like Indians, adopted some of the values of Indians, learned Indian languages, married (sometimes permanently) into Indian tribes, and came to believe in Indian religion, which was more relevant to their circumstances than the allegories of Moses and Christ. When the first missionaries came, they saw instantly that the mountain men were more Indian than white. By the 1840s, to say "I took 'ee for an Injun" was a compliment to a trapper, though an abhorrence to an emigrant.

The story of the settling of the West is, in part, a saga of physical conquest of a resistant land, in part a tragedy of the destruction of one culture by another. It is also a moral drama: The values and ways of civilization rooted out the values and ways of the mountain men. It was order, institutions, agriculture, and community against wildness and the love of wild land, personal freedom, and lusty individualism. The emigrants defeated the mountain men as surely as they defeated the Indians. And, by that time, the mountain men had developed a spiritual brotherhood with the Indians, not the settlers.

In a rare reversal of historical process, the Indians had won the mountain men, relatively, to their ways, not vice versa. And prominent trappers like Tom Fitzpatrick and Kit Carson, after the era of trapping had ended, turned Indian agent and gave the Indians what understanding and sympathy they could.

The conquistadores in the West were not the mountain men, but the settlers and the missionaries. The settlers wanted land, and got it. The missionaries had a much more deadly goal: They wanted souls. They found out that to get a man's soul, if it is deeply alien, you first have to destroy it. And where they got a firm enough hold, destroy it they did.

X

Alpenglow

NO SEGMENT OF HISTORY ENDS WITH A SINGLE NEAT period. Though the era of Rocky Mountain trapping was gone under by December of 1843 when Jim Bridger turned in his traps, a good number of free trappers kept working the creeks, taking their plews, and roaming the mountains. They didn't take to greenhorns or green ways; nor did the greenhorns take to them.

Here comes Joe Meek, for instance, tongue-lashing his animals through South Pass on a hot July day in 1838, just after the Popo Agie rendezvous. Joe is trying to ride down his Nez Percé wife. After Mountain Lamb got rubbed out in a scrap, he married this girl and she gave him a daughter. But back at rendezvous, she got her dander up and took off for home. Wal, Joe will show her some plain and fancy lodge-poling. He is carrying liquid refreshment in the form of rendezvous whisky in a kettle on his saddle-horn. Since he has indulged more than a little too much, his head feels like overripe fruit about to bust open, and he is using the hair of the dog to cure it. Not a good moment for a mountain man to trip over greenhorns.

But there they are, stopped, a man and a woman, the man flopped on the ground. A bad place to be taking a pause. Not a breath of wind here on the plain. The sun feels scorching even to Joe's burnt-leather skin. The buffler grass is parched and drooping on the dry, sandy earth. In the heat mirage, the Pass takes on an unreal look—the hills slightly detached from the plain, just floating there, the occasional antelope or buffler seeming to trot through a strange, shiny medium that will make you hope for water, unless you know better.

When he gets up to them, he recognizes the missionaries from rendezvous, Reverend and Mrs. Smith. The Reverend is going through the rigamarole of declaring himself dead of thirst. The Missus cries out to Joe as providential assistance and begs for water. Wagh! Joe doesn't have any water, but he'll gladly share the contents of his kettle with the Reverend. No, protests the holy man, death itself would be preferable to partaking of alcohol.

Joe ponders the situation for a moment. This pious greenhorn is giving up, going under, deliberately not making a man's try. And he is abandoning his woman besides. Some religion he must have. (Trapper religion holds the second a grievous sin, and the first a cardinal one.) So Joe lets him have it. The lady who later wrote down Joe's life from his dictation tried to make the wording acceptable, though it certainly wasn't:

You're a—pretty fellow to be lying on the ground here, lolling your tongue out of your mouth and trying to die. Die if you want to, and go to h—l, you're of no account and will never be missed. Here's your wife, who you are keeping standing here in the hot sun: why don't she die? She's got more pluck than a white-livered chap like you. But I'm not going to leave her waiting here for you to die. That's a band of Indians behind me on the trail and I've been riding like h—l to keep out of their way. If you want to stay here and be scalped, you can stay; Mrs. Smith is going with me.[1]

He shoves her up on his horse against her objections, tells the Reverend she can find plenty of men better than him, and takes off. The damned female weeps behind him, begging to be allowed to die with her beloved. A mile on he looks over his shoulder and sees the Reverend standing up there in the sagebrush. A while after Joe and the Missus catch up with the missionary party, the preacher walks in. But Joe moves on. Missionaries smell sulphur on him; he smells prissiness on them.

Civilized people didn't cotton to Joe. The next year a settler described him as an Indian: "The same wild, unsettled, watchful expression of the eye, the same unnatural gesticulation in conversation, the same unwillingness to use words when a sign, a contortion of the face or body, or movement of the hand will manifest thought; in standing, walking, reading, in all but complexion, he was an Indian."[2]

Joe, like most of the trappers, was unsuited to civilized doin's, but he tried them anyway—went on to Oregon, finally, and turned his guns to trying to keep the law there. Tom Fitzpatrick guided Frémont and emigrant trains for a while, and then settled into a post as government Indian agent. Andrew Drips did the same, though he ruled the Indians partly for the profit of the Company. Carson also got around to being an Indian agent after a while. These men understood Indians, cared about them in a certain way, and tried to protect them against the unreal idealism, the stupidity, and the greed of the government and the settlers. They failed.

Fitzpatrick, Carson, Meek, Bill Williams, and many others had become Indians in more than appearance and manner. Frémont "explored" the West in the 1840s, and got nationwide credit for his daring. In fact, he was patiently guided over every inch of what he explored by Carson, Fitzpatrick, Bridger, Williams, and other men like them. And guiding was a traditional Indian function.

After the Company quit backing hunts, in 1839, the free trappers went on about the trade they knew. They moved partly out of their old stomping grounds, and kept more and more to Colorado and other spots not too close to what was becoming the Oregon Trail. Brown's Hole became a crossroads, and Bayou Salade, or South Park, became the mountain-man paradise. For trading they turned more and more to Bent's Fort on the Arkansas.

In the mid-1840s, for instance, two trappers might cross trail with another and have a little shop talk:

"Where from, stranger?"

"The divide, and to the Bayou for meat. And you are from there, I see. Any buffalo come in yet?"

"Heap, and seal-fat at that. What's the sign out on the plains?"

"War-party of Rapahos passed Squirrel at sundown yesterday, and nearly raised my animals. Sign, too, of more on left fork of Boiling Spring. No buffalo between this and Bijou. Do you feel like camping?"

"Well, we do. But whar's your companyeros?"

"I'm alone."

"Alone? Wagh! . . ."

"What's beaver worth in Taos?"

"Dollar."

"In Saint Louiy?"

"Same."

"Hell! Any call for buckskin?"

"A heap! The soldiers in Santa Fe are half froze for leather; and moccasins fetch two dollars easy."

"Wagh! How's trade on the Arkansa, and what' doin to the Fort?"

"Shians at Big Timber, and Bent's people trading

smart. On North Fork, Jim Waters got a hundred pack
right off, and Sioux making more."

"How's powder goin?"

"Two dollars a pint."

"Bacca?"

"A plew a plug."

"Got any about you?"

"Have so."

"Give us a chaw; and now let's camp."[3]

Beaver selling for a dollar a pound? Tobacco, a plew
for a plug? A far cry from the old days. But the mountain
men stuck at it. Listen to a free trapper—any free trapper
in the mid-1840s—as he crosses his legs in front of a fire,
the light showing his browned and reddened face and
his glints of eyes, nearly closed from years of sun, while
he talks about why:

Thirty year have I been knocking about these mountains from Missoura's head as far sothe as the Starving
Gila. I've trapped a heap and many a hundred pack of
beaver I've traded in my time, wagh! What has come of
it, and whar's the dollars as ought to be in my possibles? Whar's the ind of this, I say? Is a man to be
hunted by Injuns all his days? Many's the time I've said
I'd strike for Taos, and trap a squaw, for this child's
getting old, and feels like wanting a woman's face
about his lodge for the balance of his days; but when it
comes to caching of the old traps, I've the smallest
kind of heart, I have. Certain, the old State comes
across my mind now and again, but who's thar to remember my old body? But them diggins gets too over-
crowded now-a-days, and it's hard to fetch breath
amongst them big bands of corncrackers to Missoura.

Beside, it goes aginst natur to leave buffler meat and feed on hog; and them white gals are too much like picturs, and a deal too fofarraw. No; darn the settlements, I say. It won't shine, and whar's the dollars? Hows'ever, beaver's bound to rise; human natur can't go on selling beaver a dollar a pound; no, no, that arn't a going to shine much longer, I know. Them was the times when this child first went to the mountains: six dollars the plew—old 'un or kitten. Wagh! but it's bound to rise, I says again; and hyar's a coon knows whar to lay his hand on a dozen pack right handy, and then he'll take the Taos trail, wagh![4]

And he knocks the ashes out of his pipe and gazes about at his partners.

But he knew that beaver warn't about to rise, that the dollars never would stuff his possible sack, and that he'd never take that trail to Taos. He waded into half-frozen creeks at dawn and flashed powder on Indians at night because he loved the life, nothing more nor less. But a child didn't put tongue to them feelings.

What they did put tongue to was their impatience, sometimes jovial and sometimes bitter, at the newcomers. In 1843, these came in trains that stretched as far as the eye could see, and were later referred to as the Great Migration. In 1847, the Mormons headed west, and that was a spectacle to rouse the full scorn of the mountain men. Around that campfire where the two trappers and the stranger sat down for the night, one is talking about that holy people:

The doins of them Mormon fools can't be beat by Spanyards, stranger. Their mummums and thummums you speak of don't shine whar Injuns are about; nor pint out a trail, whar nothin crossed but rattlersnakes since it fust snow'd on old Pike's Peak. If they pack along them profits, as you tell of, who can make it rain hump-ribs and marrow-guts when the crowd gets out of the buffler range, they are some, now, that's a fact. But this child don't believe it. I'd laugh to get a sight of these darned Mormonites, I would. They're no account, I guess; and it's the meanest kind of action to haul their women critters and their young 'uns to sech a starving country as the Californys.[5]

And in mistaking prophets for profits, the old coon accidentally names a crucial difference between the old Westerner and the new.

Or listen to another trapper, Long Hatcher, sound off about *mangeurs de lard*:

This child hates an American what hasn't seen Injuns skulped or doesn't know a Yute from a Shian mok'sin. Sometimes he thinks of makin' tracks for the white settlement but when he gits to Bent's big lodge on the Arkansa and sees the bugheways, an' the fellers from the States, how they roll thar eyes at an Injun yell worse nor if a village of Camanches was on 'em, an' pick up a beaver trap to ask what it is—just shows whar the niggurs had thar brungin' up—this child says, "a little bacca ef it's a plew a plug, an' Dupont an' G'lena, a Green River or so," and he leaves for the Bayou Salade. Darn the white diggins while thar's buffler in the mountains.[6]

So the trappers went farther and higher into the mountains, chasing the beaver that were already thin and the buffler that the settlers, the army, and the Indians were starting to butcher by the thousands. When they did show

their hides at white diggin's, like the forts that were springing up all over the plains, they were damned as stinking,
useless, dangerous eccentrics. They spoke a language no
more comprehensible than hieroglyphics. They had ways
no man could understand. And they seemed to tolerate
Injuns as well as white folks. So they kept to themselves
and retreated into still wilder places. A lot of them had
Indian wives, half-breed children, and were adopted sons
of tribes. Some of these simply pitched their tipis with
their Indian brothers and settled into the pattern of migrating after the game in summer and wintering in warm
valleys with plenty of water, wood, and meat. They even
stretched on long enough to watch or fight as the relentless
oncoming of settlers wiped out their friends, their families, and their way of life. They were only holding on,
waiting to see whether they would die before they were
rubbed out by civilization.

That life was not for Jim Bridger, though. He was a considerable man, and could be of particular service to his
country and the white race. Considerable men did not just
disappear into the mountains and spin out their lives in
quiet.

Jim had the map that the atlas makers knew nothing
about right in his head. He passed his information on to
emigrators as they came through his Black's Fork post.
He guided their trains. He led surveyors and detach-
ments of official exploration teams. He had his fort taken
by force by Mormons, whom he had befriended and directed to their Promised Land in Utah; Brigham Young
didn't want an infidel in his territory. Then he leased it to
the U.S. government. But when the time came for him to
get it back, they slyly asked for his deed of ownership—a
deed of ownership in a country with no land offices, a
country where a man's title was never more than his gun

and the other fellow's honor. So he was cozened by the institution that used him.

He lived on to become a scout for the army. He advised against military stupidity and arrogance and cruelty as often as he could. When he couldn't, he tried to make the damnfool plans work so that they'd lead to as little trouble as possible. Though he continued to mate up with Indian women, and was loved, feared, and respected by every tribe in the Rockies, he ended by leading military expeditions against the Indians. Had to make way for white progress. And wherever gold was discovered, that land suddenly switched from permanent Indian territory to the white man's property.

He was only thirty-nine when he set up shop at Fort Bridger. He lived to be seventy-three, mostly blind, having to be taken care of by his mixed-blood children and grandchildren in Missouri.

He didn't call back, then, the times after all the green-horns came West. He had seen enough of that—South Pass filled with Conestoga wagons as thick as railroad cars. The Oregon Trail, rutted and barren of grass and hard as granite, so repellent to the buffler that they wouldn't even cross it, but staved on one side.

He recollected back to when he was young and his blood ran swift and he first went to the Rockies. When the land was so new that he could see a little valley and believe he was the first man ever to see it. When he could look at a place so new he could give it a name. When a man could feel he was the first ever to piss against a tree, the first ever to dip his head into a stream and drink its coldness.

The last twenty-five years it hadn't been the same. It changed when you knew someone else had camped by a spring before you. It changed when you had memories that flooded in along with the sight of Pierre's Hole, like ghosts inhabiting the land. It changed when you knew that an official party had recently "discovered" Yellowstone, where you had stood in fresh amazement decades ago. It wouldn't do, it didn't shine.

So Jim, among his grandchildren, Bill Sublette, among his zoo animals, and Captain William Drummond Stewart, among his formal parks filled with "bison," can only remember the Rocky Mountains: The creak of saddle leather, the acrid smell of alkali dust kicked up by the mules in front of you, the bellowing of buffler in starvin' times. The pungent smell of buffler chips making fire, the sharp taste of raw liver dipped in bile, and then the good meat smell of hump ribs roasting.

Jim has those memories in the muscles and tendons of his forearms, in his tongue, in the legs that forked a cayuse for too many years. He can feel the rhythm of the big back muscles and the flank muscles as the horse walks slowly, or the quick flexing as it rushes for water. When he cannot sleep, he sees a party of Indians ride up full speed, scalps flying from lance-poles, and stop suddenly to greet friends and collect tribute. He can hear the shrieking of a brave over a kill. He can feel the sticky blood of a scalp just torn off.

They come on him at sudden moments, the memories, by surprise: The burning of alkali in his nostrils when he can see rain on a ridge just over there. The feel of an Indian arm around his shoulders in false friendship. The madness and then the easing with his squaw in buffler robes. The fiery taste of whisky improved by red peppers and molasses. The prime flavor of boiled beaver tail, or roasted dog.

He can't see down here in the flat. Maybe getting old, but he could always see in the Rockies: The still soar and then the quick lift of a watching eagle; the flat light of the sagebrush desert, helping the heat to distort things so much that the hills off to the left seem to be swimming; the motionless blue of Jackson Lake, looking like it had been there forever and would never even move; the gold of aspen in fall; the boiling rush of a little creek pretending to be a river; the V made by a beaver head easing across the surface of the water behind a dam.

He remembers, too: Jed Smith, who went under on the Cimarron, setting out for Californy with a look on his severe face more determined than any missionary's; Tom Fitzpatrick, exhausted and happy, when he came in starved and naked after a skirmish with the Blackfeet; Black Harris telling a whopper across a fire; and himself, in a bullboat he couldn't steer, careening down the rapids of Bear River like a damn fool and coming out on a lake or ocean that stretched as far as he could see. Again, in memory, he sticks his finger in the water, and he can still taste the salt.

He thinks of the Indian legends about the waters of the Rockies. He calls back one of the thousands of the springs they told about—a tiny spring that seeps out of the ground in a cool, mossy place, trickles over the stones to a ledge, and then throws itself into the air, falling, glittering, arching in a fine spray through space until it splashes into a small, clear pool. Sometimes, he just looks at it for a long spell. He goes close to feel the spray in his upturned face. He stoops, and cups his hands to drink. On his knees he sticks his head into the water and opens his eyes to peer through the radiant liquid. The Indian poets say that these waters have magical powers. They claim solemnly that once a man drinks of such waters, he must someday return to drink again. Old Gabe knows with all his heart that the Indians speak with a single tongue.

In the late afternoons, he sits in the yard of his Missouri farm facing west, into the setting sun. His dimming eyesight blurs the red-yellow of level fields stretching to the horizon. His mind brings back the Rockies at this time of day: In the setting sun the stone of the mountains glows warmly, flushed with a delicate rose color, an odd luminosity called alpenglow. Jim sees it clear, and holds it. But then he blinks, and raises his lids on a flat Missouri pasture graying in the dusk.

APPENDIX A

Chronology of the Fur Trade

1806: John Colter, a member of the Lewis and Clark expedition, decides not to return to the settlements with the rest of his party, but goes back to the mountains to trap.

1807: Manuel Lisa brings the first large commercial venture to the mountains for fur, using Colter as a guide. Lisa builds the first post of the mountain fur trade at the mouth of the Big Horn River.

1807–1808: Colter, sent to befriend the Crows and secure their trade, makes a lone exploration of the valleys of the Big Horn and Wind Rivers, crosses the continental divide twice, sees what is now Yellowstone National Park, and returns to the fort.

1809–1810: Lisa, Pierre Chouteau, William Clark, and Andrew Henry form the Missouri Fur Company to take beaver from the area of the upper Missouri River. Henry constructs a fort at the Three Forks of the Missouri, in Blackfoot country, but is driven out by the Blackfeet.

1811: John Jacob Astor founds Astoria to compete with the British for fur. Part of his forces goes to the mouth of the Columbia River by ship; the other part crosses the mountains under the leadership of Wilson Price Hunt. Missouri Fur abandons Fort Lisa and reduces its upper-river efforts.

1813: Astor gives up Astoria to the Northwest Company, which later merges with the Hudson Bay Company.

1822: William Ashley and Andrew Henry become partners in the fur trade. Henry, the field leader, builds a fort at the mouth of the Yellowstone.

1823: Ashley, taking reinforcements to Henry, is defeated and driven downriver by the Arikaras. When the combined forces of the trappers and the United States Army fail to chastise the Arikaras for their attack, the Missouri River is closed to traders. Ashley sends Henry to the Yellowstone post by land, and another party, under Jedediah Smith, directly to Crow country.

1824: Smith leads the Ashley-Henry men across South Pass and begins the American exploration of the interior of the West. Henry retires. Ashley, guided by Tom Fitzpatrick, takes new forces to the mountains by the new Platte River route. Jim Bridger and Etienne Provost independently discover the Great Salt Lake at about the same time.

1825: Ashley holds the first rendezvous on Henry's Fork of the Green River. Jed Smith becomes Ashley's partner in the trade.

1826: At the second rendezvous (the first full-blown one), Ashley sells out to Smith, David Jackson, and Bill Sublette; he becomes their banker and sales agent. Smith pioneers the land route to California, by way of south-central Utah, northwest Arizona, and the Mojave Desert.

1827: Smith, leaving most of his men, crosses the Sierra Nevada Mountains and the states of Nevada and Utah on his way to rendezvous. The American Fur Company, headed by Astor, incorporates Missouri Fur and the Columbia Fur Company with a view to competing in the mountain trade. Smith, on his way back to California, has half his party massacred at the Mojave villages.

1828: Smith's brigade is massacred on the Umpqua River in modern Oregon, four men escaping. His competition, Hudson Bay Company, helps him to recover some of his property.

1829: Smith returns to rendezvous after a two-year absence and great losses. The firm makes an extensive and productive hunt. American Fur, getting into competition seriously, builds Fort Union.

1830: Smith, Jackson, and Sublette, having made substantial profits, but becoming wary of the Trust, sell out to Tom Fitzpatrick, Jim Bridger, Milton Sublette, Henry Fraeb, and Jean Gervais. The new partners, trappers more than businessmen, call themselves the Rocky Mountain Fur Company. American Fur succeeds in opening trade with the Blackfeet.

1831: Jedediah Smith, venturing into the Santa Fe trade, is killed by Comanches on the Cimarron River. For the first time since 1825, no rendezvous: Neither Rocky Mountain Fur nor American Fur get their supply caravans to the mountains in time. The Trust steps up competition with RMF.

1832: American Fur establishes forts in Crow country and in Blackfoot country. Nathaniel Wyeth and Benjamin Bonneville start their trapping efforts. The Sublette-Campbell train wins the race with the Trust to rendezvous and RMF gets most of the fur. Trust brigades follow RMF through the mountains.

1833: Campbell again wins the race to rendezvous for RMF. William Drummond Stewart comes to the mountains with Campbell for big-game sport. Wyeth, having lost his brigade, makes plans to supply rendezvous from the mouth of the Columbia. Joe Walker leads an outfit to California for Bonneville. The Trust gains on RMF, absorbing big losses to get fur.

1834: Bill Sublette makes a deal with American Fur, giving up his river posts in exchange for the Trust's temporary withdrawal from the mountains. At rendezvous, Sublette uses RMF's debt to persuade the partners to buy goods from him rather than Wyeth; Wyeth's plans are blasted. RMF goes out of business; the new partners, Fitzpatrick, Bridger, and Milton Sublette, make a deal with the Trust rather than with Sublette-Campbell for supplying next year's rendezvous. Competition for mountain fur is effectively ended. Jason Lee comes west with Wyeth as missionary to the Indians.

1835: Fitzpatrick and Bridger give up their facade of competing with the Trust and become its partisans. Two more missionaries, Marcus Whitman and Samuel Parker, come west. Trappers are discouraged by the low price of beaver.

1836: Four missionary couples come to rendezvous, making the first appearance of white women in the mountains. Smallpox debilitates the Blackfeet. The price of beaver is still down.

1837: Stewart takes an artist west, and Alfred Jacob Miller makes the first visual records of mountain life.

1838: The market for beaver fur is still diminished. Chouteau, Pratte (which has taken over from American Fur) sends only a small train to rendezvous and declines to outfit another year's hunt. Bridger journeys to St. Louis and finds backing for a two-year hunt. Trappers work mostly in small, free-lance groups. During the next few years, the rendezvous system is abandoned. Free trappers work in small numbers and take their furs to trade at the fixed forts, which have proliferated. The market for beaver continues to be depressed; it will never recover. Bridger keeps leading substantial brigades with no particular success. Emigrants start making their way west in wagons, often led by former trappers. John Charles Frémont, guided by Kit Carson and Tom Fitzpatrick, begins his "exploration" of the West. Bridger builds Fort Bridger on Black's Fork.

1843: Stewart, back in the mountains, finances one last rendezvous himself. Bridger, after another unsuccessful hunt, shifts from trapping to trading with the emigrants who pass Fort Bridger. The Great Migration begins on the Oregon Trail. Though some trappers will continue to work the mountains for some years, it is the end of an era.

APPENDIX B

Glossary

ABSAROKA: Crow territory. The Crow word means "Land of the Sparrow-Hawk People."

APISHEMORE: Saddle pad.

ARWERDENTY: Liquor. A corruption of the Spanish.

BLACK YOUR FACE AGAINST (TO): To be at war with. From the Indian custom of blacking the face to show the tribe is on the warpath.

BOUDINS: Buffalo guts, a treat for the mountain gourmet.

BUG'S BOYS: Children of Satan; the familiar name for the Black-feet.

BULLTHROWER: Rifle, usually of Hawken make.

CACHE: To hide or conceal; applicable either to one's self or one's goods. Also used as a noun: the hidden goods; from the French.

CHILD, COON, CRITTUR, BEAVER, NIGGUR: Interchangeable terms for person, either one's self or someone else. They did not necessarily carry a charge of denigration; the term niggur was applied freely to white, red, and black men.

COME (TO MAKE SOMEONE): To kill a person or animal, as in "I made two of the varmints come that day."

COUNT COUP (TO): To execute a coup (to do a brave deed such as killing someone, scalping him, or striking him with a coup-stick); or to relate one's brave deeds in a formal manner.

DUPONT: Gunpowder. From the name of the manufacturer.

ENGAGÉ: A hired hand, sometimes French-Canadian. Of lower social status than a free trapper or a trapper contracted for part of his take; from the French.

FOOFURAW: Trinkets, doodads, decorative trivia fancied by women, especially Indian women. By extension, the quality of having a fancy for the same, as in. "She was a deal too foofuraw to suit me."

GALENA: Lead for balls.

GO UNDER (TO): To die or be killed, usually the latter. *Gone beaver* was used in the same sense, but only in that past participle form.

GREEN RIVER: A knife. From the name of the manufacturer, not the name of the river. *To shove it in to the Green River* meant to shove the knife in to the hilt, where the trademark of the manufacturer was engraved. By extension, to do anything up to *the Green River* meant to do it to the full.

HA'R OF THE B'AR: To say that a man had the ha'r of the b'ar in him was a supreme form of praise. The expression probably came from the Indian belief that a man could become more brave by eating the hair of the grizzly bear.

HAWKEN: A rifle. The most valued rifle in the mountains was the flintlock model made by the Hawken brothers.

HUMPRIBS: The small ribs that support the hump of the buffalo. See also *meatbag*.

LEVÉ, LECHÉ LEGO: Wake up, turn out. Usually used in combination. (A corruption of French?)

MANGEUR DE LARD: Literally, eater of pork in French. Figuratively, an inexperienced man. Said of a man who is used to the diet of the settlements (which would include pork) and not of the mountains (almost exclusively buffalo meat). Always a term of denigration.

MEATBAG: Stomach, of an animal or human being. The trappers frequently applied the terms they used for buffalo anatomy (fleece, humpribs, boudins) to human beings.

OLD EPHRAIM: Grizzly bear.

ON THE PERAIRA: Free. As in "he gave me a rifle on the peraira." Peraira is a dialectical version of *prairie*.

PLEW: Beaver pelt. A corruption of the French plus.

POOR BULL, FAT COW: Figuratively, poor eating, living, or times, as opposed to good eating, living, or times. A trapper might mention that he was forced to eat crickets and comment, "That was poor bull, sure." To *know poor bull from fat cow* was to know what was what, what was bad and what was good, to understand mountain ways. Derived from the fact that, except at calving time, the meat of the bull would be more muscular and less fatty than the meat of a cow, therefore tougher and less enjoyable.

POSSIBLES, POSSIBLE SACK: Equipment; sack for carrying equipment.

SHINE (TO): To suffice, to be suitable or good. As in, "City ways don't shine." *Shinin'* suggested fine or splendid, as in, "Them was shinin' times."

SHOT IN THE LIGHTS (TO BE): To be shot in the vitals.

SOME: Remarkable, admirable. "That Jed was some, now. He had the ha'r of the b'ar in him. Wagh!"

TAOS LIGHTNING: A potent liquor.

VIDE-POCHE: Literally, empty-pocket. Usually said of French-Canadians, French speakers of Indian-white descent, etc. Figuratively, the equivalent of worthless no-good.

VOYAGEUR: Boatman, usually French-Canadian. Voyageurs did the hard pulling (cordeling) to get a keelboat upriver. They were widely thought to be cowards and therefore held in contempt by the trappers.

WAGH: An exclamation of surprise, admiration, etc. Sounded like a grunt.

THE WAY THE STICK FLOATS: To know the way the stick floats was to know what's up, what's what. Only an experienced mountain man would be said to know the way the stick floats. The expression came from the use of a float stick attached to a beaver trap to indicate where the trap was if the beaver swam away with it. Its meaning was extended to suggest knowing the ways of the mountains.

NOTES

I. *The First Mountain Man*

1. Thomas James. *Three Years among the Indians and Mexicans,* Philadelphia and New York: J. B. Lippincott Company, 1962, p. 35. (First edition published 1846.)

A good general source for Colter's life is Burton Harris's *John Colter: His Years in the Rockies.* New York: Charles Scribner's Sons, 1952. See also Hiram Chittenden's *The American Fur Trade of the Far West.* New York: The Press of the Pioneers, 1935 (first edition published 1902); and accounts of the Lewis and Clark expedition. In reconstructing Colter's escape from the Blackfeet by his celebrated run, I have relied on accounts by two men who heard the story directly from Colter: In James, pp. 29–34; and in John Bradbury's *Travels in the Interior of America in the Years 1809, 1810, and 1811,* Liverpool: Sherwood, Neely, and Jones, 1817, pp. 18–21 (and quoted in full in Chittenden).

Interlude: The Great American Desert

1. Bernard DeVoto, *Across the Wide Missouri,* Boston: Houghton Mifflin Company, 1947, p. 3.

II. *Mountain Skill, Mountain Luck*

1. This first part of Glass's story rests on the recollection of a trapper named Yount, who knew Glass and later had his memories of the West set down. See Charles L. Camp. ed., *George C. Yount and His Chronicles of the West*, Denver: Old West Publishing Company, 1966, pp. 197–199. John Myers Myers has written a life of Glass— *Pirate, Pawnee and Mountain Man: The Saga of Hugh Glass*, Boston: Little, Brown and Company, 1963.

2. My version of Glass's epic year is based on five main authorities: the *Yount Chronicles*, in which Yount claims to have heard the story from Glass and his companion Dutton; Alphonso Wetmore's "The Missouri Trapper," an article which first saw print in the Philadelphia *Port-Folio*, March 1825, pp. 214–219, and was reprinted in the Missouri *Intelligencer*, June 18, 1825; Philip St. George Cooke's *Scenes and Adventures in the Army*, Philadelphia: Lindsay & Blakiston, 1857, pp. 137–152; Edmund Flagg's "History of a Western Trapper," Dubuque *Iowa News*, November 2, 1839; and Myers's discussion and composite of these first four sources.

The evidence that Jim Bridger was the "kid" who stayed behind with Glass is not rock-solid (it needs a little help from oral tradition), but now seems generally accepted.

III. *Falstaff's Battalion*

1. James Clyman, *James Clyman, Frontiersman, 1792– 1881*, ed. Charles L. Camp. Portland, Oregon: Champoeg Press, 1960, p. 7

2. This episode, the overland crossing from Fort Kiowa to the Wind River valley, is based principally on Clyman, pp. 15–20.

3. Washington Irving, *The Adventures of Captain Bonneville, U. S. A., in the Rocky Mountains and the Far West,* ed. Edgeley W. Todd, Norman: University of Oklahoma Press, 1961, p. 127.

4. Clyman, pp. 21–23.

5. Clyman, pp. 23–25. It is likely that other whites had crossed South Pass previously (for instance, the members of the Astoria expedition). But Smith had no benefit from their knowledge. His was the effective discovery of South Pass; he established it in the minds of other trappers and ultimately of the public; he integrated it into a wider knowledge of the West. See Dale L. Morgan, *Jedediah Smith and the Opening of the West,* Indianapolis and New York: The Bobbs-Merrill Company, 1953, p. 101, on this point and on most events in this chapter.

6. Clyman, pp. 28–29. This lone journey is narrated in Clyman, pp. 25–29.

7. Etienne Provost came on Salt Lake at about this same time, so there were two independent discoverers of Salt Lake.

Interlude: Yarning

1. George Frederick Ruxton, *Life in the Far West,* Edinburgh and London: W. Blackwood and Sons, 1849, pp. 7–9. Ruxton, in turn, had taken it from a St. Louis newspaper.

2. Lewis H. Garrard, *Wah-to-yah and the Taos Trail,* New York: A. S. Barnes & Company, 1850, pp. 209–229.

IV. *The Quest for the Buenaventura*

1. *The Life and Adventures of James P. Beckwourth,* New York: Harper & Brothers, 1856, was taken down by T.D. Bonner from Beckwourth's dictation. Bonner added

what he thought of as the proprieties of style, with an effect at once false and comic. And Beckwourth, besides getting chronology mixed up, lied a lot. I have used the book cautiously and skeptically.

2. Beckwourth, p. III.

3. The rest of this chapter is drawn from the letters and journals of Smith and Rogers (which are printed in Harrison Dale, *The Ashley-Smith Explorations and the Discovery of a Central Route to the Pacific, 1822–1829,* Cleveland: The Arthur H. Clark Company, 1918, and in Maurice S. Sullivan, *The Travels of Jedediah Smith,* Santa Ana: The Fine Arts Press, 1934) and from Morgan's fine synthesis of the same events.

4. Smith's letter to William Clark, printed in Morgan; see p. 336.

5. Rogers's journal, printed in Dale; see pp. 220–221.

6. Smith's letter to the United States plenipotentiary in Mexico, printed in Morgan; see p. 332.

Interlude: Rendezvous

1. Irving, pp. 155–156

v. *Starvin' Times*

1. Beckwourth, *Life and Adventures,* p. 124.

2. Alfred Jacob Miller, *The West of Alfred Jacob Miller,* Norman: University of Oklahoma Press, 1951, p. 67.

3. Morgan, pp. 218–220

4. See Sullivan, *Jedediah Smith,* p. 21. This account of the desert journey from the present Nevada-Utah border to Salt Lake is closely based on Smith's journal.

5. Sullivan, p. 22.

6. Sullivan, p. 23.

7. Sullivan, p. 25.

Interlude: The Buffalo—Cuisine Première

1. Ruxton, *Adventures in Mexico and the Rocky Mountains,* London: J. Murray, 1847, pp. 268–269.

2. Ruxton. *Life,* p. 78.

3. DeVoto, *Wide Missouri,* p. 41.

VI. *Rescue in Californy*

1. Sullivan, p. 54. The Smith expedition material in this chapter is taken from his letters and the journals of Rogers; see also Morgan's composite of these events, pp. 236–269.

2. Dale, p. 245.

Interlude: Mountain Craft

1. See DeVoto's superb essay on mountain craft, *Wide Missouri,* pp. 158–160.

VII. *A Choice of Allegiance*

1. Letters in the Hudson Bay *Archives*; reprinted in Sullivan, pp. 109–111.

2. Frances Fuller Victor, *The River of the West,* Hartford and Toledo: R. W. Bliss & Company, 1870, p. 76.

3. Jedediah Strong Smith Collection Kansas State Historical Society, pp. 350–351.

4. Jedediah Strong Smith Collection Kansas State Historical Society, pp. 353–354.

5. Morgan, p. 304.

6. Charles Keemle, St. Louis *Beacon,* November 4, 1830.

7. Printed in Morgan, p. 358.

8. The anonymous eulogy was published in *Illinois Monthly Magazine,* June 1832, pp. 393–398. My view of Jed Smith's character and motives differs from the views

of Sullivan and Morgan, the scholars who have worked most fully on his life. I see Smith as a man torn by conflicting allegiances—the values of his church and of his society, and the values that he learned and lived by in the wilderness. The evidence of his letters to his family seems to be that he judged his life as a mountain man to be wicked; that conviction seems to have been deep and sincere. He seems to have damned himself for his love of wildness in the same way that settlers would later damn most mountain men for it. So he went home in an attempt to live by the beliefs he professed.

Smith himself says nothing about his decision to return to the mountains in 1831. Though it was only a partial turning back to his former way of life, I think it expressed a strong-felt need, a need he probably chastised himself for. So what is remarkable here, to me, is the conflict between professed values and the values he actually lived by. When his anonymous eulogist said that Smith made his altar the mountaintop, he meant that as a tribute to Smith's ability to live in Christian fashion in the mountains. The irony may be that Smith made the mountaintop his altar in a different sense—that he replaced, symbolically, the altar of the Christian Church with the mountaintop as an object of worship.

I believe that Smith, had he lived, would have been unable to stick to his decision to become a respectable citizen of the settlements.

Interlude: Mountain Mating
1. Ruxton, *Life,* pp. 245–246.

VIII. *War in the Mountains*
1. Victor, *River of the West,* pp. 138–140.
2. This discussion owes much to Don Berry, *A Major-*

ity of Scoundrels: An Informal History of the Rocky Mountain Fur Company, New York: Harper and Brothers, 1961 (pp. 347–353), who first offered this interpretation of Sublette's leverage. The pervasive debt of this chapter is to DeVoto.

3. Berry, p. 359.

4. Berry, pp. 363–364.

5. Berry, p. 364.

IX. *Invasion*

1. DeVoto, *Wide Missouri,* pp. 8–9.

2. DeVoto, p. 9.

3. DeVoto, p. 201. This discussion of Lee and the Flathead mission is based on DeVoto's excellent treatment.

4. See DeVoto, pp. 259–261.

5. Gilbert L. Wilson, "Hidatsa Eagle Trapping," *Anthropological Papers of the American Museum of Natural History,* Vol., XXXIII, Part IV, 1928.

6. This entire sequence of incidents is taken from Ruxton's *Life,* pp. 142–176. The dialogue is Ruxton's, verbatim, except for some of his typographical idiosyncrasies.

7. DeVoto, p. 346.

8. Gene Caesar, *King of the Mountain Men: The Life of Jim Bridger,* New York: Dutton, 1961.

X. *Alpenglow*

1. Victor, *River of the West,* p. 240.

2. DeVoto, p. 383.

3. Ruxton, *Life,* pp. 47–49.

4. Ruxton, *Life,* pp. 17–18.

5. Ruxton, *Life,* pp. 273.

6. Garrard, *Wah-to-yah,* p. 43.

BIBLIOGRAPHY

Since this book is intended for general readers rather than scholars, it seems more useful to append a guide to further reading about the mountain men than a formal bibliography. (References which I have relied on in a relatively direct way are listed below.)

The premier book about the mountain men is still Bernard DeVoto's *Across the Wide Missouri* (Boston: Houghton Mifflin Company, 1947). Primarily following the travels of William Drummond Stewart in the West, DeVoto evokes the period with a striking feeling for its realities. Though he deals only with the years 1832–1838, his is the single invaluable source about the period. Perhaps the ideal supplement to DeVoto is A. B. Guthrie's *The Big Sky* (New York: William Sloane Associates, 1947), published in the same year. Guthrie captures fictionally the life of a characteristic mountain man.

John G. Neihardt's *A Cycle of the West* (New York: Macmillan Company, 1949) remains the most ambitious attempt to render the eras of the mountain men and the Indian wars as grand epic poetry. Neihardt deserves a much wider audience than he has yet found.

If the reader wants to push further, he should turn to the first-hand material about the trappers, the books written or dictated by the men who were there. The liveliest and most accurate of these are George Frederick Ruxton's *Life in the Far West* (Edinburgh and London: W. Blackwood and Sons, 1849) and Lewis H. Garrard's *Wah-to-yah and the Taos Trail* (New York: A. S. Barnes & Company, 1850). Frances Fuller Victor's life of Joe Meek, *The River of the West* (Hartford and Toledo: R. W. Bliss & Company, 1870) is great fun, though Meek is not reliable about dates; James P. Beckwourth's autobiography, *The Life and Adventures of James P. Beckwourth* (New York: Harper & Brothers, 1856) is outrageously entertaining and untrustworthy.

The best sources for the life of Jed Smith are Dale L. Morgan's *Jedediah Smith and the Opening of the West* (Indianapolis and New York: The Bobbs-Merrill Company, 1953), a notably intelligent and thorough biography of Smith and history of mountain trapping. 1822–1831; Maurice S. Sullivan's *The Travels of Jedediah Smith* (Santa Ana: The Fine Arts Press, 1934), which prints important parts of Jedediah's journal, previously undiscovered; and Harrison Dale's *The Ashley-Smith Explorations and the Discovery of a Central Route to the Pacific, 1822–1829* (Cleveland: The Arthur H. Clark Company, 1918), which prints the other known parts of Jedediah's journal, the journal of his clerk Harrison Rogers, and some of Jedediah's letters.

Don Berry has provided an engaging history of the mountain-man period from 1822–1834 in his *A Majority of Scoundrels: An Informal History of the Rocky Mountain Fur Company* (New York: Harper and Brothers, 1961).

Hiram Martin Chittenden laid the base for scholarship about Rocky Mountain fur trapping seventy years

ago in *The American Fur Trade of the Far West* (second
edition, New York: The Press of the Pioneers, 1935).

My own large debts are to DeVoto and Morgan, from
whom I have borrowed shamelessly.

References

Beckwourth, James P. *The Life and Adventures of James
P. Beckwouth,* ed. T. D. Bonner. New York: Harper &
Brothers, 1856.

Berry, Don. *A Majority of Scoundrels: An Informal
History of the Rocky Mountain Fur Company.* New
York: Harper & Brothers, 1961.

Bradbury, John. *Travels in the Interior of America in the
Years 1809, 1810, and 1811.* Liverpool: Sherwood,
Neely, and Jones, 1817.

Caesar, Gene. *King of the Mountain Men: The Life of
Jim Bridger.* New York, Dutton, 1961.

Camp, Charles L., ed. *George C. Yount and His Chronicles
of the West* Denver: Old West Publishing Company,
1966.

Carter, Harvey Lewis. *'Dear Old Kit': The Historical
Christopher Carson.* Norman, University of Oklahoma Press, 1968.

Chittenden, Hiram Martin. *The American Fur Trade of the
Far West.* New York: The Press of the Pioneers, 1935.

Cleland, Robert Glass. *This Reckless Breed of Men: The
Trappers and Fur Traders of the Southwest.* New
York: Alfred A. Knopf, 1950.

Clyman, James. *James Clyman, Frontiersman, 1792–
1881,* ed. Charles L. Camp. Portland, Oregon:
Champoeg Press, 1960.

Cooke, Philip St. George. *Scenes and Adventures in the
Army.* Philadelphia: Lindsay & Blakiston, 1857.

Dale, Harrison Clifford. *The Ashley-Smith Explorations and the Discovery of a Central Route to the Pacific, 1822–1829.* Cleveland: The Arthur H. Clark Company, 1918.

DeVoto, Bernard. *Across the Wide Missouri.* Boston: Houghton Mifflin Company. 1947.

Favour, Alpheus H. *Old Bill Williams.* Chapel Hill: University of North Carolina Press, 1936.

Flagg, Edmund. "History of a Western Trapper," Dubuque *Iowa News,* November 2, 1839.

Garrard, Lewis H. *Wah-to-yah and the Taos Trail.* New York: A. S. Barnes & Company, 1850.

Harris, Burton. *John Colter: His Years in the Rockies.* New York: Charles Scribner's Sons, 1952.

Irving, Washington. *The Adventures of Captain Bonneville, U. S. A., in the Rocky Mountains and the Far West,* ed. Edgeley W. Todd. Norman: University of Oklahoma Press, 1961.

James, Thomas. *Three Years Among the Indians and Mexicans.* Philadelphia and New York: J. B. Lippincott Company, 1962.

Miller, Alfred Jacob. *The West of Alfred Jacob Miller.* Norman: University of Oklahoma Press, 1951.

Morgan, Dale L. *Jedediah Smith and the Opening of the West.* Indianapolis and New York: The Bobbs-Merrill Company, 1953.

Myers, John Myers. *Pirate, Pawnee and Mountain Man: The Saga of Hugh Glass.* Boston: Little, Brown & Company, 1963.

Neihardt, John G. *A Cycle of the West.* New York: Macmillan Company, 1949.

———. *The Splendid Wayfaring.* New York: Macmillan Company, 1920.

Russell, Osborne. *Journal of a Trapper.* Boise: Syms-York Company, 1921.

Ruxton, George Frederick. *Adventures in Mexico and the Rocky Mountains.* London: J. Murray, 1847.

———. *Life in the Far West.* Edinburgh and London: W. Blackwood and Sons, 1849.

Sullivan, Maurice S. *The Travels of Jedediah Smith.* Santa Ana: The Fine Arts Press, 1934.

Sunder, John E. *Bill Sublette: Mountain Man.* Norman: University of Oklahoma Press, 1959.

Victor, Frances Fuller. *The River of the West.* Hartford and Toledo: R. W. Bliss & Company, 1870.

Wetmore, Alphonso. "The Missouri Trapper," Philadelphia *Port-Folio,* March 1825, 214–219.

INDEX